Dat

CULTURE, COMMUNICATION, AND DEPENDENCY
The Tradition of H.A. Innis

COMMUNICATION AND
INFORMATION SCIENCE

A series of monographs,
treatises, and texts

Edited by
MELVIN J. VOIGT

University of California, San Diego

HEWITT D. CRANE • The New Social Marketplace: Notes on Effecting Social Change in America's Third Century
RHONDA J. CRANE • The Politics of International Standards: France and the Color TV War
GLENN FISHER • American Communication in a Global Society
BRADLEY S. GREENBERG • Life on Television: Content Analyses of U.S. TV Drama
JOHN S. LAWRENCE AND BERNARD M. TIMBERG • Fair Use and Free Inquiry: Copyright Law and the New Media
ROBERT G. MEADOW • Politics as Communication
WILLIAM H. MELODY, LIORA R. SALTER, AND PAUL HEYER • Culture, Communication, and Dependency: The Tradition of H. A. Innis
VINCENT MOSCO • Broadcasting in the United States: Innovative Challenge and Organizational Control
KAARLE NORDENSTRENG AND HERBERT I. SCHILLER • National Sovereignty and International Communication: A Reader

In Preparation

HERBERT S. DORDICK, HELEN G. BRADLEY, AND BURT NANUS • The Emerging Network Marketplace
ITHIEL DE SOLA POOL • Retrospective Technology Assessment of the Telephone
CLAIRE K. SCHULTZ • Computer History and Information Access

CULTURE, COMMUNICATION, AND DEPENDENCY
The Tradition of H.A. Innis

WILLIAM H. MELODY
LIORA SALTER
PAUL HEYER
Simon Fraser University
Editors

Ablex Publishing Corporation
Norwood, New Jersey 07648

Printed in the United States of America.

Library of Congress Cataloging in Publication Data

Main entry under title:

Culture, communication, and dependency.

  (Communication and information science)
  Bibliography: p.
  Includes index.
  1. Innis, Harold Adams, 1894–1952—Addresses,
essays, lectures. 2. Communication—Addresses, essays,
lectures. 3. Economics—Addresses, essays, lectures.
I. Melody, William H., 1937–   II. Salter, Liora, 1941–
III. Heyer, Paul, 1946–   IV. Series.
HB121.I6C84   330'.092'4   80-21189
ISBN 0-89391-065-1

Ablex Publishing Corporation
355 Chestnut Street
Norwood, New Jersey 07648

CONTENTS

PREFACE

Harold Adams Innis (1894-1952) was a Canadian scholar of international reknown. He was approaching the pinnacle of his career when cancer claimed him prematurely, denying him the opportunity to deliver his presidential address to the American Economic Association—one of many honors he received for his pioneering work.

Although educated as an economist, economics was far too narrow a discipline, even then, to contain the scope of his interests and the range of his abilities. Innis was a Renaissance scholar at a time when the social sciences were being fragmented into ever narrower specializations. Whether writing about regional economic issues in Canada or the impact of communication technology on the course of world history, he was thorough and imaginative. He brought together the canons of sound historical scholarship, the theoretical concerns of social science and a humanist commitment.

Innis' greatest legacy is an enormous body of unfinished work, rich in detail and deep in insight. Although most of his ideas reached published form, many were not fully elaborated. Nor were they adequately interpreted and criticized by his contemporaries and successors. The broad swath he cut across the social sciences and humanities makes his work fertile ground for the growth of new insights and research opportunities. Also, in much of his work Innis was not a clear and lucid writer. Often he packed his ideas too densely and assumed that connections between them—perhaps obvious to him—did not need be spelled out. By its nature, his work requires interpretation, criticism and extension.

To a significant degree, Innis spent his career sowing seeds and laying foundations for the study of very large societal issues, not putting the finishing touches on definitive specialized works.

Today, societies throughout the world are challenged by issues of natural resource extraction, the dependency of minority cultures created by economic development, the effects of introducing new capital intensive technologies and the consequences of extended communication systems—all of which concerned Innis. Events of the last decade have made his writings particularly relevant today. His work provides no final answers, but it raises important questions and offers revealing insights.

Reflecting the enormous breadth of his scholarship, Innis was alarmed at the tendency of academic disciplines and modern scholars to fragment their fields of study and to isolate the work of certain popular authors, while ignoring completely major contributions by their lesser known precursors and contemporaries. Little did he realize that his own major contributions were to be relegated by academic specialization to the background of the social sciences for the quarter century following his death.

In recent years, scholars in many disciplines have begun to rediscover the work of Innis. This volume is an acknowledgment of his contribution. It is an attempt both to recognize the significance of his work in its own time and to stimulate the fresh mining of this motherlode of social science research, Canadian in origin and global in its ramifications. It is time for a new generation of scholars to interpret and to critically assess Innis' work in light of today's social realities.

The editors of this volume have received their academic education in different social sciences—economics, sociology, anthropology. The course of our work has led us beyond the confines of our traditional disciplines. We have been drawn together in an interdisciplinary Department of Communication at Simon Fraser University that is directed to the systematic study of communication patterns, processes, institutions and policies and their implications. As social scientists working in the Innis tradition, albeit in quite different ways, we found ourselves in agreement regarding the need for an inclusive assessment of the Innis legacy, one that would involve an examination of his work as comprehensive scholarship, not merely as a set of artificially fragmented contributions to specialized academic disciplines.

After discussions with colleagues both inside and outside the university community, we decided that a major conference was warranted. The conference would assess: (1) the significance of Innis' work a generation after his death; and (2) current research that follows directly in the Innis tradition. The Department of Communication, in conjunction with

Continuing Studies, sponsored a Symposium at Simon Fraser on March 29–31, 1978 entitled "Harold Adams Innis: Legacy, Context, Direction." Attendance at the Symposium exceeded all expectations. It included a surprising number of participants from several different disciplines, a healthy delegation of active students and a significant representation from outside the university community. The event precipitated enthusiasm from both panelists and audience. It led to a lively exchange of ideas and strong encouragement to pursue further many of the issues raised for discussion and study.

Extending the experience of this Symposium into the present volume became the exciting next step. Most papers from the Symposium were revised and included in the book. A few additional papers were requested from scholars who could provide unique contributions supplementing those presented at the Symposium.

Like the Symposium that spawned it, the format of the book is designed both to introduce Innis to those not already familiar with his contribution and to highlight the debates that have been inspired by aspects of his research. This task would have been impossible without the substantial assistance of many people. In the planning and conduct of the Symposium, Jo-Lynne Hoegg, Carol Knight and Ann Cowan of Continuing Studies and Joan Homer of the Department of Communication played major roles. Many students, staff and faculty in Communication performed well the innumerable tasks necessary to make the Symposium run smoothly. Simon Fraser University provided essential financial assistance.

In the final preparation of material for the book, Glennis Zilm has been a most thorough, but understanding copyeditor. Linda Clark typed endless drafts of material for both the Symposium and the book with her customary outstanding efficiency. Finally, we must acknowledge the extra time and effort devoted by Liora Salter in assuming primary responsibility for the day-to-day co-ordination of activities throughout this project.

WILLIAM H. MELODY
LIORA SALTER
PAUL HEYER
Burnaby, British Columbia

CULTURE, COMMUNICATION, AND DEPENDENCY
The Tradition of H.A. Innis

I
ASSESSING
THE CONTRIBUTION

1

INTRODUCTION

WILLIAM H. MELODY
Simon Fraser University

> The universities should subject their views about their role in civilization to systematic overhauling and revise the machinery by which they can take a leading part in the problems of western culture.
>
> —Innis

This book is a collection of papers in the tradition of Harold Innis. The papers are organized into three major sections. The first provides an assessment of the Innis contribution by major scholars in social research, history, communication and political economy. The second examines Innis' work in light of several current debates on issues centering in political economy, development and dependency. The third focuses on the concern with communication, culture and the interdisciplinary perspective that characterized his later work.

Preceding the three major sections is a special paper prepared by the eminent Canadian historian Donald Creighton. It highlights the personal reflections of someone who was to Innis both a colleague and a close personal friend. Creighton is the author of *Harold Adams Innis: Portrait of a Scholar* (Toronto: University of Toronto Press, 1975). His paper was presented originally as the Keynote Address of the Symposium on H. A. Innis: Legacy, Context, Direction held at Simon Fraser University, March 29–31, 1978.

In this introduction, the main themes of Innis' work are briefly outlined as background to the papers. This summary is not comprehensive and excludes a great deal of important work by Innis in other areas. It is intended only as a quick overview for those who have read Innis, and an initial exposure to whet the appetites of those who will be reading Innis as a result of this volume. Hopefully, it will facilitate a more complete understanding of the papers that follow.

STAPLE RESOURCES AND DEVELOPMENT

Innis began as a student of Canadian economic history. He published *A History of the Canadian Pacific Railway* in 1923, which showed how the westward expansion of Canada was influenced by an extension of the transport and communication system to meet economic and political objectives. From here he sought the antecedents of Canadian industrialism. In *The Fur Trade in Canada*, 1930, he described the conditions underlying the development of the transport system of canals and railways as well as the characteristics of industrialism resulting from coal and iron, wheat and tariffs. He showed how Canada's development was influenced by the demand for furs in Europe, Canada's unique geographical characteristics and the drive of technology to exploit this staple resource. In this and later work, Innis developed what is now called a "staple thesis." Regional development often serves only the interests of the major centers of power because it exploits the staple, or natural, resources of the region. This creates instability and distorted development in the region and dependency of the region on the centers of power. Innis concluded that "the economic history of Canada has been dominated by the discrepancy between the center and the margin of western civilization."

In *Cod Fisheries: The History of an International Economy,* 1940, Innis broadened his examination to encompass the impact of machine industry upon the exploitation of staple resources in outlying regions. He addressed the broader implications of technological change upon development and began to examine the factors underlying the extension of power by empires such as the British and American.

Canada is still very much a staples economy; it still is a region at the margin of western civilization. In addition to mining, fishing, pulp and paper, electric power, grain, water and other resources, the current issues surrounding the pipeline development for delivery of oil and gas to United States' markets run disturbingly parallel to the oft-repeated history that began with the delivery of furs to Europe. Today, many developing countries and regions within countries throughout the world find themselves in the position of being staples economies, very heavily dependent on their natural resources, located at the margin of western civilization. For them, as for Canada, and particularly the Canadian North, the work of Harold Innis is especially relevant.

COMMUNICATION TECHNOLOGY

It was apparent in Innis' work that the exploitation of staple resources in outlying regions and the extension of the power of empires

4

depended on effective systems of communication. Canada developed in directions and at a pace permitted by the waterways, railways, and telegraph. The geographical limits of empires were determined by the possibilities for effective communication. Historically, changes in the technology of transport and communication permitted vast changes in the possibilities for the extension of empires.

Innis turned his attention to mechanized communication, beginning with printing, publishing, and the implication of mass communication. He showed how the enormous expansion of a commercially based printing industry, and an emphasis on freedom of the press, favored the growth of monopolies, the entrenchment of biased viewpoints and the extension of compulsory education. He argued that these developments tend to intensify nationalism, constrain freedom of speech, and resist the power of thought. The press and radio broadcast to the world; they do not address the individual or facilitate dialogue.

Once again, the issues posed by Innis are with us today. Monopolization in the press is increasing as more and more localities are served by a single newspaper. A great proportion of the news we receive ultimately comes from one or two international wire services. The Canadian Department of Communications and the federal regulatory agencies (Canadian Radio-television and Telecommunications Commission) are worried about bias in television programming and minimum quotas of Canadian content in all mass media. The future satellite delivery of pay television is of great concern for Canada because of the consequences for Canadian culture (and Canadian broadcasters) of a quantum jump in United States programming. Here, too, many Third World nations find themselves with parallel concerns about the mass communication content that permeates their societies. Innis did not live to see the development of television or satellites in Canada. Nevertheless, there is much in his work that is instructive for addressing today's policy issues in communication.

COMMUNICATION AND THE EXTENSION OF EMPIRES

Finally, Innis broadened his scope of inquiry far beyond Canada to a study of the history of communication in the development of civilizations. He focused particularly on the role communication systems have played in extending the power of "empires." Innis argued that in any society the media of communication greatly influences the forms of social organization, and thereby the patterns of individual association. New competing communication media alter the forms of social organization, create new patterns of association, develop new forms of knowledge and often shift the centers of power. The technology of communication, he concluded, is central to all other technology.

Innis observed that any medium of communication is "biased" in terms of its tendency to permit control over extended periods of time or over extended geographical space. His books *Empire and Communications,* 1950, and *The Bias of Communication,* 1951, specifically address these issues. He argued that media used in ancient civilizations such as parchment, clay and stone were durable and difficult to transport. These characteristics are conducive to control over time, but not over space. These media are time-biased. Paper is light, less durable, and easily transportable with reasonable speed. It is spatially biased; it permitted administration over great distances, and therefore, the geographical extension of empires.

In cultural terms, time-biased communication media are associated with traditional societies that emphasize custom, continuity, community, the historical, the sacred and the moral. They are characterized by stable, hierarchical social orders that tend to stifle individualism as a dynamic for change, but permit individualism in the rich expressiveness of language and the range of human emotion. Time-biased communication systems are found in societies with rich oral traditions or with sophisticated writing technologies where access is limited to a privileged few.

Space-biased communication media have an orientation toward the present and the future, the expansion of empires, an increase in political authority, the creation of secular institutions, the growth of science and technical knowledge. They are characterized by the establishment of systems of information exchange and mass communication that are extremely efficient, but which cannot convey the richness, diversity and elasticity of the oral tradition. The modern media of print, telephone, radio, and television are all space-biased.

Innis concluded that the media of communication, depending upon their bias, conferred monopolies of authority and knowledge on religion, through sacred order and moral law, or on the state, via the technical order and civil law. An overemphasis or monopoly of either time- or space-biased modes of communication was the principal dynamic of the rise and fall of empires. The bias toward time or space produced instability in society. A stable society was possible only with the development of mechanisms that preserved a balance between the time and space orientations. Innis concluded that the flowering of ancient Greece was made possible and maintained by a balance between the time bias of the oral tradition and the space-bias of writing on easily transportable documents.

Today, the rapid development of communication technologies such as satellites, computers and sophisticated communication terminals makes possible instantaneous communication throughout the world, and the extension of empires into space itself. Modern technology indeed has introduced a powerful spatial bias into modern communication.

Some recent communication studies argue that the extention of power and empires in the future will no longer result from military battles, but from battles for control of the communication environment. Many developing nations are now in the process of establishing modern telecommunication systems and domestic mass communication institutions. Some of these countries have adopted policies attempting to limit the bombardment of communication originating from external sources. A major United Nations debate continues to rage on the issue of the scope and limitations of the international flow of information.

Does the space bias of modern communication technology point to the expansion of empires and the creation of instability in the future? If so, what can or should be done to restore the balance of time and space bias needed for stability? Innis observed: "The ability to develop a system of government in which the bias of communication can be checked and an appraisal of the significance of space and time can be reached remains a problem of empire and of the western world."

FUNDAMENTAL CONCEPTS COMMON TO INNIS' STUDIES

It can be argued that underlying Innis' many studies is a common theoretical framework. But one must make some large inferences if an Innisian theoretical structure is to be derived. Innis' method of research emphasized inductive analysis almost to the exclusion of abstract deductive theorizing. He engaged in thorough, painstaking, and detailed research, and preferred to let his ordering of the massive array of detailed facts provide an understanding of the system and processes under investigation. He was not seeking generalized principles or high theory and he was suspicious of attempts in this direction.

As a result, some students of Innis' work, such as Ian Parker, have sought to dig out and expose the theoretical consistancy and continuity in his work. Others, such as Dallas Smythe, see in it not much more than a Rorschak ink-blot test; the interpretation is unique to the interpreter and it is not evident from Innis' writings. Most readers will find Innis' work somewhere between these positions. Studying Innis is a collaborative exercise between Innis and the reader. Understanding comes from the interaction of the detailed descriptive analysis and analytical insights of Innis, and the knowledge, experience and interpretive abilities of the reader. Innis' writings do not preach. They work with you in acquiring understanding. But to get the most out of Innis, the reader must work. And even then, one is never sure whether all there is to be gained has been extracted from any given text.

Nevertheless, there are certain fundamental concepts pervading Innis' work that are worthy of mention at the outset and that uniquely characterize the approach adopted for all of his major studies. In contrast to most social science research of his generation and even in the quarter century since his death, Innis adopted an holistic perspective. His concern was understanding macro-social systems and developmental processes. His study of Canadian economic history was not limited to Canada. Rather it addressed the role of Canada in the international political-economic system. And his studies of communication technologies focused on their implications for the global evolution of societies and civilizations.

Despite his broad systemic perspective, Innis had a preoccupation with the detailed study of historical developments. For him, the source of understanding regarding the nature of the larger systems and processes had to be derived from a detailed study of events and relationships. Only the study of detail could provide the necessary information about the specific character of events, their context, relationships and interactions. It provided the richness necessary to interpret and understand parts of the larger system, which ultimately led to a better understanding of that system.

Innis viewed the developmental processes that he studied as extremely complex. They evolved as they did because of unique patterns of interaction in a dynamic process. He addressed himself particularly to the contextual constraints and influences of geography, space and time. He examined the evolution of the dominant institutions, particularly the economic and political. He focused on conflicting forces and on action/reaction sequences as part of his own form of dialectic analysis.

Innis paid particular attention to the implications of industrial production methods and changes in technology. Major technological changes disrupted inherited societal structures and relationships, with significant long-term consequences. Innis examined the nature of the disruptions and attempted to trace out their implications.

Underlying much of Innis' work is a concern for the maintenance of balanced relations in whatever system or process he was studying. In contrast to the overwhelming emphasis that economics has come to place on optimization conditions, Innis' objective was to understand the set of relations under balanced conditions, and the implications of disturbances from balanced conditions. This led him to direct his attention to disruptions in a balanced social system, such as new technology; to instabilities, such as massive overhead costs; and to rigidities, such as monopoly power.

It was within this general framework of analysis that Innis—paying particular attention to the economic circumstances of Canada, economically dependent initially on Britain and then on the United States—developed his detailed analysis of market relations. To Innis, economic markets were not simply aggregations of buyers and sellers that exchanged goods in independent transactions that could be studied without regard to context, history, and the larger set of relations among the institutions involved within the total system of which the market was only a part. Market price at any point in time may be important to clear away the quantities supplied, but it does not address the overall character of the aggregate set of market relations between areas, regions and countries. It is these relations that establish the conditions within which market exchanges take place. Market relations between the large central, dominant areas and outlying areas at the periphery of larger economic systems will result in very different consequences for the dominant center than for the outlying areas. Efficiency and stability in the central areas may be traded off for dependency and instability in the outlying areas. This detailed conception of market relations permitted Innis to develop a much more comprehensive understanding of Canada's economic development than abstract market theory could possibly provide.

THE RELEVANCE OF INNIS' WORK TODAY

Innis' approach to social studies conflicted directly with the dominant trend in social science analysis over the past quarter century: the artificial division, specialization, and separation of disciplines within the social sciences, and the focus on small scale, abstract theorizing and very narrowly defined empirical analysis. Because of its breadth, Innis' work did not fit any single social science discipline. In an age directed to the pursuit of high theory, mathematical analysis, and narrow empirical rigor in the social sciences, Innis' examination of the detailed history of institutions, within a context of macro-social systems, was certainly not in academic fashion.

This is the primary reason why Innis' early work on economic history generally is regarded as an entirely different subject from his later work on communication. Economists have examined his economic history and debated the staples thesis within a narrow framework of analysis constrained by the more limited scope of economics today. His communication studies have been interpreted, for the most part, by scholars from the humanities, emphasizing the cultural and humanistic aspects of his analysis. Thus, the distinction between the early and the late Innis is largely the result of the limitations of his interpreters.

In his communication studies, the resource examined was not fur, fish, wheat or rail transport. It was communication systems and the long-term societal implications of technological change in those systems. The focus was not Canada's relations within an international economic system, but the role of communication technology upon the course of development of ancient civilizations. The methodology was not a detailed examination of facts and relationships drawn from field trips, interviews, and the review of primary documents. It was a detailed examination of a vast range of secondary material about ancient civilizations. This shift in source and reference material is fundamental and carries great import for assessments of the quality of the research, the validity of the insights and the conclusions drawn from it. However, it was a shift necessitated by the problem under study, not by any major shift in Innis' perspective or approach. Finally, Innis did emphasize cultural and humanistic implications more in his communication studies. There are two reasons for this. First, his secondary source materials were drawn heavily from the humanities. Second, his analysis concluded that cultural and human consequences were of greater significance than in his earlier studies. But even in his economic studies, Innis did not ignore cultural and human implications. It was his economic interpreters who tended to ignore these implications, just as his humanist interpreters tended to ignore the economic implications in his communication studies.

Fortunately, in at least a few areas, the trend to fragmentation and separation in the social sciences is coming to a close. Interdisciplinary study is on the ascendence. It is being recognized in more and more circumstances that a narrow reductionist analysis simply assumes away all the relevant issues and problems. Now, a new generation of researchers is directing its attention to holistic and systemic kinds of analysis. It has taken a long time, but the social sciences finally are beginning to move in the direction followed by Innis many years ago.

Over the past quarter century we have learned the weaknesses and failures of the traditional paradigms of both economics and communication for meeting the problems of development, particularly in societies that have not been industrially and technologically "modernized." As separate and distinct sets of paradigms, the theories and models in economics and communication have been unrelated and often incompatible. As a result, studies of economic development and communication and development have had little or nothing to contribute to one another. In these two specialized fields a fundamental reason for this failure has been because each ignored the other. Economic development models have ignored essential communication and information aspects, while the communication and development models have ignored essential economic aspects.

Innis was unique among his contemporaries in recognizing the high degree of interrelationship and interdependence between economics and communication. He noted that communication patterns and information flows are central to economic development. He argued that communication technologies are the building blocks for most other technologies in the economic system, and are clearly the most important. At the same time he recognized that economic incentives and market forces have powerful influences on communication patterns and information flows, which cannot be ignored in any realistic analysis of communication and development.

Today, Canada finds itself in the anomolous position of being the world's most modern developing country. It is an advanced industrial society, pioneering in the development of telecommunications technologies—space-biased technologies that encourage the extention of empires. But it also has all the problems of developing nations. Its history has been one of dependency upon the British and American empires. The dominant forces influencing the course of direction of the Canadian economy are United States economic policy and the decisions of multinational corporations that control Canada's branch plant economy. Canada continues to operate primarily as a supplier of natural resources at the margin of the world economic system.

Although at the frontier of telecommunication technology, Canada has been, and continues to be, a major victim of the consequences of space-biased technology. Communication technology has permitted the Canadian communication environment to be permeated by United States content. Canada is already several steps down the road toward cultural colonization via communication. Thus Canada, and its role in the world economic and communications systems, may provide the most appropriate living laboratory for building on the global implications of the work of Harold Adams Innis.

2

HAROLD ADAMS INNIS— AN APPRAISAL

DONALD CREIGHTON
University of Toronto

Some little time ago, the head of one of the University of Toronto's new colleges put a sudden and very general question to me. What, he said in effect, is the importance of Harold Innis? I must admit that I was surprised and slightly annoyed by this abrupt inquiry and I made no serious attempt to answer it. I might have replied that Harold Innis had been the Head of the Department of Political Economy and the Dean of the Graduate School, that his published works in history and political economy numbered more than a dozen, that he had sat on several Royal Commissions and that his advice was almost invariably sought, during a large part of his career, on every important university issue and appointment in Canada. I might have made an answer along these lines, but I decided not to. I was repelled by the idea of summing up Harold Innis in what would have sounded like a short paragraph out of *Who's Who*. Besides, I could not help suspecting that my questioner was not likely to be much impressed by any brief answer I might make. His inquiry was not an honest request for information, but a disguised expression of disbelief. He probably knew little about Innis and his works, and he was not disposed to accept the Innis legend on trust. He rather brusquely invited me, a friend and a known admirer, to justify my faith in it.

It seems to me that this little incident makes a point, or raises a question of some importance. Has the time come for a reexamination, a reinterpretation, even a reappraisal of Innis and his work? The twenty-fifth anniversary of his death occurred in November 1977 and frequently this particular anniversary prompts a critical backward look at the work of a formerly popular author or prominent scholar. Harold Innis deserves such a retrospective review as much as any Canadian scholar and more than most; but the twenty-fifth anniversary came and went unmarked by any special effort at commemoration. The University of Toronto Press at first planned to publish a memorial volume of essays in his honor, but in the end this project fell through and only my own short biography, *Harold Adams Innis: Portrait of a Scholar,* was reissued in paperback. This absence of a special remembrance was perhaps unfortunate, but it by no means implies a decline in the high evaluation of Innis' work. The very existence of a symposium held early the next year, more than half a continent away from the city where he lived and wrote, is in itself a significant proof of the enduring vitality of his ideas. And in Toronto, the Innis Foundation, which for some years devoted itself to the task of converting the old Innis farm into a study and conference center, has now returned to its original and main purpose, which is encouragement and promotion of studies about Innis and his ideas.

It would be difficult to think of another Canadian scholar whose stature equals or approaches that of Harold Adams Innis. Banting won a Knighthood and the Nobel Prize. Wilder Penfield has been, so far, the only nonpolitical Canadian to become a member of that highly select body, the British Order of Merit. But these brilliantly creative scientists and medical men left behind them no great body of written work for the instruction and delight of their fellow Canadians. Harold Innis did, and the bulk, as well as the brilliance, of that work forces upon us the difficult but fascinating task of investigating the origins of the complex mind that conceived it.

The farm, in which he was born and grew to manhood, and the First World War, in which he almost lost his life, were the two most important early influences in his life. Both were to have important and permanent aftereffects; but the farm, the home, and the Baptist faith and morality, which pervaded it, were probably basic and primary. It was a complex varied influence and Innis' own attitude to it was extremely ambiguous. He hated its stultifying labor and was only too glad to escape from it forever, but he never forgot its seasonal rhythms or its complex daily operations. It taught him also, for his father's farm was a relatively poor one, the need and practice of hard work, and, throughout his entire academic career, he was repeatedly forced to increase his small income with student teaching. The farm gave him the directness and simplicity of his approach to people and things, his insatiable interest in significant detail, his capacity for hard sustained labor, and his enormous powers of endurance.

It also exercised, through the religious and cultural interests of the farm household, a direct and powerful influence on Innis' standards and values. The Innises were Baptists, "hard-shell" Baptists, their neighbors called them, who believed in adult baptism by total immersion and who lived a simple, narrow, and devout existence. Innis had not yet undergone the formidable rite of baptism when he left Otterville to join the Canadian army, but he was still a professed Christian, and he told his sister solemnly he did not believe he would have volunteered if it had not been for his Christian faith. How much of that faith survived the horrors of World War I is uncertain, but certainly there was none of it left in his later years. He had ceased to be a Baptist, but he clung tenaciously to certain convictions and values that have always been characteristic of his sect. He believed in the independence, dignity, and self-sufficiency of the individual, and he utterly rejected any compromise with his high standards in scholarship or teaching. Many people, when they are angered by an unjustified slight or an unmerited favor to others, go as far as to threaten resignation. Harold Innis did not threaten to resign; he just resigned. He resigned when a junior was appointed over his head in the Department of Political Economy at Toronto: He withdrew his resignation only when he was promoted to the same higher grade in the academic hierarchy. Years later, at the height of his career, he angrily resigned from the Royal Society of Canada on the ground that one of its awards had been bestowed on an unworthy fellow, and the academic world of Canada was confronted by the astonishing spectacle of one of its most distinguished members openly boycotting the proceedings of its most prestigious society!

There was still another important but negative influence of the Innis household: its undeniable cultural poverty, which, in my view, profoundly affected Innis' development. The *Family Herald* was the only periodical that arrived regularly at the farm; no metropolitan newspaper entered the home until Innis, who, like the rest of his family, was then a stout political Liberal, subscribed to the Toronto *Globe*. The family's speech was slovenly and ungrammatical, and Innis learnt his first big words from reading Borden's and Laurier's speeches on the Naval Bill in the House of Commons. There may have been a small library in the farmhouse, but, if so, its existence is not recorded. The young Innis no doubt gulped down a good many books, but they were books which, in the main, bore directly on the academic courses he was taking at Woodstock Collegiate Institute or McMaster University in Toronto. Even at McMaster, he never seems to have plunged into that fascinating debauch of extracurricular reading to which so many undergraduates succumb. At McMaster, he was known not as a bookworm, but as a debater, a powerful opponent in intercollegiate debates. And his success made him think of law as a career.

It was not until a good deal later, when Innis went to Chicago and fell in love with Mary Quayle, that he became dimly aware of this great, gaping hole in his general education. Mary Quayle was, as she later proved, a writer herself, and well versed in modern and contemporary English literature. During her engagement to Innis, she lent him a novel by Willa Cather, the leader of an early twentieth-century group of mid-western novelists in which she was interested. Innis later admitted that he had read the book, but had, if I remember correctly, nothing what-ever to say about it; if the loan of Cather's *My Antonia* was intended to start him off on an extended course on the modern novel, it was a total failure! Years later, when Harold and Mary visited our Muskoka cottage, I tried to create a diversion from endless academic gossip, by reading some of the pieces from Stephen Leacock's *Nonsense Novels* or *Sunshine Sketches of a Little Town*. Innis was immensely amused and laughed up-roariously, but it was obvious that this was the first time he had encoun-tered Leacock! He had never even heard his name before!

Years later, in a series of lectures on prominent Canadian histor-ians and economists, which was sponsored by the Department of Political Economy and the Department of History at Toronto, Innis gave a paper on Stephen Leacock. With laughable professional complacency, he at-tributed the vividness and accuracy of *Sunshine Sketches of a Little Town* to the fact that Leacock was an economist! In the entire history of English literary criticism there is probably no more hilarious absurdity than this inept remark. It was Leacock's inspired novelist's insight into the charac-ters and circumstances of his little town—the gifts of a born storyteller—and not the laboriously acquired knowledge of an economist that gave his *Sunshine Sketches* their freshness and authenticity. What Harold Innis badly needed—and what he never took the trouble to acquire—was a thorough knowledge of the realistic and naturalistic novelists, French and English, of the nineteenth and early twentieth centuries. A thorough course of reading in Balzac, Flaubert, Zola, Trol-lope, Bennett, and Galsworthy would have shown him clearly how far novelists excel economists in depicting the social circumstances and class relationships of a given country and period.

There is one last formative influence on the development of the early Innis—World War I and its effects—that remains to be explored. When he left the Innis farm in South Norwich to join the Canadian artillery, he had felt himself to be a Christian soldier engaged in a holy crusade; when he came back, war had, for him, turned into a monstrous, sickening mixture of blood, filth, and stench. His experience left him with an enduring sense of sympathy and comradeship with the men who had actually risked the peril of front-line fighting; for everybody else supposedly engaged in the war, he had nothing but uncompromising contempt. As an economist, he might have been expected to realize that modern warfare was a vast, complicated enterprise in which thousands of noncombatants played essential parts, but, in fact, he was even more unwilling to apply Adam Smith's dictum about the necessary division of labor to World War II than he had been to World War I. In his view, noncombatants were simply bureaucrats who risked nothing and battened on the war's emoluments of money, prestige, and power. Bureaucracy meant regimentation and centralization and all the other evils of big government, which Innis instinctively hated. And World War II, directed and controlled by a triumvirate of War Lords, was an even more monstrous example of centralization. Innis simply endured it. He watched young university teachers go off to Ottawa, or London, or Washington, without interest and with barely concealed contempt. In his opinion, their real place was in their universities, guarding the threatened traditions of scholarship.

EARLY ACADEMIC CAREER

For Innis, World War I was a horrible but comparatively brief interlude in a life increasingly devoted to academic study. He had refused to take advantage of McMaster University's dubious offer of a free degree to fourth year students who enlisted before the end of the year and had stayed stubbornly on to write his examinations. In June, 1917, when he was stuck in the trenches at Vimy and there appeared not the remotest prospect of his release from fighting, he wrote to McMaster University asking for information about the requirements for the Master of Arts degree. A month later, a severe wound in his knee took him back to England and eventually to the Canadian General Hospital at Basingstoke. There he started in to read the formidable list of books Professor Duncan McGibbon had provided him and to write an M. A. thesis on his own chosen subject, "The Returned Soldier." He reached his home at Otterville at the end of March, 1918, and within only two days he was back again in Toronto, conferring with McGibbon. There was time for only a last fortnight of frantic study: On April 19, he wrote his examinations. Only a few days later he was honorably discharged from the army and on April 30, in Walmer Road Baptist Church, McMaster University's Annual Convocation awarded him the M.A. degree.

It was an astonishing record, carried out in an incredibly brief space of time. In only a little more than six months, a convalescent soldier, distressed by occasional periods of pain and weakness, had shown extraordinary powers of grim determination and compulsive speed. He had passed all the barriers now, academic and military; he richly deserved a holiday, but now, as always, he was in a hurry. There was the problem of his future career. In vain his mother renewed her old pleas that he become a Baptist clergyman. He himself had vaguely considered the law a profession; now he finally decided upon a legal career. His professional training at Osgoode Hall in Toronto was to begin in September, 1918, but before that happened, there were five empty months to be filled. Most young returned soldiers, if they had been academically as far advanced as Innis, would have welcomed a summer of comparative idleness, but Innis was not among their number. He discovered that the University of Chicago, to which McMaster was accustomed to send its most promising students for further study, had a graduate summer school. He decided to attend.

That summer at Chicago was decisive for Innis in a number of important ways. He made up his mind he would win his doctoral degree at Chicago and seek an academic career as a teacher of economics. He was launched on the study of Canadian economic history through the choice of his thesis subject, the Canadian Pacific Railway. Through an elementary course in economics, which he taught at this supervisor's request, he met, and soon fell in love with, one of his students, Mary Quayle. There was no doubt whatever about a job, for in both Canada and the United States the veterans were returning to their studies, and universities all over the continent were busily recruiting staff. A variety of academic openings were available, but Innis wanted to teach in Canada and preferred a senior and recognized university. Very quickly his hopes were realized, for Toronto offered him a position as lecturer in economics at a salary of $2,000 a year. In the autumn of 1920, he began to teach in the department of political economy and, in the spring of the following year, he married Mary Quayle.

Obviously, the first definite period in Innis' academic career begins with his appointment at Toronto in 1920, is neatly bisected by the publication of *The Fur Trade in Canada* in 1930, and ends with the appearance of *The Cod Fisheries: the History of an International Economy* in the early winter of 1940. For both Innis and his chosen subject, economics, it was a period of rapid advance and steady enlargement. In 1937, when he had been only seventeen years in the department, he was appointed its head. Those seventeen years witnessed an amazing increase in the range and depth of Canadian studies in economics. The revival of the Canadian Political Science Association in 1931 was followed four years later by the founding of the *Canadian Journal of Economics and Political Science*. The publication of the two volumes of Canadian Economic Documents, edited by Innis, and Innis and Arthur Lower, gave students for the first time an opportunity of getting at the roots of their subject. The launching of those two large scholarly enterprises, *Canadian Frontiers of Settlement* edited by W. A. Mackintosh, and *The Relations of Canada and the United States* edited by James T. Shotwell, gave senior scholars in economics, history, political science, and sociology more opportunities for publication than they had ever had before.

In contrast with the second period of Innis' career, which began in 1940, the first was essentially Canadian, North American in character. It was not, of course, that he carefully avoided contact with England and Europe. During the 1920s and early 1930s, he made perhaps half-a-dozen trips to England and the continent, chiefly in the guise of an economic geographer, which was the academic role he liked to assume at the time. He attended geographical conferences and made an investigation of German methods of teaching geography, but he never stayed long, never did any serious research in England or Europe and never attempted to learn a European language. By an odd coincidence, I encountered him myself on one of his brief European visits. In the summer of 1928, I was working at the Bibliothèque National on a subject in French Revolutionary history. At that time Innis and I knew each other slightly, but he showed a friendly interest in my researches and we went out together for a light luncheon, which probably consisted, as mine invariably did in that summer of abject poverty of "un sandwich au jambon." I remember that as we passed the guardian at the gate of the library, he muttered the one word "retourner." I never heard him speak a sentence or even a lengthy phrase in French. He may have come back again to the library, as he told the guardian he would, but I never saw him again that summer.

The brevity and infrequency of these European visits provide a striking contrast with the steady and unflagging zeal with which he explored Canada. The famous journey down the Mackenzie River in the summer of 1924 was only the most exciting and dangerous of his many travels. In those first ten crowded years at Toronto, he could be said to have realized the motto of the Canadian coat-of-arms: "He shall have Dominion from sea to sea, and from the river unto the ends of the earth." He became intimately acquainted with the land, its regions, resources, and industries. He got to know its universities, their principal scholars, and promising juniors. Through J. Bartlet Brebner, who had left Toronto for Columbia University, he became acquainted with James T. Shotwell, one of the directors of the Carnegie Endowment, and through him with Joseph Willits and Anne Bezanson of the Rockefeller Foundation, and Henry Allen Moe of the John Simon Guggenheim Foundation. These influential American associations were vital to Canadian scholarship in those days, for the establishment of the Canada Council was decades in the future. I had gone to Paris in 1928 on my own meager savings, but in 1940 I won a Guggenheim Fellowship, through, I am sure, the influence of Harold Innis.

The fact that Innis became a power in Canada and a potent influence in the United States was the result mainly of the two major works he produced during this period, *The Fur Trade in Canada* and *The Cod Fisheries: the History of an International Economy.* Both these books were applications of what came to be called the staples approach to Canadian economic history. Innis was not the sole inventor of this approach, but in the final chapter of *The Fur Trade in Canada,* which was one of the strongest chapters he ever wrote, he gave the classic exposition of the general theory upon which the staples approach was based. The migrant to a new country such as Canada, he assumed, was desperately dependent on the importation of manfactured goods from the homeland for the maintenance of the culture to which he or she was accustomed. For these, the migrant could pay only by the discovery of a native commodity or staple, which was available in fairly large quantities in the colony, was light enough to be carried for long distances in the little ships of the period, and was either unknown or scarce, and consequently desirable, in the Motherland. For Canada, the first two of these staples were fish and furs.

The *Fur Trade* and the *Cod Fisheries* are excellent examples of the way in which Innis carried out the application of this theory to Canadian economic history. His method of composition was unusual, highly distinctive and, at times, extremely exasperating. A large amount of the task of understanding his books was left to the reader. He insisted on including large chunks of original documents in an undigested and sometimes almost indigestible form. All too often his sentences were awkward collections of words, with a series of huge abstract nouns and a few rather feeble and frequently repeated passive verbs carrying the main action of the narrative or the chief burden of the argument. This dense, leaden exposition might go on for paragraphs, or even pages, when it could be suddenly interrupted by a brilliant generalization, a short paragraph that simply but superbly summed up pages of exposition, or a final chapter that suddenly seemed to open up vast horizons of understanding to the reader.

In those superb features of his work, the *Fur Trade* is surely the better of his first two books. Perhaps he tired in the end of the endless involutions of the story of the fisheries. Perhaps the sheer weight of his material overwhelmed him. At any rate, the vast untidy manuscript he finally sent down to New York was too much for James T. Shotwell, the general editor of the series on the *Relations of Canada and the United States.* He succeeded in persuading Innis that considerable revision was essen-

tial and Arthur W. MacFarlane, an old friend of Shotwell, came to Toronto and for more than a year worked with Innis over the revision. It
was he who supplied the appendix to Chapter II, which explained the
coins and money values of the period—a complicated subject Innis had
majestically ignored.

Innis' uncompromising attitude to his readers had its origin in his
conception of economics. He believed that it was a science, a difficult
science certainly, with serious limitations, which invited study and exploration but definitely precluded any final, dogmatic conclusions. No word
appeared more frequently in his work—it was part of the title of one of
his collections of essays—than the word "bias." No man was ever more
acutely aware of the fact that everybody, including the most supposedly
detached economist, was a creature of his own generation and environment and deeply affected by its values, assumptions, and beliefs. Such
arguments, carried to their logical extreme, could end only in complete
relativism; they could mean only that an objective economic science was
logically impossible. This absolute conclusion Innis refused to accept.
Bias was the social scientist's greatest danger, but paradoxically it also
was the best hope of salvation. Bias, he seemed to say, is an historical
phenomenon that is always with us and can be studied and analyzed just
like any other historical phenomenon. And through such study the
economist could discover the cumulative force of biases, and their effect
on institutions.

This was a modest defense of economics as a difficult science without dogmatic conclusions. It also provided a useful retort to the radical
reformers of the 1930s, who suddenly appeared as a result of the world's
worst depression and who were always demanding drastic economic or
political changes and insisting economists should direct and aid the
politicians in carrying them out. The League for Social Reconstruc-
tion—the very name was abhorrent to Innis—was founded early in the
1930s; the first Canadian Socialist Party—the Co-operative Commonwealth Federation, with a manifesto stuffed with huge economic and
social generalizations—followed shortly after. Innis had nothing to do
with either of these organizations. He dealt with them only when he was
attacked by one of their members, or when the League for Social Recon-
struction produced a book, *Social Planning for Canada*, which purported
to be a serious intellectual exposition of its socialist principles. Innis gave
this pretentious effort a highly critical review in the *University of Toronto
Quarterly* a year later, at the first meeting of the revived Canadian Political Science Association, when F. H. Underhill denounced the Canadian
economists as "the intellectual garage mechanics of the Canadian economy" and urged them to throw aside their timid academic scruples and

join the holy crusade for a socialist Canada. Innis made such a devasting reply that thirty-five years later, George Ferguson, the editor of the Montreal *Star,* was still marveling over it!

For Innis all social planning on the grand scale was bad, but the social planning proposed by Canadian socialists was particularly bad because it assumed the federal government as the chief agent of social change. In sharp contrast with today, when a chorus of pious Canadians propose to save Confederation by pulling it to pieces or cutting it into shreds, the constitutional reformers of the 1930s were all strong federalists. It was their federalism almost as much as their socialism, which aroused Innis. He had nothing to do with the great federal Doomsday inquiry of the 1930s, the Royal Commission on Dominion–Provincial Relations. The only economic investigation of the 1930s in which he took part was Nova Scotia's Provincial Economic Inquiry of 1934 and even here he was careful to assert his own intellectual independence. The two other Commissioners signed the main report; Innis wrote a separate report, a complementary report he called it, that was mainly an economic history of Nova Scotia, with a few, relatively small specific recommendations tacked on.

LATER CAREER

The second and final period in Innis' career started with the real beginning of the World War II in the spring of 1940 and the commencement of his researches in the history of paper, printing, and the press, in the summer of the same year. This second period, which lasted only twelve years, differed markedly from the two decades that had preceded it. The range of Innis' work grew vastly larger and more ambitious. Before, his studies had been largely confined to North America; now, he seemed to appropriate the whole world and travel freely up and down the centuries of its history. He became much more deeply involved in the economic, political, and social issues of his time than he ever had been before and his criticism took on a much more pessimistic and intransigent tone. He had always dealt occasionally in generalizations and epigrams. Now the generalizations grew more frequent and sweeping, the paradoxes more daring, the conjunction of ideas and the association of events more unexpected and startling.

It seems to me that it is possible to explain the later Innis, the angry, gloomy, obscure, and overconfident Innis of the postwar period, and that the explanation is to be found partly in the radical change in his own researches and partly in the revolutionary transformation of the postwar world itself. It is difficult for historians and political scientists who now occupy the senior positions in Canadian universities to appreciate the profound impact this revolutionary transformation in world affairs had upon Innis. He lived through it all. He witnessed the British Empire's last desperate effort and the beginnings of its rapid decline. He saw the rise of the three great new Empires that were to dominate the postwar world—the United States, the Soviet Union, and the Republic of China. Canada, he realized, was passing inevitably from the light and easy obligations of an old empire to the uncompromising orders of a new one. During the war, this control took the form of an armed occupation of the Canadian North by American forces, virtually uncontrolled by the Canadian government. During the peace, it changed into a heavy diplomatic pressure that forced Canada to support American imperialistic policies in the Far East and eventually took us into the Korean War. The United Nations, under peremptory American direction, justified the Korean War and in those days Lester Pearson and the Canadian Department of External Affairs regarded the United Nations as a divine institution, created by God for the preservation of collective security and peace. Looking back now, after a lapse of nearly thirty years, we can realize how wonderfully correct they were in their confident expectations, can't we? In their eyes, the Korean War was a noble crusade for the collective system. Innis saw it for what it was, an American imperialist war decked out in a pious cloak of United Nations respectability!

These profound changes in world politics affected Innis deeply, but there was another important influence, the scope and nature of his new research, which also radically altered his outlook. Originally, pulp and paper had no doubt been conceived as another study of a Canadian staple industry, not unlike the fur trade and the fisheries; as time was to show fairly quickly it was, in fact, radically different. The fur trade and the fisheries had fairly definite limits in time and place, but once Innis had passed from pulp and paper to printing, the press and communications generally, he had entered an almost illimitable field. Communications was, in fact, an open-ended subject. It streched back into remote historical times and forward into the present and future. It was an enormous, monstrous subject and the fundamental difficulty Innis faced in tackling it was that he was almost as ignorant of the immediate present as he was of the remote past. He was no great newspaper reader, found little interest in popular periodicals, rarely listened to the radio and, of course, never saw television. His ignorance of Latin and Greek was more abysmal than his unfamiliarity with French and it is probable that before the early 1940s he had barely heard of the Greek poets, dramatists and philosphers he quoted so freely in the fourth chapter of *Empire and Communications.*

Inevitably, the new, vast work he had undertaken forced him to adopt new methods that differed radically from the old. In the past, his work had always been based on a careful study of the available documentary evidence and on comprehensive knowledge of the geographical setting. Now, neither of these solid foundations could possibly be built. It was just as impossible for him to gain a detailed knowledge of the geography of Europe and the Middle East as it was for him to acquire an intimate acquaintance with the world's modern journalism. He had no time to turn himself into a Greek or Roman historian or an Egyptian archaeologist, and he could not spend his life reading daily newspapers. What he read, in fact, was *not* daily newspapers, or Greek philosphies and dramatists, or Latin historians, but books *about* them. Every night he arrived home with a bulging briefcase. He gulped down books like a man dying of hunger and thirst. He devoured what to other scholars would have been whole libraries.

As he worked, a theory rapidly developed. The *Fur Trade* and the *Cod Fisheries* had both produced a system of assumptions, which had come to be called the staples theory, but the staples theory applied only to colonial times and to limited areas. The new communications theory that Innis now rapidly elaborated was far more grandiose in conception: it was both global and eternal in its significance. The media of communications, he came to believe, were central to the history of organized society and changes in the character of the media meant alterations, often drastic, in institutions, social organizations, and cultural values. Two main classes of media had existed from the beginning of time, each with its different qualities and influences. A heavy, durable medium, such as stone, clay-baked tablets or parchment, emphasized stability, permanence, or time. A light, easily transported material like papyrus or paper meant rapid dissemination over distance or space. A medium of communication that favored time, he believed, emphasized local initiative, respect for antiquity, and religious observance. A space-based medium encouraged secular attitudes, centralized, bureaucratic government, imperialism, and technocracy. Like Oswald Spengler and Arnold Toynbee, Innis was attempting to explain the rise and fall of civilizations, the growth and collapse of empires; unlike Toynbee and Spengler, who found complex explanations laden with diversified historical evidence, Innis relied on a simple mechanical determinant, expressed in the twin categories of space and time. He did not openly predict the downfall of western civilization, as both Spengler and Toynbee had done, but from the angry despair with which he wrote of modern times, we can hardly doubt what he believed its inevitable end would be.

In June, 1946, Innis received a letter from the administrators of the Beit Fund at Oxford University, inviting him to give six lectures on any subject in the economic history of the British Empire. Innis had nothing new that he wanted to say about the economic history of the British Empire, but he was burning to deliver himself of the great new theory of communications that had been maturing rapidly in his mind for the last few years. The Beit lectures were given two years later, in the Trinity Term of 1948, but even before that Innis had crammed the substance of his great new theory into his presidential address to the Royal Society in the spring of 1947. In the next few years, he seemed to proclaim it everywhere. He lectured at the University of Nottingham and the University of London; he gave the Sesquicentennial lectures at the University of New Brunswick. In the last six years of his life, four books of his essays and lectures were published. It was as though he was driven by the desperate necessity of compulsion to deliver his last message to a sick and troubled world. And then, the cancer, which was to end all these efforts forever, began inexorably to destroy his life.

He was that rarest of all beings in Canadian history, a genius—not a flawless and immaculate genius, but a genius whose characteristic weaknesses and imperfections, the flaws of his upbringing and training, seem almost to heighten and intensify his special and unique brilliance.

3

THE CONTRIBUTION OF H.A. INNIS TO CANADIAN SCHOLARSHIP

S. D. CLARK
University of Guelph

This paper is concerned with the contribution of Harold Innis to Canadian scholarship over a very broad front. I leave to others the assessment of his work in Canadian economic history and in the field of communications. The interest here is in the role Innis played during his lifetime in the Canadian academic community, in his teaching within the classroom and without, in encouraging and determining the direction of work in the social sciences, in establishing throughout the Canadian scholarly community standards of excellence and, finally, in defending the autonomy and freedom of action of the individual scholar and the university community. An assessment of his contribution along such lines involves a consideration of his personal qualities as a scholar even more than his work as such.

If a count were made of the number of scholars who might have been described as belonging to "the Innis School," or, as it was called, "The Toronto School of History," the number would not be great, certainly, if excluded from the count were those social scientists who in recent years have come to be influenced by his work. Only within the last six or seven years of his life were there any great number of graduate students in the Department of Political Economy at Toronto and few of those did their doctoral work under his supervision. He had little contact with graduate students in history where his influence might have been expected to be the greatest. I have often felt it was unfortunate that because of the departmental structure of the university Innis spent his years teaching students, the vast majority of whom, in economics, commerce, and finance, had little interest in economic history. The result was that no great number of students came out of Toronto over these years as followers in his line of work. Most of them, indeed, went off into the business world. Of those who pursued further study, and entered upon an academic career, many of them engaged in work in the area of economic theory or political science.

Yet it was just here, in his undergraduate course in economic history, that he came to have over the years a profound and widespread influence as a university teacher. His was a course required of all honor students in economics, political science, commerce, finance, and sociology. It came to number in the hundreds. Gathered in the front rows of the large hall in which he lectured were those with an interest in the course, while filling the back rows was that large body of students who suffered through what they thought were horribly dull lectures only because they could not graduate if they failed to gain credit for the course. Had student evaluations been in vogue at the time, Innis' course would surely have got a very low rating!

Yet many of these very students who at the time had so little interest in what Innis was teaching them came in later years to think of him as their greatest teacher. At social gatherings made up largely of business people, when the conversation turned to the University of Toronto, the first name almost invariably that came forward was that of Innis. What was evident was not only how much such former graduates of the university came to realize they had learned in Innis' course but also that from this course they had gone out with a deep respect for the university scholar. If the university of the 1930s and 1940s enjoyed the high regard of a great number of influential people in the Toronto community, that regard was owing more than a little to Innis' influence as a teacher. For these people Innis represented very much what was truly a university.

For most of these students the contact with Innis extended over no more than one year. In the years after World War II, however, the number of students going on to graduate study in the Department of Political Economy vastly increased, and most of the students enrolled in the doctoral program took Innis' graduate seminar. The seminar sessions seldom varied in format. Papers were prepared and presented by various students in turn. Vigorous discussion ensued. Yet throughout Innis said very little. There was no expounding on his part; no effort to present, certainly in any systematic manner, his ideas. A pointed remark now and then constituted what appeared to be his total contribution to the discussion. It was, however, his very presence that made participation in the seminar a unique intellectual experience. Every student in the seminar felt called upon to put forward his or her best. It was here, perhaps more than anywhere else, that the graduate student learned what was involved in the exercise of scholarship.

It is in terms very similar that can be assessed Innis' contribution as a teacher at large during the slightly more than thirty years he was at the University of Toronto. He did have students occupying the front rows of the hall in which he lectured because of their interest in what he was teaching. It was here, certainly in the classroom that one gained the fullest appreciation of the range of his thought. There was no flippancy, either in what he said or in his manner of presentation. Indeed, I recall on one occasion he prefaced what he wanted to say with the remark, "At the risk of making this lecture interesting. . . ." The message he clearly conveyed was that scholarship was a serious business, involving hard work and hard thinking. It was in no sense a game for dilettantes. Perhaps no instance more vividly illustrated how seriously he assumed his obligation as a teacher than the occasion when a twenty-three-inch snowfall brought all transportation in the city to a halt and he showed up at his lecture, having walked the three miles from his home, and, as related by one of three or four students in attendance, proceeded as if nothing out of the ordinary had occurred.

Innis was a shy man, awkward of manners, who was little given to light conversation. While, in the company of men, he loved to tell the off-color joke, he almost invariably muffed the punch line. In social gatherings, particularly in his own home, he stimulated and directed conversation by asking questions, very seldom himself entering into discussion. He had little capacity to state abstract ideas coherently. Thus, in conversation with him, one was almost always left somewhat puzzled about what he was getting at. It was a matter of seizing upon particular remarks and attempting to relate them to what appeared to be the general trend of his thinking. To some extent, this difficulty in communicating ideas may have accounted for the fact that he developed about him no body of disciples. He set out no clear blueprints that could be followed by others. In truth, however, the very last thing he would have wanted was to build up a body of disciples. His every effort was directed to encouraging one to think on one's own. To him any espousal of a cause, or subscribing to an ideological position, imposed limits upon independence of thought. The result was an extreme reticence on his part to give expression to his own ideas. The freedom to think, without constraints of any sort, was to him the necessary condition for true scholarly effort. It was his continuous encouragement of such intellectual inquiry that made him, for all who came in contact with him, a great teacher.

Innis the teacher had all the diffidence of the scholar, never with such a feeling of certainty about his ideas that he was prepared to press them on others. Innis the social scientist, however, accepting a responsibility for the development of the social sciences in the country, was far from diffident about expressing, and, indeed, pressing his views. It was a very different kind of Innis one encountered in discussions relating to what scholars were worthy of support in their research endeavors, who should be brought on in the way of appointment or promotion, how the involvement of certain persons in political activity or the search for the good life had led to their abandonment of scholarly effort. In such discussions there was a forthrightness that could be almost brutal in the assessment of people. Modest to an extreme when engaged in intellectual discourse, he recognized nevertheless the simple fact that he was the leading scholar in the social sciences in the country and as such had a responsibility to exert his influence in their development. He was conscious of his power, and had no hesitation in using it, as he frankly admitted in many conversations I had with him over the years.

There were not a great number of distinguished scholars about whom the social sciences in Canada could boast back in the 1930s. H. F. Angus in British Columbia, G. A. Elliott in Alberta, R. MacG. Dawson in Saskatchewan, R. McQueen in Manitoba, H. A. Logan in Western Ontario, A. Brady with Innis in Toronto, W. A. Mackintosh in Queens, C. A. Dawson in McGill came close to comprising the total list of economists, political scientists and sociologists who had made their mark in Canadian academic circles. Certainly, no great body of work had come forward in the social sciences, particularly work relating to Canada. Before Innis, the writings of Adam Shortt stood out as the single important contribution to Canadian economic history. Mackintosh was almost alone in the development of a concern about problems of the Canadian economy, as was R. MacG. Dawson in the development of a concern about problems of the Canadian political system. What certainly was much wanted was the kind of leadership Innis could offer.

It would not be correct to say that the great move forward in the development of the social sciences in Canada in the 1930s was wholly owing to the leadership Innis provided. The two major projects of the decade, Canadian Frontiers of Settlement, and Relations of Canada and the United States, grew out of the efforts of a number of scholars of whom Innis was only one, and it was these projects and, later in the decade, the Royal Commission on Dominion–Provincial Relations in which Innis was in no way involved, that stimulated in an important way research in the social sciences. Nevertheless, it was with this development in the social sciences in the 1930s that Innis' position of influence was firmly established. He became recognized by the Carnegie Endowment for International Peace and the Rockefeller Foundation as the scholar in

Canada to turn to for counsel in the distribution of research funds in the country, and these strengthening connections with research foundations and other bodies outside the country led to a strengthening of his influence within the country. Some universities came to rely almost wholly upon his advice in the staffing of their departments of economics and an increasing number of scholars became heavily indebted to him for his support, whether with respect to their appointment or promotion or their receipt of research grants.

Not everyone, it has to be said, took kindly to this growing influence of Innis in Canadian academic circles. In his own university, outside the department of Political Economy and within, and in more than one university across the country, there was no little resentment about the kind of power he came to wield. Talk within University of Toronto circles of "the Bloor Street Empire," or in academic circles beyond of Toronto pretensions to a position of dominance had pointed reference to the influence Innis had come to exert in the area of university politics. It was no easy row he undertook to hoe in his determined effort to raise the standard of social science scholarship in the country. Harsh judgments about the worth of particular scholars or social science departments were not calculated to endear him to those who failed to win his favorable regard.

Not always was the resentment directed at Innis motivated by the feeling that he had been unfair in his judgments. There was among many scholars an honest questioning of the direction he was pushing the social sciences. He remained firmly committed to the concept of political economy; it was he, on becoming head, who had changed the name of the department from that of Political Science to Political Economy. He thus vigorously resisted any effort to detach economics (and sociology) from an historically oriented social science that embraced economic history and political theory. Within the department, and even more in economic departments in some of the other universities, there was a strong feeling that the influence exerted by Innis had the effect of crippling the development of the discipline of economics.

Certainly, whatever the consequences, Innis succeeded in making the department of Political Economy in Toronto during his lifetime a distinguished center of economic history scholarship. Given his presence in the department, it could scarcely be otherwise. As well, he gave to the department a character that made it congenial for scholars in other disciplines who had an historical or philosophical orientation in their approach, such as V. W. Bladen in economics, C. A. Ashley in commerce and finance, A. Brady and C. B. Macpherson in political science, and myself in sociology.

How sociology in Toronto became a part of the department of

Political Economy is revealing of the kind of influence exerted by Innis in the development of the social sciences. Sociology in Toronto could well have followed the direction taken by sociology at McGill, with its close ties with the University of Chicago. Had the views of E. A. Bott, head of the Department of Psychology and a member of the committee in charge of the honors program in sociology, prevailed, such was the direction it would have taken. E. J. Urwick, however, the founder of the sociology honors program and chairman of the committee, had all the disdain of the English scholar for American sociology and when the first full-time appointment in sociology was to be made he, with Innis' strong support, succeeded in securing my appointment over a University of Chicago trained sociologist sponsored by Bott. The attachment of sociology to the Department of Political Economy the year after my appointment assured that the direction of its development would be determined largely by Innis.

Elsewhere I have commented on the consequences of this tie of sociology in Toronto to the Department of Political Economy.[1] Suffice it here to say that it was owing largely to Innis' sponsorship that sociology in Canada began to assume an image of respectability. The Canadian academic community was not yet ready to accept the kind of Chicago-oriented sociology represented by McGill, and thus it was to Toronto that such universities as Manitoba, Saskatchewan, and New Brunswick turned in making sociology appointments during the 1940s. Though Innis came to appreciate the work being carried on by C. A. Dawson in McGill, he continued to the end to view with disfavor American sociology as he had come to know it. As his own interest in sociological problems strengthened, as reflected in the program of reading for his graduate seminar in economic history, it was the sociology of scholars such as Weber, Pareto, Mosca, and Mannheim that commanded attention.

By the mid-1940s, Innis certainly had become the dominant figure in the social sciences in Canada. Even those social scientists who resented the kind of influence he at times exerted recognized his scholarly preeminence and hastened to seek his opinion and, they hoped, his approval of work on which they were engaged. It was just here, in the establishment of standards of excellence in scholarly performance, that Innis' influence in the development of the social sciences in Canada had its greatest impact.

His contribution to scholarly work in Canada, however, went far beyond the social sciences. It was Innis the scholar, not Innis the economic historian, who came to be known and regarded with respect throughout a large part of the Canadian academic community. The academic community was not as large in his time as it is now. There were few scholars in the humanities and even, indeed, in the sciences who did not know him. He stood out in more ways than height at gatherings of the Royal Society of Canada, the Canadian Political Science Association, and the Canadian Historical Association. If only a small number of persons at such gatherings could fully comprehend what he was expounding in a paper he may have presented—his "Minerva's Owl," for instance, presented as his presidential address to the Royal Society—his stature as a scholar was never questioned. In informal meetings on such occasions, his opinion and advice were sought, whether about a scholarly work or a matter of university administration.

Innis, it has to be said, could be generous in the time he devoted to the concerns of others because of his capacity to work with amazing speed. He could read and make meticulous notes on a lengthy book in a few short hours. There were not many people who could have engaged in their lifetime in the critical appraisal of the work of so many scholars and still have accomplished what he did. I would question whether anyone who ever requested Innis' opinion about a manuscript they had prepared failed to get it back within two or three days with detailed criticisms. Very often, on his own campus, a lengthy manuscript delivered to him one day would be returned the next morning. It would be impossible to estimate the number of scholarly works, papers, and full-length manuscripts, in economics, economic history, political science, history, sociology, and the humanities, that over the years were subjected to Innis' critical appraisal.

The kinds of criticisms he made of such work could range all the way from corrections of mistaken spellings to identification of the faulty expression of ideas. They were always helpful. It was not here, however, in his detailed criticisms of other scholars' work, that his unique contribution to Canadian scholarly activity was to be found. I can think of many colleagues whose criticisms of things I had written were more helpful than those made by Innis. What was sought from Innis was his opinion of the worth of the work being subjected to appraisal. I do not believe it is possible to exaggerate the importance of this role played by Innis. It was a young Canadian academic community in Innis' time. What was much needed was a standard by which scholars could measure the worth of their work. Innis provided such a standard. His judgments, of course, were not infallible. If anything, perhaps he erred on the side of generosity. Certainly I can recall at least one occasion when he came later to realize that the good opinion he had expressed about a particular study was not warranted. It could be, however, a rigorous test of the worth of their work, which scholars subjected themselves to in seeking Innis' opinion. The great move forward in Canadian scholarly work during Innis' lifetime was owing not a little to the high standard of performance he established.

It was, however, beyond simply the quality of scholarly work that Innis made his influence felt. He offered in his person a model of the true scholar, dedicated to the advancement of scholarly work and jealous of any interference, whether from university administrations or governments, with the free pursuit of knowledge. On issues relating to academic freedom he held strong views and never hesitated to give expression to them. He could, for instance, meet the president of his university of the campus and, while still thirty feet off, greet him with "God damn you," repeated over and over again until the two men came together. Or, on another occasion, it took only a one-sentence letter to make known to the chairman of a committee of the Canadian Social Science Research Council how strongly he disapproved of a particular action taken by the committee. The letter in its entirety read: "I don't like what your god-damned committee is doing and I hereby resign from your god-damned committee."

The scoldings administered on these two occasions related to issues about which Innis felt deeply. Not always was the language he used so strong, but however expressed no one could be left in doubt about his views. Over the years, university presidents, faculty deans, department heads, directors of foundations, persons in the public service all anxiously sought his opinion on various matters. However cryptic might be the comment of his on a particular question, all of those who became associated with him learned the true meaning of scholarship and the proper role of the university in society. Any biographer of Sidney Smith would be bound to take account of how much Smith owed to Innis in his growing stature as a university president. In my very last conversation with Smith he offered a testimony of his debt.

In these terms one cannot help but think how sorely a scholar such as Innis was wanted during those troubled years in our universities after 1968. Any reflection along such lines, however, leads almost inevitably to the conclusion that the events of those years would have come near destroying him. Almost everything that occurred in the university ran sharply counter to those principles of scholarly conduct to which he so passionately adhered. Perhaps no development of recent years would he have found more distasteful than the effort to seize upon his work to further the claims of a particular ideological position in the social sciences. I wonder, indeed, what he would have thought of a book such as this one, seeking to make more of his work than he would have felt it warranted.

I return to the opening theme of this paper, but now on a note of a more personal character. I first met Innis sometime in the year 1932–33 on the occasion of a trip he made to London, England. I invited him to a debate between Professors Laski and Webster at the London School of Economics on something to do with Hobbes. On attending the debate I was distressed to find that Hobbes was not the political theorist but an English cricket player and that Laski and Webster had reversed their ideological positions, with Laski arguing for the preservation of traditional values respecting an issue relating to some sort of change of cricket rules. Innis thoroughly enjoyed the debate. This was a side of Innis only those people who got to know him well could fully appreciate. He was in his way a fun-loving person. He was, also, very much a person with warm human feelings, enjoying to the full the companionship of friends, of whom he had a great many. In the end, no full assessment of his contribution to Canadian scholarship can be made without taking account of his personal qualities as a man. If he won great respect for himself as a scholar, he won no less respect for himself as a person.

NOTES

[1]In a paper presented to a seminar at Carleton University, March 17, 1978, entitled "The Changing Image of Sociology in Canada."

4

THE AMBIVALENT VERDICT: HAROLD INNIS AND CANADIAN HISTORY

WILLIAM WESTFALL
York University

Any evaluation of the place of Harold Innis in Canadian history must consider carefully two closely related themes that run through his work. One is tied directly to the study of the history of Canada. Innis' own research and writing articulated new ways of perceiving Canada and consequently opened new fields of study for Canadian historians. Writing in 1929, Innis lamented the fact that Canadian scholars did not have a "philosophy of economic history or economic theory suited to Canada's needs."[1] The "Staples Thesis" filled this vacuum not only for Innis and economic historians but also for writers in a number of academic disciplines. His success in this area of his work was witnessed by the way the staples thesis entered into the mythic levels of Canadian thought and helped to reorganize the way Canada was understood as a nation.

The second theme is more general. Innis was vitally concerned with history, research, and scholarship as questions in themselves. Here his work centered on what he termed "bias," especially the impact of bias on the social sciences and the university. He tried to confront a major theoretical problem in the social sciences and, although his solution was not totally compelling, it was nonetheless provocative. Innis also assumed a major presence in the day-to-day life of scholarly writing in Canada. He helped to establish journals, academic organizations, and research institutes. His help as an editor, supervisor, and friend must have placed a whole generation of younger scholars in his debt.[2]

The importance of his contribution in both areas of his work was confirmed by the unique and powerful position that Innis attained within the institutional structure of Canadian academic life. As chairman of the Department of Political Economy in the University of Toronto, and then as Dean of the Graduate School in the same institution, Innis was able to initiate, oversee, and in large measure, control the course of research within a wide area. At a time when Toronto had almost no rivals in Canada at the graduate level, he tried to make the university live up to what he regarded as a national duty to expand research, to create Canadian scholars, and to place these scholars in Canadian institutions. While the phrase "Toronto School" would become something of a term of disapprobation (especially in the hinterlands), the institutional reality that sustained it was largely the creation of Innis.[3]

At the time of his death in 1952, many of Innis' colleagues acknowledged in their praise the substantial contribution that he had made. His work, John Bartlet Brebner testified, laid "the cornerstone of a new structure in Canadian intellectual life."[4] "Beyond his writings," W. A. Mackintosh added, "his interest in and generosity toward other and younger scholars have left a heritage which will increase and spread through the years."[5] Writing almost twenty-five years later, Carl Berger portrayed Innis as one of the most creative and original figures in the history of Canadian intellectual life.[6] Innis seems to have been able to alter the context of which he was a part, leaving a new starting point for those who would come after.

Yet the Innis inheritance in the field of Canadian history is a decidedly ambivalent one. He has remained something of an icon: his influence is at times ritualistically acknowledged and of late he has enjoyed the honor of being born again.[7] When one looks more closely at what has become of the Innis contribution, one is forced to stress the discontinuity that seems to characterize the relationship between Innis and those who came after him. His methodologies and insights have neither been systematically developed nor rationally criticized; his work on the nature of history, scholarship, and the university has been almost totally ignored while his way of seeing Canada itself has been altered and then replaced. He has been avoided rather than followed. Innis' work and his institutional position gave him a commanding prospect from which one might have expected him to influence the course of Canadian academic life but his inheritance is comparatively meager. Canadian history chose to follow a different path.

Innis' place in Canadian history rests to a large extent upon what has become known as the "staples thesis." Although the thesis deserves to be scrutinized very critically, it was in Innis' hands a sophisticated and complex instrument that was able to integrate and explain a wide variety of historical material. It stressed the way a particular physical environment—the characteristics of the staple and the system used to exploit it—had impressed a certain pattern on Canadian development. The thesis also provided a way of examining the relationship between various elements in the historical process, especially social structure, politics, and the economic system. It located all these elements within a dynamic imperial system characterized by a disequilibrium between metropolitan centers and their hinterlands.

The breadth of the thesis also emphasized the need for a large measure of unity within Canadian scholarship. Staples illuminated the ties between government, business, and society, and consequently linked economics to geography, political science, and sociology. And it tied all of them to the study of Canadian history.

The staples approach had important implications for both the content and the structure of the interpretation of Canadian history. By focusing upon the features of the material environment, staples tried to get below the surface of the political and constitutional narrative in order to find the more substantial dynamics that underlay Canadian history. In this sense the staples thesis substituted a material narrative for an idealistic one. Instead of recounting the gradual unfolding of an idea or a series of ideas (such as political liberty, responsive government, and autonomy) in a constitutional or biographical framework, it turned history toward the study of the on-going ramifications of a body of material factors in a geopolitical and economic setting. Cold facts and determinism seemed to replace grand ideas and romance.

The staples thesis also altered the way historians might organize this material. The traditional themes in Canadian history were political in character and national or imperial in outlook. The story that they told was divided into parts by a number of key events (for the most part of a constitutional nature), and was then organized within a progressive framework. The conquest, responsible government, confederation, national expansion, and Dominion status marked the progress of Canada from a primitive beginning to a mature present. Staples did not reject this structure completely. The same political events often remained, but now they could be explained as reflections of a deeper commercial process. The succession of staples themselves—fish, fur, timber, and wheat—became an important (if somewhat hidden) organizing device. In addition, the staples narrative did not rely on the march of progress in the same way as the older story. Growth and development did not necessarily mean improvement. One could not categorize the early period as a dark age when it set the pattern for the whole story. In addition, the pattern of staple production itself was highly vulnerable. The transition from one period to the next was neither simple nor straightforward. A staples system would spring up, race ahead, and then come crashing down. There were often periods of great depression and dislocation before the cycle might begin again.

The staples thesis also contributed to a new understanding of the nature of Canada itself. It seemed to provide academics and a larger public with a new raison d'être for the existence of the Canadian nation–state. For many years, conventional wisdom maintained that Canada was created in defiance of the physical features of the North American continent. The academic roots of this attitude lay in part with the anti-Canadian thesis of Goldwin Smith,[8] in part with the type of environmentalism that one associates with the frontier school. On a popular level, this view of Canada reflected the longevity of the Gothic spirit that often associated physical nature with human nature. The ability of man to suffer through the wilderness of a harsh physical climate became a metaphor of salvation: a historical representation of the ability of man to escape from the wilderness of his own fallen nature. Consequently, the struggle against a hostile enviromnent (the north) was a positive feature of Canadian life, and the triumph over the obstacles thrown up by nature (by the building of railroads) proved conclusively the righteousness of the national undertaking.[9] Innis himself had worked within certain elements of this older national mythology when he wrote his *History of the Canadian Pacific Railway.*

The final twenty pages of *The Fur Trade in Canada*, however, altered this mythic structure. By reworking the relationship between Canada, nature, and historical time, Innis seemed to demonstrate that the Canadian nation was a "natural" geographic unit—the logical sequel to the economic system that the fur trade has worked out over a century before. He justified the existence of Canada by appealing to history, nature, and science; and science provided for that generation a more secure foundation than romance for a credible national mythology.

Many of the implications of the staples approach for the interpretation of Canadian history were pursued during Innis' lifetime or shortly after his death. The staples trades themselves provided an obvious starting point for historical scholarship. From staples, the focus could expand to the relationship between staple development, national social and economic policies, and political protest movement.[10] Staples also supplied the foundation for new theories of social creation that in turn provided a number of insights into the sociology of radical political parties and religious organizations.[11] Staples even had a hand in literary criticism. The European penetration into the center of a continent that accompanied the fur trade presented one noted critic with at least a symbolic explanation for the unique psychic matrix that colors so many of the central concerns of Canadian literature.[12]

Under the influence of Innis' work, Canadian historical writing in

general shifted away from a north–south orientation in order to empha-
size more emphatically the importance of the east–west dimensions of
Canadian development, both within Canada and in her relations with
Europe.[13] The spine of this east–west dimension, the St. Lawrence–
Great Lakes system, became a new organizing metaphor in Canadian
historiography. The early work of Donald Creighton, especially his book
The Commercial Empire of the St. Lawrence, established most forcefully this
"Laurentian" interpretation.[14] Here Creighton was able to integrate geography, politics, and economics within a broad staples framework, to
move from seemingly insignificant material facts to draw out their transcontinental implications and then to document the rise and fall of an
entire cultural system. The work stands as one of the fullest and most
eloquent testimonies to the value of Innis' work for Canadian history.

The power of this dimension of Innis' contribution was also
marked by the way staples drew Canadian scholarship as a whole into a
common orbit. In the last decade of his life, it is singularly difficult to
distinguish clearly between Canadian political economy, history, sociology, and cultural anthropology. All were historical in orientation and all
relied on approaches that rested on some of the insights that Innis had
provided.

By the time of Innis' death, as academics reworked the implications
of Innis' scholarship and moved away from the general thrust of the
staples approach, this sense of unity began to break down. The course of
Canadian historical writing is most instructive. The "Laurentian" approach, which had become something of a new orthodoxy of Canadian
history, secured itself on one idea that it credited to Innis and moved
away from other elements of his canon. Laurentianism stressed above all
else the geographical unity of Canada and became essentially "rivers and
streams" history. In Creighton's later work on both John A. Macdonald
and Confederation, the word "Laurentian" seemed to connote a vision
of national unity in search of becoming a political reality. It served as a
criterion against which one could judge the significance (and moral hon-
esty) of the central players. Those who saw the possibilities of Canadian
geography merited praise; those who did not deserved the severest criticism.

The work of Professor J. M. S. Careless expanded Laurentianism
into "metropolitanism" in order to draw ideological and cultural elements into the European–British North American axis. But in this transformation, the links to Innis' own work were blurred. Metropolitanism
appeared to tie into the metropolis–hinterland relationship that was so
vital to Innis; yet, metropolitanism was primarily a theory of social, political, and cultural development that focused on the center (the process of
urban expansion) rather than the edge (the impact of the city on the

hinterland). The link between metropolis and hinterland (the staple economy) and the imbalance between these two elements were not central to this revised methodology.

More significantly, the form of Canadian historical writing changed. The main work of Creighton and Careless, the two historians whose presence seemed to dominate historical scholarship in the post-Innis period, was biographical in nature. Creighton's *Macdonald* and Careless' *Brown* were without doubt outstanding achievements, but they also represented a movement away from the material elements of political economy to the lives of men, and especially politicians. It was this biographical focus that would characterize to an incredible degree the new historical work of the generation who would come into prominence in the 1960s. With a few exceptions, all the doctoral theses in Canadian history that were successfully passed in the Department of History at the University of Toronto in the years after Innis' death were political in orientation and most often biographical in focus. This, of course, does not mean that all of them eschewed Innis but, in the department where one might have expected Innis to have had a sustained and powerful influence, his inheritance was, in practice, relatively weak.[15]

In sum, the shifts in the interpretation of Canadian history that one associates with Innis' work were significant, not only for historians but for scholars in other disciplines as well. Nonetheless, these shifts were limited in both time and extent. The material thrust of political economy did not find a secure place in Canadian history. Staples were acknowledged, but they were integrated into another type of story; history used staples without the staples thesis. When one looked into the near future, one saw an older past. The implications of the Innis contribution were wide-ranging but his inheritance was much more restricted.

The second broad dimension of the Innis contribution to Canadian history shared a similar fate. In addition to his commitment to research into the specific features of Canadian history, Innis was also deeply concerned with the craft of history itself, especially with questions of historical scholarship and the problems that scholarship had to confront in the modern university. The answers he tried to present to these issues represents a significant contribution to the theoretical levels of Canadian history. But his inheritance is once again an ambivalent one. Canadian historians in general have neither used his methods nor attempted to develop his insights. In fact, they have rarely even addressed the same question.

Innis' work here focused on what he termed "bias." He began with a specific problem and ended with what was almost a theory of social and cultural analysis. This was the issue. The world that one studied could not be regarded as simply a conglomeration of facts that one could analyze objectively according to the traditional methods of the social sciences. "Facts" reflected a series of values; facts were biased by a level of cultural factors that were subjective in nature. Furthermore, the social scientist was personally biased by the cultural assumptions of the environment.[16]

In a broader perspective, this problem was one aspect of a larger philosophical and methodological issue—the shortcomings of rational empirical science especially in relation to the study of religious phenomena—that a number of disciplines were trying to confront.[17] Innis, like many others, had to deal with his problem on both an abstract and a personal level. He sought to establish a methodology that would allow the social sciences to study the world objectively, and he tried to find a way for the social scientist to escape the pull of the social environment so that he or she might gain a measure of freedom in order to be able to employ the methodology that Innis was trying to develop.

In many respects the issue of "bias" was a singularly appropriate one for the son of a devout Baptist household who was always intrigued by theological questions and seriously considered answering a call to the ministry. The emphasis that he gave to determinism, objectivity, and rigorous self-examination seems to form a pattern. Carl Berger has suggested that Innis tried to understand the extent of bias so that he might understand the areas of freedom.[18] If one were to read predestination for bias, and free will for objectivity and freedom, then Innis' concern with bias becomes a secular reflection of the way Protestants, and especially Baptists, have devoted one of the central questions in their faith—what was the place of individual free will in God's plan for the history of the world.

Innis tried to solve the problem of bias by making the problem itself into a part of the solution. He made necessity into a virtue. He accepted the fact that both sides of the subject/object relationship were shaped by bias, but, he then made bias the subject matter of social scientific analysis. There were patterns, Innis argued, in the way that bias influenced cultures. These patterns provided the elements of continuity and predictability that were so essential for constructing scientifically sound statements. To rescue objectivity, one should study the shape of subjectivity: The only element in society that was not relative, Innis seemed to argue, was relativity itself.

These patterns of bias, Innis continued, were themselves a reflection of another series of relationships that were tied to social processes that could be studied empirically. His representation of the social system was constructed on hierarchy of levels. Below the visible surface of social reality was a system of bias, and below this system of bias was a set of what might be called primal cultural factors. Contemporary society, for example, was biased by a certain attitude toward time that in turn could be understood in relation to a system of communication. And from the bias of communication one could range over the entire history of man.

This approach provided a way of dealing with bias in the external world but, as Innis realized, this represented only one half of the solution. It did not address directly the difficulties presented by the impact of bias on the observer. The fact that one studies bias does not make one immune from it. Consequently, Innis incorporated into his analysis of bias a study of the specific context in which the observer existed and in which scientific analysis took place.

For Innis this context was the university, or more specifically the graduate school. Consequently, he continually argued that these academic institutions must be able to withstand all the social, political, and economic influences that bias the structure of knowledge. The university must remain an unbiased haven so that the objective study of bias might flourish within it. He invested in the university the same sacred character that his Victorian ancestors had placed in the institutions of Ontario Protestantism. The graduate school, like the church, might be in the world, but it was not of it. It drew its essence from a source of knowledge that was above time and place.

Innis' solution to the problem of bias contains a number of difficulties, but the analytical correctness of his position is not at issue. What is singularly important here is the way Innis emphasized, in his study of bias, the value of history as a discipline. Within the discipline there was little awareness, Innis believed, of the historical forces that underlay and continually altered that structure.[19] It dealt with bias by saying in effect that the problem did not exist.

Innis' own work stressed most emphatically the cultural significance of historical time. His epistemology was evolutionary in structure and his understanding of man emphasized the way man was subject to the processes of historical environment. He tried to examine the patterns that underlay contemporary events, and he used history to try to provide a unified approach to the study of Canada—her geography, politics, economic development, social structure, and culture.

When one turns from the work of Innis in this area to the work of the Canadian historians who followed him, one finds again a very ambivalent inheritance. Perhaps some of his conclusions deserve to be passed over for they were bound to enjoy only a limited lifetime. Even if one were to make allowances for the time in which they were set down, some of his pronouncements still seem naive. He invested so much in the ability of the university to withstand external forces and in the unsullied determination of scholars to pursue truth (as he understood it) that he was bound to be disappointed.

In another sense, when Canadian historians ignore this aspect of Innis' work, they are abandoning a coherent, and at times, rich body of insights into the craft of history and its role in society. In Canadian culture the study of history has served an important role as a vehicle for social analysis and social criticism. Innis tried to refurbish and strengthen this relationship by placing contemporary issues in a complex historical context; by using history both as the subject matter for study and as a tool for social analysis; and by examining the relationship between history, historians, and culture. His conclusions might not have been compelling but they were systematic.

At the present time this type of question is scarcely even addressed. History has been removed from social analysis and social criticism. Few discuss the cultural role of the university in any depth. Scholarship has become a singularly promiscuous notion. It has been abstracted from a systematic view of society, knowledge, and man; it has become synonymous with specialization and departmentalization within a professionalized university. We have succumbed to the very pressures that Innis had worked so hard to oppose.

The bridges that Innis had built through history to a number of disciplines were also dismantled. The attacks came from statistics and static models of social analysis. Economics tended to follow the former away from history toward quantification; sociology, in spite of the spirited sorties of S. D. Clark on the structural functionalism of Talcott Parsons,[20] succumbed to the latter. History lost its place as the discipline that was to organize the study of Canada as a whole. It moved away from both a theoretical and a generalist orientation. It retreated into a commonsense empiricism—a display of the facts so that they might speak for themselves.

The question of bias lives on in Canadian historical scholarship in a unique and somewhat ironical form. Only in Canadian intellectual history, and more specifically in Canadian historiography, does one find more than an echo of the Innis methodology. This type of historical scholarship acknowledges the fact that history is an interpretive discipline. It accepts cultural bias as an eternal feature of the scholarly process, and it employs bias as a vital tool for historical analysis. It also seeks to find the deeper patterns—the systems of thought—that underlie the surface of the written record.[21] Innis was continually turning his analysis of bias upon his own assumptions. It is perhaps fitting then that many of his techniques and orientations should be turned by intellectual historians upon both the man and his work, and that this approach should lead to one of the most balanced assessments of the man and his work.[22]

Some might regard the fact that intellectual historians have descended upon the corpus of Innis' work as a sure sign of the death of national history in general and Innis' contribution in particular. Certainly, the Innis inheritance is a very ambivalent one. The historical synthesis and the methodology that he presented might well deserve to be criticized for being simplistic or premature. His statements on history, bias, and scholarship could well be criticized for being incomplete or impossibly demanding, but the Innis contribution met a different fate. For the most part it has been avoided or passed over.

This ambivalence of the Innis inheritance in Canadian historical scholarship reflects, at least in part, the changing relationship between the historian and the subject matter, between the writers of national history and the Canadian nation–state. At the start of Innis' career, the two seemed to be in harmony and their prospects were very bright. Along with a number of others in his generation, Innis tried to rework the structure of the national mythology in order to explain in contemporary language the character of this rising nation. In many respects he was singularly successful. He articulated a philosophy of development and propagated a methodology that a number of disciplines could use to explore various features of Canada's history. He was also able to support Canadian scholars and to provide the institutional apparatus that could promote Canadian scholarship on an on-going and systematic basis.

In the 1950s and 1960s, however, the national orientation in Canadian history underwent a number of changes. The national mythology altered its focus, and then the national dimension of the mythology began to pass slowly out of fashion. In 1954, when Professor J. M. S. Careless published his seminal historiographical article, "Frontierism, Metropolitanism, and Canadian History,"[23] he was able to list and analyze a series of national schools (including Laurentianism) and then outline with confidence yet another national school, metropolitanism, that he regarded as an extension and an elaboration of the staples approach. The broad pattern of the development of national history appeared to be self-evident; national schools would rework earlier national schools in an unending evolutionary pattern.

The new pattern did not hold. Metropolitanism did not become the new national synthesis that Professor Careless had anticipated. Historians turned away from articulating broad interpretive frameworks such as the staples thesis. The national impulse was still in evidence, but in an altered form. The national content of national history was no longer to be found in the interiors of social and economic structures but in the realm of psychology. It shifted from the study of staples to the search for a national identity, from the analysis of the nation's political economy to the study of the lives of her political leaders.

At that time the national impulse itself came under attack. Professor Careless, along with other Canadian academics, challenged some of the central assumptions that underlay national historiography, at least in its biographical form. He wondered whether there was such a thing as a single national identity, and suggested that much of the work written from this point of view was teleological rather than historical. Our national character, he suggested, might reside in out limited identities, and he pointed scholars toward regional studies as an alternative to national ones.[24] In addition, many historians simply began to ignore the whole debate. They implicitly rejected either national or regional frameworks, because their scholarly interests were not served by these categories. Research went in a number of directions as historians turned to social questions such as class, women, education, religion, ethnicity, and violence.

The decline in the power of the national orientation in Canadian historical scholarship was matched by a rapid change in the character of Canada itself. The exploitation of certain staples, Innis argued, had created Canada. He also knew that the exploitation of different staples might destroy it. Canada itself—the staple of national history—proved to be, in Innis' eyes, a very vulnerable enterprise. A national historian had to witness the subject matter separating itself from his or her own interpretative structure, the historian had to witness what was perceived to be the imminent collapse of his or her own social and cultural context. In fact, the historian tried to analyze this process personally by studying communications and culture. The pessimistic tone that pervades this part of Innis' work is indicative of the nature of his outlook on the future.

This pessimism, nevertheless, has proved to be one of the few enduring features of the Innis inheritance. Innis tied systems of communication to the growth of empires, and he saw the impact of these forces in cultural and humanistic terms. His own bias, as he so often stated, valued a culture characterized by balance, order, and the oral tradition. His analysis of the problem and his attachment to these human, nontechnological values set a course that a number of Canadian nationalists would follow. He beheld the decline and fall of a meaningful culture, and he was bitter as he faced defeat. One can hear the echoes of his lamentations in the work of George Grant, Donald Creighton, and Dennis Lee.[25]

The discussion of the place of Harold Innis in Canadian history should not end on a pessimistic note. While the Innis inheritance is an ambivalent one, he still remains one of the few God-like figures in Canadian scholarship. He is the type of person that each generation should come back to on a number of different levels. His contribution still stands as an extraordinary, if relatively unused, resource for Canadian historians.

It is a resource that some of the "new" directions in historical scholarship would do well to consult. The recent outbreak of regional studies provides a good example. Regionalism seems to begin from a position that is the antithesis of the one set out by Innis. It is often antinationalist in intent; it focuses on the parts of Canada rather than the whole; and it tends to argue that regions predate the nation–state both historically and culturally. In Canada, we have strong regions with strong regional identities and a weak nation–state with weak national identities. The regional picture of Canada is, in fact, quite similar to the one Goldwin Smith set down in 1891—Canada was a land of regions separated by physical barriers, in which the regions share very little with one another.

While the Innis inheritance has been associated with the "discovery" of the geographical unity of Canada, his work in fact provides many important insights into the structure of Canadian regionalism. It is especially valuable in an area in which the new regionalism is quite weak—the historical relationship between the regions of Canada and the Canadian nation–state. The unity of Canada, Innis argued, was not tied to the physical features of the land, but to a way certain features of landscape could be used in relation to a specific type of economic enterprise. Other types of enterprise could lead to different "geographical" configurations. Boundaries—whether national or regional—were not "in the land" but rather tied to the character of staple production. Furthermore, Innis stressed the way economic and social systems developed in relation to metropolitan centers of capital and enterprise, and how the metropolitan centers were able to control the character of the social, political, and economic development in their hinterlands.

These insights, far from denying the existence of regions in Canada, suggest a way of constructing the regional framework on a more analytical basis. If one sees regions in terms of hinterlands, then it is hard to maintain that regions developed in relative isolation, or that the national government was weak. It seems especially true that the regional character of the west was shaped by the power of forces external to it. Railroads, tariffs, and immigration were imposed on the area. The existence of strong regions, then, might connote a wealth of power rather than weakness at the national level. National policies may in fact have been regional policies.

Innis' work also places the "new regionalism" in its proper cultural context. Both the new regionalism, especially in literature, and the old nationalism of Harold Innis share a common starting point. Both begin with question of myth and identity. Regional writing is presently preoccupied with the relationship between form and place, especially within a colonial context. Writers such as Kroetsch, Mandel, and Harrison are searching for ways to tell the story of the West in its own terms.[26] They reject what they regard as imported forms and language. Innis sought a paradigm that would accomplish the same purpose for the history of Canada as a whole. He found that paradigm by focusing upon the tensions that defined the problem itself—the tension between the metropolis and the hinterland, the tension between what was inside and what was outside. As Innis did so often, he fashioned from the problem the key to solving it. The same insight might be valuable for the people trying to come to grips artistically with regional cultures and regional identities. The tension that sparked the interest in regionalism might provide the metaphors for understanding the regional experience.

The task of locating and reworking the myths of our culture is performed by each suceeding generation. Innis began his search more than fifty years ago. It is important that we remember that someone of his stature has passed over this gound before us.

ACKNOWLEDGMENT

I would like to acknowledge the encouragement and help that Carl Berger of the University of Toronto gave to me at the start of this enterprise, and the criticisms and comments with which Joe Ernst of York University was able to help me complete it.

NOTES

[1]Innis, Harold. "The Teaching of Economic History in Canada." In Mary Q. Innis, (Ed.), *Essays in Canadian Economic History*. Toronto, University of Toronto Press, 1956, p. 3.

[2]See: Jane Ward, "The Published Works of H.A. Innis," *Canadian Journal of Economics and Political Science*, May 1953, pp. 234–244.

[3]The history of Innis' role as Dean of the Graduate School should be examined carefully, especially the way his institutional reforms continued to influence graduate work well after his death. See: School of Graduate Studies, Report of the President's Committee on Graduate Studies, 1947; SGS, University of Toronto, Statute Number 1844, Passed May 9, 1947; and H. A. Innis, "The Problem of Graduate Work," *The Canadian Social Science Research Council Third Annual Report, 1942–1943*, Ottawa, Canadian Social Science Research Council, 1944, pp. 16–19.

[4]University of Toronto Archives, Innis Papers, J. B. Brebner, "Innis as Historian," p. 6.

[5]Mackintosh, W. A. "Innis on Canadian Economic Development," *The Journal of Political Economy*, June 1953, p. 164; see also: Donald Creighton, *Harold Adams Innis: Portrait of a Scholar*, Toronto, University of Toronto Press, 1957.

[6]Berger, Carl. *The Writing of Canadian History: Aspects of English–Canadian Historical Writing, 1900–1970*. Toronto, Oxford, 1976, p. 85.

[7]There has been a recent public revival of Innis, tied in part to the twenty-fifth anniversary of his death. See: Daniel Drache, "Rediscovering Canadian Political Economy," *Journal of Canadian Studies*, August 1976; *Journal of Canadian Studies*, Winter

1977, special issue on Innis; and *Queen's Quarterly*, Winter 1977. At times one is not certain exactly who this rediscovery is rediscovering. More substantial certainly and more a part of the Innis framework is Viv Nelles, *The Politics of Development*, Toronto, Macmillan, 1974.

⁸Smith, Goldwin. *Canada and the Canadian Question*. Toronto, Hunter Ross, 1891.

⁹For example: G. M. Grant. *Canada and the Canadian Question: A Review*, Toronto, C. B. Robinson, 1892[?]. See also: Carl Berger, "The True North Strong and Free," in Peter Russell, (Ed). *Nationalism in Canada*, Toronto, McGraw-Hill, 1966.

¹⁰For example: G. E. Britnell, The Wheat Economy, Toronto, University of Toronto Press, 1939; V. C. Fowke, *The National Policy and the Wheat Economy*, Toronto, University of Toronto Press, 1957; C. B. Macpherson, *Democracy in Alberta*, Toronto, University of Toronto Press, 1953.

¹¹See: S. D. Clark, *Church and Sect in Canada*, Toronto, University of Toronto Press, 1948; S. D. Clark, *Movements of Political Protest in Canada, 1640–1840*, Toronto, University of Toronto Press, 1959.

¹²Frye, N. "Conclusion." In Carl F. Klinck, Alfred G. Bailey, Claude Bissell, Roy Daniels, Northrup Frye, and Desmond Pacey, (Eds). *Literary History of Canada: Canadian Literature in English*. Toronto, University of Toronto Press, 1965.

¹³This reorientation can be seen within the Carnegie Series on the Relations of Canada and the United States. See: Carl C. Berger, "Internationalism, Continentalism, and the Writing of History: Comments on the Carnegie Series on the Relations of Canada and the United States." In R. A. Preston, (Ed.), *The Influence of the United States on Canadian Development: Eleven Case Studies*. Durham, Duke University Press, 1972, pp. 50, 84; and Creighton, *Harold Adams Innis*, pp. 78–80.

¹⁴Creighton, D. G. *The Commercial Empire of the St. Lawrence*, 1760–1850. Toronto, Macmillan, 1937.

¹⁵See: Judy Mills and Irene Dombra, (Eds.). *University of Toronto Theses, 1897–1967*, Toronto, University of Toronto Press, 1968; and SGS, *University of Toronto Doctoral Theses, 1968–1975: A Bibliography*, Toronto, University of Toronto Press, 1977. There were about twenty-seven doctoral theses in the department of History dealing with Canadian topics between 1953 and 1968. Only six of these were not specifically political and almost all the political topics were also biographical. The exceptions to the political and biographical trend are still significant and they include the work of Morris Zaslow, F. H. Armstrong, Carl Berger, and Michael Cross.

¹⁶See especially: H. A. Innis, "The Role of Intelligence: Some Further Notes," *Canadian Journal of Economics and Political Science*, 1935, pp. 280–286; and Leslie A. Pal, "Scholarship and the Later Innis," *Journal of Canadian Studies*, Winter 1977, p. 34.

¹⁷See: Raymond Aron, *Main Currents in Sociological Thought*, London, Weidenfeld & Nicolson, 1968, especially the introduction to Part Two.

¹⁸Berger, *The Writing of Canadian History*, p. 111.

¹⁹For example: H. A. Innis, "The Penetrative Powers of the Price System," *Canadian Journal of Economics and Political Science*, 1938, pp. 299–319.

²⁰See: S. D. Clark, "Sociology, History and the Problem of Social Change," *Canadian Journal of Economics and Political Science*, November 1959, pp. 389–400; and S. D. Clark, *The Developing Canadian Community*, Toronto, University of Toronto Press, 1962, especially Part IV, "Sociology and History," pp. 269–313.

²¹See: A. B. McKillop, "Nationalism, Identity, and Canadian Intellectual History," *Queen's Quarterly*, Winter 1974, pp. 533–550.

²²Berger, *The Writing of Canadian History*.

²³Careless, J. M. S., "Frontierism, Metropolitanism, and Canadian History." *Canadian Historical Review*, March 1954, pp. 1–21.

²⁴Careless, J. M. S., "Limited Identities in Canada." *CHR*, March 1969; "Somewhat Narrower Horizons," CHA Report, 1968, pp. 1–10. See also: Ramsay Cook, "Canadian Centennial Celebrations," *International Journal*, Autumn 1967; Northrop Frye, *The Bush Garden: Essays on the Canadian Imagination*, Toronto, Anansi, 1971, pp. i–ii.

²⁵Grant, George. *Lament for a Nation: The Defeat of Canadian Nationalism*. Toronto, McClelland & Stewart, 1965; Donald Creighton, *Canada's First Century*, Toronto, Macmillan, 1970; Dennis Lee, *Civil Elegies and Other Poems*, Toronto, Anansi, 1972.

[26]See: Robert Kroetsch, (Ed.), *Creation*, Toronto, New Press, 1970; Eli Mandel, "Writing West," *Another Time*, Erin, Ont., Press Porcepic, 1972; Dick Harrison, *Unnamed Country: The Struggle for a Prairie Fiction*, Edmonton, University of Alberta Press, 1977.

5

THE STAPLE THEORY REVISITED

MEL WATKINS
University of Toronto

The substantial contribution of Canadian economic historians, and others, to the study of Canadian economic history is the staples approach. Indeed, it is Canada's most, if not only, distinctive contribution to political economy, and the occasion of the formal recognition of the existence of the latter by the Canadian Political Science Association is an appropriate time to reexamine the staples approach.

Let me begin by reference to a previous paper on this topic published in 1963.[1] That paper attempted to pull out of more diffuse historical writings, notably by Innis, an explicit theory of economic growth appropriate to Canada and other "new" countries. At least in retrospect, its contribution was to give legitimacy to the staples approach—by showing that it was respectable within orthodox economics—but this was bought at the high price of constraining the theory to the very limiting paradigm of orthodox economics in general and the theory of international trade in particular.

In revisiting the theory,[2] it seems appropriate to review in particular the literature that has appeared since 1963 that is of *analytical* interest.[3] That literature can be conveniently classified under four heads: (1) quantitative testing of the staple theory under the influence of the new economic history; (2) studies on the closely related topics of foreign ownership and the structure of Canadian industry, to the extent that they are concerned with the evident bias toward staple export on the one hand, and a retarded industrial structure on the other hand; (3) historical and contemporary analysis of resource policy, with particular respect to the further processing of staples, the appropriation of economic rents from staple production, and the North; (4) work based on the Marxist paradigm.

The bias of the paper is toward the Marxist paradigm. This reflects the straightforward fact that, in quantitative terms and, in my opinion, in qualitative terms as well, it is scholars working out of the Marxist paradigm who are now predominant in the literature on the staples approach. This presumably is the result of a general resurgence of scholarly interest in Marxism that is, of course, not confined to Canada.

That Marxists should be attracted specifically to the staple approach is wholly understandable and should give no offense.[4] While its leading proponents were certainly liberals, at least in the beginning, it was clearly political economy and at least in the hands of Innis it was about dependence—and these latter two characteristics are, of course, central to Marxists. Innis in particular was a liberal with difference, who saw the dark underside and the gross contradictions and this makes him susceptible to an approach that specializes in such matters.[5]

Beginning in the late 1950s and thereafter, the postwar quantitative bias of American scholarship spread from economics into economic history, and the resulting new economic history penetrated the study of Canadian economic history in some part through the work done by American scholars and Canadian-born scholars resident in the U. S. The latter is indicative of the difficulties of transplanting the new phenomenon to Canada and suggests that its contribution is likely to be second-order. Nonetheless, worthwhile contributions have been made, directly by Bertram[6] and Caves,[7] and indirectly by Chambers and Gordon[8] in a joint article so scandalous as to compel reasoned defense of the staples approach.[9]

Bertram's first article, appearing simultaneously with my own in 1963, demonstrates the gradual but steady filling in of the manufacturing sector around the impetus generated by staple exports. The two articles have much in common in terms of giving not only the staples approach but the Canadian staples-oriented economy a relatively clean bill of health, but Bertram goes further in the second respect. Drache has recently suggested[10] that there are not one but two (non-Marxist) theories of capitalist development based on the staple theory, the steady-progress view of Mackintosh and the dependency view of Innis. Bertram, and the other writers in the new economic history, opt wholeheartedly for the more laundered Mackintosh approach.[11] MacDonald in his critique of Naylor[12] (of which more below) makes an analogous distinction between two branches of the staples approach: first, metropolitanism, or the commercial penetration of the hinterland positively viewed, as evidenced by (the early) Creighton and Ouellet;

and, second, the entirely different principle that a dominant trade might organize an economy inexorably around itself and lead to stagnation. MacDonald puts my 1963 article in the second category—as well as the writings of Fowke, Pentland, Dubuc, and Ryerson.

Caves' first article enhanced the legitimacy of the staple model for orthodox economists by showing its formal similarity with the unlimited-supply-of-labor model in the literature on economic development, that is, both were "vent for surplus" models of trade and growth rather than models based on growth through more efficient allocation of an existing stock of employed factors of production. Caves focuses narrowly on the linkages of the staple sector to other sectors, while urbanely noting in passing that there was "of course, the whole field of possible influences of the pattern of industry upon social and political development" [p. 112]. He sensibly concludes that the staple model, at least in its simple form, "probably yields no normative conclusions" [p. 113], and that both vent-for-surplus models "received their respective laurels and brickbats as a source of guidance for policy on the basis of what the linkages have or have not done in a particular case" [p. 114].

But he is very much of the Mackintosh cast of mind. As well as staple-induced growth, there will be "an underlying steady swell of neo-classical growth" such that "export-based growth may explain a large part of the *variation* in the aggregate rate of growth . . . whether or not it explains a large part of the average level of that growth rate" [p. 102]. Following Baldwin,[13] he recognizes the possibility of staple production having unfavorable effects on the character of factor supplies and the resulting distribution of income and hence on the composition of final demand, but dismisses it as improbable. "The staple version includes no . . . likely appearance of a maldistribution of income, especially if the rents accruing to natural resources [in the staples region] are allotted somewhat randomly among the erstwhile workers and capitalist elements of the population . . . [A] happy partnership of immigrant labor and capital is further cemented by windfall gains to the fortunate finders of natural resources" [p. 115]. While Caves is basically correct with respect to the overall distribution of income, his facile comments on rents—in both this, and to a lesser extent, his second paper—denied him an important insight that others have shown can be derived from the liberal paradigm, and that has less happy implications for generating sustained growth (see below).

In the best—or worst—tradition of the new economic history, Robert Fogel having allegedly demonstrated the limited contribution of railroads to American economic growth, Chambers and Gordon set out to demonstrate that the opening of the Canadian West, or the wheat boom, had likewise made a limited contribution to Canadian economic growth. Had they succeeded, the staple approach would indeed be in disarray, but, in fact, they failed miserably. They asked the wrong, or at best distinctly second-order question, that is, what contribution did the export of wheat make to the growth of income per capita rather than what contribution did it make to the growth of aggregate national income. Insofar as the staple theory has always been about understanding the successive opening up of the country, or increasing the stock of land, with resultant inflows of labor and capital, or, increases in *their* stocks, rather than about reallocating fixed endowments of factors, Chambers and Gordon, whatever they were doing, were hardly testing any known version of the staple theory. (This makes it all the more unfortunate that the Canadian edition of Samuelson's *Economics*—though Canadianized by Scott, a specialist in resource economics—insists on taking Chambers and Gordon seriously.[14])

To compound their problems, Chambers and Gordon appear not only to have misspecified the mode, but to have handled the data badly. Both Bertram and Caves make new quantitative estimates which show wheat to have, in fact, made a major contribution to Canadian economic growth. Bertram confines himself narrowly to quantitative testing. But Caves shows that the staple theory, depending on the staple, does not necessarily yield easy growth. If, because of scale economies in staple production, there are large capital requirements for staple enterprises, there will be "extraregional or foreign borrowing (with no incentive for local saving), absentee ownership and no contribution to the supply of local entrepreneurial talent or profit available for local reinvestment" [p. 433–434]. On a closely related point, he notes that the drawing in of undiscovered resources vents a surplus and creates a rent [p. 408], and that "where natural-resource rents accrue as profits to foreign entrepreneurs, the critical question for national welfare is the extent to which they are recaptured in taxation" [p. 436]. Nevertheless, he makes the curious observation in a footnote that "The extent to which export-led growth possesses any special virtues in furthering sustainable growth remains to be demonstrated, but any that it possesses seems unlikely to derive from the creation of rents" [p. 409].

In sum, then, the new economic history, which has been a central obsession of economic historians in recent years to the extent it poses real questions, has upheld the validity of the staples approach—though making little or no contribution to our theoretical understanding. The staple theory has survived the worse onslaughts of Americanization and for that reason alone must be seen as hardy and genuinely Canadian.

In the postwar period, and notably in the past two decades, a very substantial literature has emerged on the structure of Canadian industry and on the closely related topic of foreign ownership. The concern of this literature has not been with the staple theory per se—and therefore there will be no exhaustive review of it here—but it is necessary to inquire to what extent that literature sheds light on the viability of the staple theory, and to what extent the staple theory might shed some light on the topics of industrial structure and foreign ownership.

The historic tendency for staple production to take place under the aegis of foreign capital has persisted, indeed accelerated. In the first substantive study of foreign ownership in the postwar period, Hugh G. J. Aitken's *American Capital and Canadian Resources* in 1961, that simple fact was the central theme. Unfortunately, it has tended to be obscured in most subsequent studies—Safarian,[15] the Watkins Report,[16] the Gray Report[17]—but it does figure prominently in Levitt.[18] The most straightforward explanation, which requires no stepping outside the liberal paradigm, is the high American demand for Canadian staples and the high capital-intensity of the new staples, which create an advantage for the typically large established American company over a potential Canadian company. Put differently, the staples approach enables us to "explain" the continuing and rising level of foreign ownership of staple production.

That begs the question of why there is *so much* foreign ownership, not only in the staple sector but in the rest of the economy too, and particularly in manufacturing proper. Putting aside the tendency of Canadian economists to claim it does not really matter, and therefore presumably needs no explanation, those who have wished to explain it have ultimately fallen back for the most part on a Schumpeterian-like argument about the inadequacies of Canadian entrepreneurship; this is true even as of perceptive a writer as Levitt. This, of course is something less than a satisfactory answer, because it merely poses the question of the cause of the deficiency of Canadian entrepreneurship. As we shall see shortly, the first serious answer is offered by Naylor,[19] but from the Marxist paradigm.

The more conventional staples approach nevertheless contains some insights, having primarily to do with the tendency toward an excessive preoccupation with staple production that inheres in staple production itself, e.g., the sucking of domestic capital into the staple sector, notwithstanding the predominance of foreign capital, and the propensity of government to see staple production as a panacea for economic growth and neglect the working out of a proper industrial strategy. We are unlikely to be able to improve on Innis' cryptic formulation:

> Energy has been directed toward the exploitation of staple products and the tendency has been cumulative. . . . Energy in the colony was drawn into the production of the staple commodity both directly and indirectly in the production facilities promoting production. Agriculture, industry, transportation, trade, finance, and governmental activities tend to become subordinate to the production of the staple for a more highly specialized manufacturing community.[20]

Work on the structure of industry proper, notwithstanding many useful insights about the minature replica effect, has concerned itself ad nauseum with the Canadian tariff as *the* source of the problem. This begs the question as to the "source" of the tariff and the answer has tended, as before, quickly to degenerate into an appeal to the inadequacies of Canadian businessmen. With respect to the narrower mechanisms of the staple theory, Naylor reminds us of one that was once well-known in the literature, namely, that the National Policy, protectionist though it was, generated a flood of government revenue that greatly facilitated the building, and overbuilding, of infrastructure for staple production.[21]

The failure of a resource base developed to meet the exigencies of staple export to lead to an industrial complex—which is, after all, the heart of the matter—has been ably described by a noneconomist, Pierre L. Bourgault, in a study not for the Economic Council but the Science Council:

> We are the world's largest producer of nickel, but we are net importers of stainless steel and manufactured nickel products . . . ; we are the world's second largest producer of aluminum, but we import it in its more sophisticated forms such as . . . precision aluminum parts for use in aircraft; we are the world's largest exporters of pulp and paper, but we import much of our fine paper and virtually all of the highly sophisticated paper, such as backing for photographic film; we are one of the principal sources of platinum, but it is all exported for refining and processing and reimported in finished forms; we are large exporters of natural gas and petroleum, but we are net importers of petrochemicals; and although we are the world's foremost exporter of raw asbestos fibres, we are net importers of manufactured asbestos products.[22]

Neither orthodox studies of industrial structure nor a staple theory focused microscopically on linkages seems quite to come to terms with this matter; we must either retreat to Innis or move forward to Naylor.

In the area of resource policy proper, two names stand out, Kierans and Nelles. A long neglected theme in the economic analysis of staple production, but one that grows logically out of the liberal paradigm, is that intramarginal "land" commands its own reward, or economic rent. The relevant questions are: What is the size of the rents? Who gets them? What differences does their distribution make to sustained economic growth? Kierans' pioneering study on the metal-mining industry in Manitoba[23] shows that they disproportionately accrue to capital which is frequently foreign. Clearly, the conventional focus on linkages has obscured an important point, that is, that the prospects for sustained and more diversified development in the wake of nonrenewable resource exploitation are decreased to the extent that rents, or "superprofits," are appropriated by the resource-capitalists, and particularly if they are foreign capitalists.

Without respect to the nationality of capital, the rents, to the extent to which they are retained by the corporations, tend to remain locked into resource exploitation, and eventually leave the region that had the resources. This is so because resource companies are generally not diversified outside the resource sector and are increasingly large multinationals prepared to exploit resources anywhere in the world. To the extent that the rents accrue, immediately or ultimately, to shareholders as dividends or capital gains on shares, the staple-producing country benefits—specifically, that small portion of its population that owns most of the shares—when the capital is domestic but not when it is foreign. To the extent governments in the staple-producing country appropriate the rents through taxation or public ownership, the country benefits—though the nature of the benefit depends on how governments spend the additional revenue and/or reduce other forms of taxation. Finally, regionally, or locally, the major consequence of losing the rents from nonrenewable resources is the well-known Canadian phenomenon of the ghost town.[24]

The addition of an analysis of economic rent to orthodox staple theory has the important result of showing how staple production can create a "blockage" to diversified development, that is, by denying the potential, create "underdevelopment."[25] In effect, the liberal paradigm can be made to yield a version of the staple approach that explains phenomena strikingly similar to what is yielded by the Marxist paradigm in which the analogous mechanism is the outward drain of surplus.

Nelles' massive study of Ontario government policy in the new staple industries of forest products, mining, and hydro-electricity over almost a century[26] is the most important descriptive work done within the context of the staple approach since Rich's monumental study of the Hudson's Bay Company.[27] He eschews economic theory, but his central concern with "the manufacturing condition" as Ontario's "little National Policy" is evidence of how staple production, at its best, leads to more of the same—in the sense of more value added within the resource sector—rather than causing a quantum leap into a diversified industrial economy under domestic control.

The Canadian North, as the new and last "frontier," is also attracting increasing attention from historians working basically around the theme of resource policy. The major writings of Zaslow[28] and Rea[29] are mostly valuable for their great detail. Rea uses a simple staple model that focuses on linkages and ignores rent. Neither shows any real grasp of the economy of the Native people, and both fall prey—and Rea explicitly so[30]—to the dual economy thesis, thereby missing the point that nonrenewable resource exploitation sets up mechanisms, which create underdevelopment for native people. Fumoleau on the history of the Treaties[31] and Asch on the economic history of the Slavey people[32] correct the bias, as does research sponsored by the Indian Brotherhood of the Northwest Territories, which is articulated around the theme of the right to alternative community-based development.[33]

In the last decade, a mere handful of Marxist writers in Canada has suddenly been joined by a small army of younger scholars.[34] At least from the perspective of the analytics of the staple approach, by far the most important contribution is Naylor's two-volume *History of Canadian Business* in the critical period from Confederation to World War 1. Indeed, his work is, in my opinion, the most important historical writing on Canada since the early Innis and early Creighton—and I am aware of what high praise that constitutes.

As we have already seen, liberal scholarship, in attempting to explain the dependent and structurally underdeveloped nature of the Canadian economy has been able to do no better than appeal to the deficiencies of Canadian entrepreneurship. Naylor saves us from this theoretical quagmire by centering our attention on the nature of capital, and specifically on the distinction between merchant capital and industrial capital and the difficulty of transforming an economy dominated by the first into an economy dominated by the second. From a contemporary perspective, his concern is with "the overexpansion of resource industries relative to manufacturing, and the drainage of surplus income as service payments for foreign investment instead of its being used to generate new capital formation within Canada" [I, p. xix].

The ties to the staple approach are obvious. Naylor writes:

> Two fundamental structural attributes of the Canadian economy in the period from 1867 to 1914 must be made central to analysis. First, it was a colony, politically and economically. In terms of commercial patterns it was a staple-extracting hinterland oriented toward serving metropolitan markets from which, in turn, it received finished goods. In such a structure, any economic advance in the hinterland accrues to the benefit of the metropole and perpetuates the established division of labour . . . Canada's commercial and financial system grew up geared to the international movement of staples, rather than to abetting secondary processing for domestic markets . . . Canada's social structure and therefore the proclivities of its entrepreneurial class, reflected and reinforced its innate colonialism. The political and economic elite were men associated with the staple trades, with the international flow of commodities and of the capital that complemented the commodity movements. . . . A second trait of the economy of the period, in part derivative from the first, was that it had only begun to make the difficult transition from a mercantile agrarian base to an industrial one. Wealth was accumulated in commercial activities and tended to remain locked up in commerce. Commercial capital resisted the transformation into industrial capital except under specific conditions in certain industries, in favour of remaining invested in traditional staple-oriented activities.[I, 3–4]

In short, the necessary origins of Canada as a staple-producer are perpetuated because of the nature of the capitalist class that emerges, and re-emerges, out of the staple trades that spring into being to serve the needs of the metropole.

Naylor, like Innis before him, provdes a wealth of detail to support his very original contribution to Canadian historiography. Suffice it here to note some of the more important specific mechanisms, which Naylor cites as to how staple production leads to the overdevelopment of the staple industries and the underdevelopment of manufacturing. The capital requirements for infrastructure to service the staple trades absorbed domestic as well as foreign capital and retarded industrial capital formation [I, p. 15]. Regionally, the Maritime Provinces were drained of surplus to finance Central Canada's development objectives in the West, thereby retarding their indigenous industrial development,[35] while Québécois industrial entrepreneurship was submerged under a wave of anglophone-controlled mergers [I, p. 15]. The Canadian banking system, and Canadian financial institutions in general, grew out of merchants' capital involved in the staple trades [I, p. 110] and took a form appropriate to facilitating the movement of staples from Canada to external markets rather than promoting secondary industries [I, p. 67]. The National Policy was a policy of industrialization-by-invitation and attracted foreign capital, and thus foreign ownership under the aegis of the multinational corporation, rather than encouraging domestic capital, which would have strengthened industrial capital relative to merchant capital within Canada and thereby facilitated a transformation out of a staples structure. Railways were built to facilitate staple production and only incidentally to create industrialization, and their operation favored international trade over interregional trade. And so on.

For Naylor, the consequence was that by the end of his period, the Canadian economy was locked into "the staple trap" [II, p. 283]. His model, then, is a Marxist version of the Innisian version.

It might be thought that the Marxist paradigm necessarily yields a dependency version of the staple model, but that is apparently not certain. There are hints in the scholarly literature—not to mention vast amounts of diatribe in the sectarian literature—that there is a steady-progress version, in this case toward the creation of a viable national capitalist class that has come to rule Canada. Ryerson, writing pre-Naylor, emphasizes the slow but steady growth of industrial capital out of merchant capital in the nineteenth century.[36] MacDonald, in his critique of Naylor, insists that "a close look at the evidence . . . shows that mercantile and industrial capital were inseparable . . ." [p. 266], but he wrote without benefit of the much closer look of Naylor's two volumes and hence he, and those who rely on the *Canadian Historical Review* for their knowledge of Canadian economic history, risk being the victims of instant obsolescence. It is not at all clear what MacDonald intends us to believe about the nature of the Canadian capitalist class, so it may be that he is of the dependency school and rejects Naylor's explanation without choosing to give us any indication of what he would put in its place. But from what he does tell us, he seriously underestimates the extent of American control of the Canadian economy by 1914,[37] and profoundly misunderstands the nature of the multinational corporation.[38] A reasonable inference therefore is that he is biased against the dependency version of the staple model.

On this murky but important question, mention must also be made of the work of Wallace Clement.[39] He understands that Canada is a staple economy and accepts Naylor's argument on the distinction between merchant capital and industrial capital and the tendency for the former to be Canadian and the latter foreign. Nevertheless, he concludes that "the Canadian economy remains controlled in large part by a set of families who have been in the past and still remain at the core of the Canadian economy" [p. 150], and that the split between the commercial and industrial capitalist classes "does not mean the total [Canadian] bourgeoisie is not powerful—indeed, it may be more powerful because of the continental context" [p. 335]. On the basis of the evidence presented in his book, and so much other published evidence to the contrary, Clement's views are unconvincing.[40]

We can look forward to further controversy around Naylor's seminal arguments, in the hope that it will illuminate whether there is one or two Marxist versions of the staple theory. For the moment, it seems to me that the dependency version will, in any event, win hands down.

So much for the capitalists themselves; what of the nature of the state that emerges out of staple production? And what is the likelihood of its showing the way out of the staple trap? Now, to transcend staple production, that is, to escape subservience to the rising American empire, would surely have required a state prepared to go well beyond the limitations of the actual National Policy.[41] But the state itself is almost a by-product of the exigencies of staple production, an argument central to Innis' analysis and now to Naylor's.

For Innis, both the Act of Union and Confederation were essentially dictated by the need to raise capital, first for canals and then railways, to facilitate the movement of staples. Creighton's *British North America at Confederation* brilliantly demonstrated the latter, and the implications for the post-Confederation period have been skillfully outlined by Dubuc.[42] For Naylor, Confederation and the National Policy reflects a state and a state policy created by the merchant capitalist class in its own image. If anything of analytic substance remains to be said on this matter, it may be that more attention should be devoted to the process by which the Canadian state successively suppressed re-emerging domestic capital within the staple sector itself, and within the manufacturing sector, in the interest of foreign capital.[43]

While none of the other new Marxist writers have matched Naylor in depth and breadth, some significant analytical gains have been made in fleshing out a Marxist version of the staple theory. The latter would require the recasting of the staple theory as a theory of class formation; this paper is only a tentative first step in that direction.

If we are to begin at the beginning, we must inquire as to the fate of the aboriginal population. How, in the most fundamental sense, do they fit into the staple theory? Innis makes the essential point, at least implicitly, when he writes "Fundamentally the civilization of North America is the civilization of Europe . . ." and again, "Canada has remained fundamentally a product of Europe."[44] The Indian way of life, indeed the Indian himself, was swept aside. Only in the era of the fur trade was the Indian functional to the Euro-Canadian, and everywhere in the long run the fur trade retreated in the face of settlement and was ultimately obliterated by it. The Indian was made irrelevant. This functional irrelevancy is dramatically demonstrated in the very terminology that is used to characterize Canada—and other like cases such as the United States, Australia, and New Zealand. Their aboriginal populations notwithstanding, they are called "new countries" or "empty lands" or "areas of recent settlement" or "undeveloped areas"—or simply "the frontier."

The analytical significance of this point can be appreciated if we imagine a very opposite situation, namely, that the aboriginal population, which we would have to assume was much larger, had not been easily pushed to the margins of society, geographically and socially. Rather than being a "colony of settlement," Canada might have been a "colony of conquest" analogous to those of Asia and Africa. Or it might have been a "white settler colony" proper, like the Union of South Africa or Rhodesia. Or it might have been a mixed case such as abound in Central and South America. In any event, Canadian development would have been different and much more difficult. A precapitalist indigenous population that could not be ignored would be reduced to underdevelopment, and either slowly converted to the capitalist mode of production or contained by massive repression and discrimination. We would not have our very high *average* standard of living, though the European stock—if it had not yet been turfed out—might be doing very well. Methodologically, there would be no special case amenable to the literal staple theory.

The aboriginal populations by being separated from the means of production have been reduced to the status of an underclass or lumpenproletariat. The historic process is outlined by Elias;[45] Brody shows the process at work today with respect to the Inuit.[46]

The aboriginal people were pushed aside; settlers poured in from the Old World; a class of capitalists emerged in the staples-region; it created a state structure and a "national policy" in its own image. What remains? Depending on the staple, the creation either of a class of commodity producers or a class of wage-earners. The distinction hinges on whether the staple activity is a trade or an industry. The great staple *trades* of cod, fur, and wheat have been extensively researched, and what has been explicitly analyzed in Marxist terms in C. B. Macpherson's classic *Democracy in Alberta.*

The independent commodity producers are capitalists, because they use capital; they are not wage-earners and do not themselves employ wage labor. The important question is not whether independent commodity production exists as a mode of production, but whether it is a dominant or subordinate mode. As a mode of production, it coexists with merchant capital and increases its sway. Hence, both in its own right but, more importantly, because it reinforces merchant capital, independent commodity production tends to retard the development of mature industrial capitalism.[47] In the case of the wheat economy, the prairie farmer was interested solely in costs of inputs to the wheat economy and hence disinterested in whether a viable industrial structure was created within Canada.

But timber and lumber were to some extent industries; the old staples created industrialization in their wake; and the new mineral staples are explicitly industries. Commodity producers are a declining class.[48] We must inquire as to the formation of the working class.

This is a critical matter neglected by Innis and thus far by Naylor. In spite of a considerable and growing literature on the history of labor, the analytical relationship between the evolution of the working class and the imperatives of staple production has yet to be definitely worked out—and this paper is not the place to attempt it.

The basic characteristics of the process were set out by Pentland some time ago:[49]

> The production for export of staples drawn from an extensive area, usually a seasonal activity in Canada, and one subject to abrupt changes in prices and profitability, is quite unfavourable to the formation of a capitalistic labour market. It is the integration of an economy—the growth of manufactures, of cities, of a home market—that provides the concentration and balance of demand for it. Construction of the transportation facilities that integrated the Canadian economy produced transitional conditions, in the direction of a domestic product market and a socialized labour market. . . . When completed, the transport systems fostered centralization of production and the growth of cities by welding the country into an economic unit. The railways promoted the growth of particular cities, through the employment of hundreds and thousands of permanent skilled workers in their extensive shops. . . . Much the same places (Montreal, Toronto, Hamilton and London) benefited from the growth of manufactures, now supported by a coherent domestic market, fostered by a new technical *milieu* and encouraged by some

> explicit protection after 1858. Early manufactures depended heavily on craftsmanship, but factory production based on machinery and unskilled labour and mass demand was a feature of the 1860s [p. 456–7].

Pentland argues as well that the raw material of the labor market came via the immigrant stream, and that this was the case both for the unskilled and the skilled:

> Many of the immigrants, moreover, were highly responsive to market incentives. But this fact produced a new hazard. The more capitalist-minded the immigrants, the more determined they were to be farm proprietors rather than wage earners. . . . It was just such a rejection of wage employment that inspired Edward Gibbon Wakefield, in the interest of capitalist development, to new barriers to the ownership of land. [p. 457]

Teeple has subsequently argued[50] that, in fact, a glut of landless labor existed in British North America by 1820, a situation he attributes not only to monopolizing land policies—an historically well-recognized phenomenon—but also, following Naylor to "the lack of industrial growth due to the presence of a mercantile ruling class" [p. 45].

In general, Pentland, from our present perspective, veered more to a Ryersonian than Naylorian view of industrialization, so we need to be on our guard. And beyond the question of class structure lies the complex matter of the nature of the labor movement, and of not only its class consciousness but also its national consciousness. Canada's dependent trade unionism has been much discussed in the literature, and the rationale and consequences have been ably stated by Robert H. Babcock, in particular:[51]

> American craft unions first invaded British North America during the middle of the nineteenth century. Older, larger, and richer than their Canadian counterparts, they were welcomed by Canadian workers who sought strike support and insurance benefits of a kind unavailable to them elsewhere. American unions willingly lent such help in order to organize the Canadian segment of a new continental product and labour market which developed at mid-century. The unions wanted to protect generally superior American wage levels and working conditions from the deteriorating effects of cheaper labour.
>
> . . . The international craft unions brought to Canada structural characteristics and policy predilections that were products of the American environment. Craft-union organization, short-term economic goals, apolitical unionism, and the pursuit of monopoly developed within the AFL. . . . [A] new impulse soon changed the rationale if not the direction of AFL policy. . . . American businessmen, seeking new markets and raw materials, turned their attention to Canada. American capital and technology began to flow northward on an unprecedented scale. . . . American branch plants flourished. . . . All these new developments seemed to demand a comparable expansion by the America labour movement into Canada. Gompers and his colleagues decided that it had become absolutely essential for them to organize Canadian workers in order to proect the North American labour and product market. . . . The structure and policies of the American Federation of Labour exerted a powerful influence upon the Canadian labour movement. . . . [T]he AFL operated as a divisive force when the Trades and Labour Congress was transformed from a body unifying Canadian unionists

> into an arm of the international crafts. In a country wracked if not wrecked by regionalism, the loss of a truly national labour institution was doubtless unfortunate. The evidence suggests that Gompers and Morrison [AFL secretary] retarded the growth of a movement linking trade unions with moderate socialist policies. . . . Still, wages and working conditions might well be less satisfactory in Canada had not the international unions exerted a constant pressure upon Canadian industry to match American standards [p. 210–216].

The full analytical relationship between dependent trade unionism and staple production needs to be pulled together from the literature. A critical aspect of this is the tendency of international unionism, directly in its own right and indirectly through its control of the New Democratic Party, to constrain Canadian nationalism and hence the potential for restructuring the Canadian economy away from its staple bias.[52]

Finally, in the process of doing all this, it would become apparent that staple production in Canada has not only generated economic growth—as emphasized by mainstream writers—but has also generated social disturbances (such as protest movements) and social rigidities (regional disparities and the social costs of regional underdevelopment).

In conclusion, then, there are clearly two liberal versions of the staple theory and one certainly, and perhaps two, Marxist versions. The continuing viability of the two dependent versions, one liberal and one Marxist and both owing much to Innis, augurs well for future work. In his one truly perceptive observation, MacDonald writes that Naylor has "synthesized, in an unprecedented way, radical and nationalist themes in Canadian economic thought" [p. 265], but he errs in his grasp of the analytical, or methodological, respectability of that "thought"—as I hope this paper has demonstrated.

Finally, here are some suggestions as to the directions in which future research might go. There is always a need for serious theoretical work; specifically, Naylor's thesis might be reexamined in conjunction with Kay's masterful treatise,[53] where the dichotomy between merchant and industrial capital, and the consequences, in his case, for the nature of Third World underdevelopment, also figures so prominently. There can, of course, be no substitute for the detailed historical writing needed to expose the pervasive and peculiar impact of each particular staple; notwithstanding Innis' *Settlement and the Mining Frontier,* some of Aitken's writings, and now Nelles' very important contribution, the new staples, of mining and oil and gas, still await definitive analysis. As previously suggested, the impact of staple production on the working class, both in terms of its existence as a class and its consciousness of its existence, is in need of sustained analysis. Finally, the staple theory is so specifically Canadian in origin and development, and yet so apparently applicable to other new countries, as to make it highly probable that its application elsewhere in a comparative context would be beneficial to its continuing utility in Canadian studies.

ACKNOWLEDGMENTS

This is a revised version of a paper presented to the Annual meeting of the Canadian Political Science Association, Quebec City, May 30, 1976; I am indebted to A. Rotstein, R. T. Naylor, and D. Drache for helpful comments on earlier drafts. I have also benefited from reading Roy T. Bowles, "The Staples School of Canadian History and the Sociological Analysis of Canadian Society," paper presented to the Canadian Sociology and Anthropology Association, Annual Meeting, Quebec City, 1976. The paper also was published in the *Journal of Canadian Studies*, Vol. 12, No. 5, Winter 1977, pp. 85–95.

NOTES

[1]Watkins, M.H. "A Staple Theory of Economic Growth." *Canadian Journal of Economics and Political Science*, XXIX, May 1963, pp. 141–58; reprinted in W. T. Easterbrook & M. H. Watkins (Eds.), *Approaches to Canadian Economic History*, Toronto, McClelland & Stewart, 1967, pp. 49–73.

[2]I have previously revisited the theory, albeit less explicitly and analytically, in "Resources and Underdevelopment" in Robert Laxer (Ed.), *(Canada) Ltd: The Political Economy of Dependency*, Toronto, McClelland & Stewart, 1973; and "Economic Development in Canada" in Immanuel Wallerstein (Ed.), *World Inequality: Origins and Perspectives on the World System*, Montreal: Black Rose, 1976.

[3]Beyond that considerable constraint, I have further defined analytical interest in such a way as to exclude writings which are explicitly analytical but use what might be called an institutional approach; with respect to the latter I have in mind the important, albeit different, institutional writings of W. T. Easterbrook and Abraham Rotstein.

[4]One response to my 1963 paper by Innisians was that it emasculated Innis. Such people may object even more strenuously to the suggestion that Innis should now be translated explicitly into the Marxist paradigm. But there are only two paradigms, and translating into both is in order.

[5]See Drache, Daniel. "Harold Innis: A Canadian Nationalist." *Journal of Canadian Studies*, IV, May, 1969, 7–12. Only last year at these meetings Drache gave an overview of the literature around the staples approach, and he cast his net much wider than mine; see his "Rediscovering Canadian Political Economy," *Journal of Canadian Studies*, XI, August, 1976, 3–18. On the narrower analytical front, see his "Canadian Capitalism: Sticking with Staples," *This Magazine* (July–August, 1975). In general, *This Magazine* has emerged as the most important forum for discussion of Canadian political economy around the theme of the staples approach.

[6]Bertram, Gordon W. "Economic Growth and Canadian Industry, 1870–1915: The Staple Model and the 'Take-Off Hypothesis,' " *CJEPS* XXIX, May, 1963, pp. 162–84, reprinted as "Economic Growth in Canadian Industry, 1870–1915: The Staple

Model" in *Approaches to Canadian Economic History;* "The Relevance of the Wheat Boom in Canadian Economic Growth," *Canadian Journal of Economics,* VI, November 1973.

[7]Caves, Richard E. " ' Vent for Surplus' Models of Trade and Growth." In Robert E. Baldwin, Jagdish Bhagwati, Richard E. Caves, Harry G. Johnson, Reinhard Kamitz, Peter B. Kenen, Charles P. Kindelberger, Fritz Machlup, Jürg Niekans, Bertil Chlin, Paul A. Samuelson, Egon Schmen, Wolfgang F. Stolper, Jan Timbergen, (Eds.), *Trade, Growth and the Balance of Payments: Essays in Honour of Gottfried Haberler,* Chicago, Rand McNalley 1965; "Export-Led Growth and the New Economic History" in Jagdish N. Bhagwati, Ronald W. Johes, Robert Mandell, and Janoslav Vanek, (Eds.), *Trade, Balance of Payments and Growth: Papers in International Economics in Honor of Charles P. Kindleberger,* Amsterdam/Oxford: North Holland Publishing Co., 1971.

[8]Chambers, E. J. and Gordon, D. F. "Primary Products and Economic Growth: An Empirical Measurement." *Journal of Political Economy,* LXXIV, 1966, 315–32.

[9]The second articles of both Bertram and Caves are responses thereto; see also J. H. Dales, J. C. McManus and M. H. Watkins, "Primary Products and Economic Growth: A Comment," *JPE,* December 1967; and Edward Vickery, "Exports and North American Economic Growth: 'Structuralist' and 'Staple' Models in historical perspective," *CJE,* VII, February, 1974.

[10]Drache, "Rediscovering Canadian Political Economy."

[11]So too do some prominent Canadian historians. The subtitle of Craig Brown and Ramsay Cooks' *Canada 1896–1921* is *A Nation Transformed,* thereby begging two questions. Certainly Innis and Creighton raise doubts as to the extent of nationhood from anything but a narrow juridical perspective, and Caves and Holton demonstrated very effectively some time ago that there was no discontinuity in this period that would justify the use of the word "transformed": see Richard E. Caves and Richard H. Holton, *The Canadian Economy: Prospect and Retrospect,* Cambridge, Mass., Harvard University Press, 1959. Yet Margaret Prang says that the sub-title of the book "could scarcely be more aptly chosen" (*Canadian Forum,* October, 1974).

[12]MacDonald, L. R. "Merchants against industry: An Idea and its Origins." *Canadian Historical Review,* LVI, September, 1975, which is a critique of R. T. Naylor, "The Rise and Fall of the Third Commercial Empire of the St. Lawrence" in Gary Teeple (Ed.), *Capitalism and the National Question in Canada,* Toronto, University of Toronto Press, 1972, pp. 1–41.

[13]Baldwin, R. E. "Patterns of Development in Newly Settled Regions." *Manchester School of Economic and Social Studies,* May, 1956, which was central to the analysis of my 1963 paper; see also his "Export Technology and Development from a Subsistence Level," *Economic Journal,* March, 1963.

[14]Samuelson, Paul A. and Scott, Anthony. *Economics,* Fourth Canadian Edition. Toronto, McGraw-Hill Ryerson, 1975, p. 679.

[15]Safarian, A. E. *Foreign Ownership of Canadian Industry.* Toronto, McGraw-Hill of Canada, 1966.

[16]Canada. Privy Council. *Foreign Ownership and the Structure of Canadian Industry.* Ottawa, Report commissioned by the Government of Canada and presented on January 12, 1968.

[17]Canada. *Foreign Direct Investment in Canada.* Ottawa, Dept. of Industry Trade & Commerce, Office of Economics, Foreign Investment Division, 1972.

[18]Levitt, Kari. *Silent Surrender: The Multinational Corporation in Canada.* Toronto, Macmillan of Canada, 1970.

[19]Naylor, R. T. *The History of Canadian Business 1867–1914,* Vol. I & II. Toronto, Lorimer, 1975.

[20]Innis, H. A. *The Fur Trade in Canada: An Introduction to Canadian Economic History.* (1930) 2nd ed. Toronto, University of Toronto Press, 1956, p. 385.

[21]Naylor, R. T. *The History of Canadian Business,* I, pp. 56–7.

[22]Bourgault, Pierre L. *Innovation and the Structure of Canadian Industry.* Science Council of Canada, Special Study No. 23, Ottawa, 1973.

[23]Kierans, Eric. *Report on Natural Resources Policy in Manitoba,* Manitoba, Prepared for the Secretariat for the Planning and Priorities Committee of the Cabinet, Government of Manitoba, Winnipeg, 1973.

[24]Northrop Frye observed in his Images of Canada television special (CBC 1976) that "Canada is full of ghost towns: visible ruins unparallelled in Europe." Bourgault goes so far as to suggest that this could happen to the whole country; he observes that Canada is becoming increasingly reliant on staple exports and that if we keep on this path "Before the children of today could reach middle age most of the resources would be gone, leaving Canada with a resource-based economy and no resources" [Op. cit. p. 126].

[26]See Russ Rothney and Steve Watson, "A Brief Economic History of Northern Manitoba" (Mimeo, July, 1975). They define underdevelopment as "Blockage of potential, sustained economic and social development geared to local human needs. In other words, the process by which economical and cultural leverage is taken or kept from the people of a region" [p. iii]. They insist on the need to pay attention to "restrictions on local social and economic development generated by institutional processes of surplus extraction in the region. These processes hinge upon specific relations between social-economic classes and between commercial metropoles and their economic hinterlands."

[26]Nelles, H. V. *The Politics of Development: Forst, Mines and Hydro-electric Power in Ontario, 1849–1941.* Toronto, Macmillan of Canada, 1974.

[27]Rich, E. E. *The Hsitory of the Hudson's Bay Company, 1670–1870.* 2 vols. London, Hudson's Bay Record Society, 1958–1959.

[28]Zaslow, Morris. *The Opening of the Canadian North 1870–1914.* Toronto, McClelland & Stewart, 1971.

[29]Rea, K. J. *The Political Economy of the Canadian North.* Published in association with the University of Saskatchewan by the University of Toronto Press; Toronto: 1968; and *The Political Economy of Northern Development,* Science Council of Canada Background Study No. 36, Ottawa, 1967.

[30]Rea, *The Political Economy of Northern Development.* p. 39.

[31]Fumoleau, Rene. *As Long as This Land Shall Last: A History of Treaty 8 and Treaty 11, 1870–1939.* Toronto, McClelland & Stewart, 1975. Fumoleau shows how the gold rush into the Klondike led to the signing of Treaty 8 in 1899 while Imperial Oil's discovery of oil near Fort Norman led to the signing of Treaty 11 in 1921; it would be difficult to find a clearer case of government policy as a response to the needs of staple producers.

[32]Asch, Michael. "Past and Present Land-Use by Slavey Indians of the Mackenzie District," Evidence before the Mackenzie Valley Pipeline Inquiry, April, 1976.

[33]Arvin Jelliss has done detailed rent calculations for the producing mines of the Mackenzie District, the Imperial Oil Refinery at Norman Wells and the Pointed Mountain gas development; see in particular his "Natural Resources Projects, Economic Rents, and Problems of Native Peoples' Development in the Mackenzie District," *ibid.* June, 1976. See also my "Resource Exploitation and Economic Underdevelopment on Dene Land," *ibid.* June, 1976; and Peter Puxley "Colonialism or Development?: The Meaning of Development," *ibid.* June, 1976.

[34]It is not my intention to classify people in a manner that may in any way be unacceptable to them. Whether or not availing oneself of the Marxist paradigm makes one a Marxist in any other sense is not relevant to scholarship. We now have it on the authority of Paul Samuelson that we all have something to gain from the use of Marxist analysis; see the most recent edition of his *Economics.*

[35]See also Bruce Archibald, "Atlantic Regional Under-Development and Socialism" in Laurier LaPierre, Jack McLeod, Charles Taylor, and Walter Young, (Eds.) *Essays on the Left: Essays in Honour of T. C. Douglas.* Toronto, McClelland & Stewart, 1971.

[36]Stanley Ryerson, *Unequal Union,* Toronto, Progress Books, 1968.

[37]For evidence on the significant level of American control of the Canadian Economy by World War I, see Glen Williams, "Canadian Industrialization: We Ain't Growin' Nowhere," *This Magazine,* March–April, 1975; and Tom Naylor "Commentary" on Simon Rosenblum, "Economic Nationalism and the English-Canadian Socialist Movement," *Our Generation* II, Fall 1975, pp. 20–21.

[38]MacDonald writes "Possibly the origin of the branch plant should be sought not in industry but in trade: from a management standpoint it was the application to manufacturing of the organizational principles of a commercial branch of a trading company" [p. 269]. It is difficult to say other than that this flies in the face of virtually all known

literature on the multinational corporation; see particularly the writings of the late Stephen Hymer, who made signal contributions successively to both the liberal and Marxist analysis of foreign ownership.

[39]Clement, Wallace. *The Canadian Corporate Elite: An Analysis of Economic Power.* Toronto, McClelland & Stewart, 1975.

[40]At the same CPSA session at which this paper was presented, Clement reported on his further researches based on his recently completed doctoral thesis. Clement appears now to be closer to Naylor; in any event, his important work needs much more extensive consideration than is possible here.

[41]See my "The 'American System; and Canada's National Policy," *Bulletin of the Canadian Association of Studies,* Winter 1967.

[42]Dubuc, Alfred. "The Decline of Confederation and the New Nationalism." In Russell, Peter (Ed.). *Nationalism in Canada.* Toronto, McGraw-Hill, 1966.

[43]This is a point that became very evident to this writer on reading the chapters in Nelles on the nickel industry; see my "Economic Development in Canada." On the subsidies to capital formation under foreign control in the period 1945–1957, and their apparent success in leading to a quantum leap in American ownership of the Canadian economy, see David Wolfe, *Political Culture, Economic Policy and the Growth of Foreign Involvement in Canada, 1945 to 1957,* M. A. Thesis, Carleton University, 1973.

[44]Innis, *The Fur Trade in Canada* (1956). pp. 383, 401.

[45]Elias, Peter Douglas. *Metropolis and Hinterland in Northern Manitoba,* Manitoba, Winnipeg, Manitoba, Museum of Man & Nature, 1975. p. 2. Elias characterizes Native people as "a totally pauperized class," "permanent state-supported class" and as being "at the absolute fringe of industrial capitalist society" [p. 8].

[46]Brody, Hugh. *The People's Land: Eskimos and Whites in the Eastern Arctic.* Harmondsworth, England, Penguin Books, 1975, p. 229. On tendencies toward the emergence of a class structure along ethnic lines in the more "impacted" Western Arctic, see the writings of Peter Usher, in particular "Geographers and Northern Development: Some Social and Political Considerations," *Alternatives,* Autumn 1974; and "The Class System, Metropolitan Dominance and Northern Development," paper presented to the Canadian Association of Geographers, Vancouver, 1975.

[47]See *Monthly Reveiw,* May 1976, for an exchange between Robert Sherry and James O'Connor on independent commodity production in early America.

[48]This is a major theme of Leo A. Johnson, "The development of class in Canada in the twentieth century" in *Capitalism and the National Question in Canada.* On the nature of Canada's capitalist class and the general issues of Canadian dependency, however, Johnson's views are confused and unreliable. At best, there is an apparent tendency to agree with everyone. At worst, there is a willingness to endorse utterly useless sectarian scribbling; on the latter, see his effusive "Introduction" to Steve Moore and Debi Wells, *Imperialism and the National Question and Canada,* Toronto, New Hogtown Press, 1975; and compare with the devastating critiques of the book by Ian Lumsden in *This Magazine,* Nov.–Dec., 1975; and Jack Warnock in *Canadian Dimension,* March 1976.

[49]Pentland, H. C. "The Development of a Capitalistic Labour Market in Canada," *CJEPS* 25, November 1969, pp. 450–461; for a fuller statement see his *Labour and the Development of Industrial Capitalism in Canada,* Ph.D. Thesis, University of Toronto (1960), which is still—incredibly—unpublished. Pentland deserves great credit for working within the Marxist paradigm when it was distinctly unusual to do so, and the tendency for his work to be ignored by the mainstream of Canadian economic historians—including myself in the 1963 article—tells us much about the limitations of orthodox economics as it impinges on economic history.

[50]Teeple, Gary. "Land, labour and capital in pre-Confederation Canada," in Teeple, *Capitalism and the National Question in Canada.*

[51]Babcock, Robert H. *Gompers in Canada: A Study in American Continentalism Before the First World War.* Toronto, University of Toronto Press, 1974. See also, Lipton, Charles. *The Trade Union Movement in Canada 1827–1959.* Toronto, NC Press, 1967; I. M. Abella. *Nationalism, Communism and Canadian Labour: The CIO, the Communist Party and the Canadian Congress of Labour 1935–1956.* Toronto, University of Toronto Press, 1973; and

the essays by Roger Howard and Jack Scott, R. B. Morris, and Lipton in Teeple, *Capitalism and the National Question in Canada.*

[52]Laxer, James. "Introduction to the Political Economy of Canada," pp. 26–41 in *(Canada) Ltd., the Political Economy of Dependency,* Robert Laxer, (Ed.) Toronto: McClelland & Stewart, 1973; pp. 37–40 are particularly suggestive.

[53]Kay, Geoffrey. *Development and Underdevelopment: A Marxist Analysis.* London, MacMillan, 1975.

6

CULTURE, GEOGRAPHY, AND COMMUNICATIONS: THE WORK OF HAROLD INNIS IN AN AMERICAN CONTEXT

JAMES W. CAREY
University of Iowa

What is it about the ponderous and often unreadable texts of Harold Innis that makes them the subject of continuing interest, indeed, of a revival of interest some twenty-five years after his death? Despite their opacity, their maddening obscurity, their elliptical quality, I find myself drawn back to these texts precisely when seeking fresh departures in the study of communications. And the texts continue to yield because they combine an almost studied obscurity with a gift for pungent aphorism, producing, thereby, sudden flashes of juxtaposition and illumination. There was to Innis a natural depth, excess, and complexity, a sense of paradox and reversal that complicates his writing and provides permanent riddles rather than easy formulas. His books, in short, are not merely things to read but things to think with.

Beyond his intellectual qualities Innis had an indispensable moral gift; this was expressed throughout his life but perhaps most ardently in his opposition to the cold war and the absorption of Canada into it and in his defense of the university tradition against those who would use it as merely another expression of state or market power. His thought and conduct defied description by terms like radical or conservative, but represented nonetheless the best of western humanism. In an age when the social studies are tepid and antiseptic, and also more powerful, his example is a source of more than intellectual inspiration.

The very opaqueness and aphoristic quality of his writing, when combined with its critical moral stance, has left his work open to be assimilated to and contrasted with newer developments in scholarship that have occurred since his death. I am thinking, in particular, of developments in cultural geography, Marxism and critical theory, and in cultural anthropology and hermeneutics.

The significance that is my theme is of another kind. For me, the significance of his work is to be found in the light of our knowledge of, and literature about, human communication and, in particular, what we effortlessly but misleadingly call mass communication. I want to insert his work into that stream of understanding to highlight the significance of his scholarship for those of us in the United States whose own work, however pale by comparison, is derivative of it.

American research and scholarship on communication began as a cumulative tradition in the late 1880s when five people came together in Ann Arbor, Michigan. Two were young faculty—John Dewey and George Herbert Mead, two were students at the time—Robert Park and Charles Cooley. The final element of the pentad was an itinerant American journalist by the name of Franklin Ford, who shared with Dewey, indeed cultivated in him, the belief "A proper daily newspaper would be the only possible social science."[1]

Like most intellectuals of the period, this group was under the spell of Herbert Spencer's organic conception of society, through not enthralled by social Darwinism. The relationship between communication and transportation which organicism suggested—the nerves and arteries of society—had been realized in fact with the parallel growth of the telegraph and railroad: a thoroughly encephalated social nervous system with the control mechanism of communication divorced from the physical movement of people and things.

They saw in the developing technology of communications the capacity to transform, in Dewey's terms, the great society created by industry into a great community: a unified nation with one culture, a great public of common understanding and knowledge. This belief in communication as the cohesive force in society was, of course, part of the progressive creed. Communications technology was the key to improving the quality of politics and culture, the means for turning the United States into a continental village, a pulsating Greek democracy of discourse on a 3,000 mile scale. This was more than a bit of harmless romanticism; it was part of an unbroken tradition of thought on communications technology that continues to this day and that Leo Marx named and I appropriated as the "rhetoric of the technological sublime."[2]

Three other features of their work are worth noting. First, methodologically they were in a revolt against formalism, in Morton White's happy phrase: They attempted to return social studies to a branch of history and to emphasize the interdisciplinary nature of social knowledge.[3] Second, they were under the spell of the frontier hypothesis or at least a certain version thereof. The significance they found in the frontier was not that of the heroic individual breaking one's way into the wilderness, but rather they emphasized the process whereby strangers created the institutions of community life de novo in the small towns of the West. This process of community creation, of institution building, was, they argued, the formative process in the growth of American democracy. Again, although there is more than a little romance with the pastoral in all this, it also led to a positive achievement. In the absence of an inherited tradition, the active process of communication would have to serve as the source of social order and cohesion. Moreover, they conceived communication as something more than the imparting of information. Rather, they characterized communication as the entire process whereby a culture is brought into existence, maintained in time, and sedimented into institutions. Therefore, they saw communication in the envelope of art, architecture, custom and ritual, and, above all, politics. And this gave the third distinctive aspect to their thought: an intense concern with the nature of public life. As Alvin Gouldner has recently reemphasized, the idea of the public is a central notion in their thought and, although they agreed with Gabriel Tarde that the public is something brought into existence by the printing press, they went beyond him in trying to work through the conditions under which the public sphere gives rise to rational and critical discourse and action.[4] In the 1920s these concerns crested and yielded a continuous stream of literature on communications, a central feature of which was a concern with the "vanishing public" or the "eclipse of the public." Despite their youthful optimism, many of the Chicago School, as they were known, came to see that although the mass media brought the public into existence, it later threatened the possibility of public life and with it the possibility of rational discourse and enlightened public opinion.[5]

Harold Innis studied at the University of Chicago when Park and Mead were on the faculty and this tradition was in full flower. Moreover, these same intense concerns with communication were ripe within the city at large: in Jane Adams' Hull House, in Frank Lloyd Wright's architecture offices, in the writings of Louis Sullivan, and, above all, in the textures of the University of Chicago.[6] At a conference a few years back, I attempted to demonstrate some of the continuity of concerns of Innis and the Chicago School but also to dispute Marshall McLuhan's claim that Innis "should be considered as the most eminent member of the Chicago group headed by Robert Park."[7] Park had no direct influence on Innis and Innis was too singular a thinker to be described as a member of any school. Innis' transcript at the University of Chicago reveals he took a very narrow range of courses, strictly limited to traditional topics within political economy. His only outside work was one course in political science on municipal government offered by the greatest Chicago political scientist of the time, Charles Merriam.[8] My only claim is this: The significance of Innis for those of us working within United States' traditions is that he took the concerns of the Chicago School and, with the unvarnished eye of one peering across the Forty-ninth Parallel, corrected and completed these concerns, marvelously widened their range and precision and created a conception and historically grounded theory of communications that was purged of the inherited romanticism of the Chicago School and that led to a far more adequate view of the role of communications and communications technology in American life.

By the time Innis started to write about communications, Chicago sociology had pretty much run itself into the sand. During the 1930s it was transformed into symbolic interactionism, a social psychology of the self and others drawn from the work of Mead. However elegant this work might be, it was also safely tucked away from the questions of politics, rationality, power, and social change that Chicago sociologists had earlier engaged. American studies in communications then came under two influences. The first came from work on psychological behaviorism initiated by John B. Watson just prior to World War I. Watson, both a professor at Columbia and a vice-president of J. Walter Thompson advertising agency, drew upon an accumulating body of work, principally from E. L. Thorndike in animal psychology, and laid down a model of human action in which mind played no part in the arrangement of behavior. Transmitted into the study of communication, this provided the basis for a program of study in which communication became a branch of learning theory, in which learning was defined as the acquisition of behaviors and in which behaviors were governed in turn by conditioning and reinforcement. By removing mind from behavior, the possibility of rational action was removed also, but this was the precise and willing price to be paid for constructing a model of human social action on the postulates of physical science. Powerfully aided by the practical research demands of World War II, behaviorism gave rise to a power or domination model of communication in which study was narrowed into a focus on the means by which power and control is made effective through language, symbols, and media.

The second influence was more indirect but came initially, I think, from the powerful demonstration effect of the Hawthorn experiments. Conducted in a Western Electric plant in the Chicago suburbs, these studies gave rise to the often noted Hawthorn effect: that worker productivity rose over the cycle of the experiments because of the experiments themselves—Hawthorn gives us Heisenberg. What is less often noted is that the experiments were presumably a test of a model derived from Durkheim: that the factory should be viewed as an integrated social system to which the worker had to be adjusted. The findings of the experiments then gave rise to a new social role, a band of ambulatory counsellors whose task it was to resocialize the workers to their grievances. That is, the major lesson of the Hawthorn experiments was the discovery of the power of communication to serve as a means of therapy in the service of social control of the worker.

These movements in thought coalesced under Paul Lazarsfeld and his students and, impelled by the war effort and coordinate developments in cybernetics, communication studies in the immediate post war years was organized pretty strictly as a subdiscipline of social psychology. Moreover, the models that guided this research yielded two alternative formulations of communication: in one model, communication was seen as a mode of domination, in another as a form of therapy; in one model, men were motivated to pursue power, in the other to flee anxiety. I characterize such models in this way to emphasize one simple point: these models were not merely models of communication, representations of the communication process. They were also models for the enactment of the communication process, powerful models of an actual social practice.[9]

Finally, the growth of these models within the intellectual community and the marriage of this social science to imitations of the physical sciences signaled a shift in the nature of American social scientists in general and communications students in particular. I refer here to the transformation of social scientists from a prophetic to a priestly class. It signaled the ingestion of social science into the apparatus of rule and a surrendering of the critical function of independent intellectuals.

One final development should be noted. The transformation of communication studies into a branch of psychology not only ended the essentially interdisciplinary character of it in the United States but also separated it from historical studies. Conceived now as a natural science, communication studies could send historical studies elsewhere, implicitly into the humanities where they might retain curiosity value, but could not make claims as a form of knowledge of pertinence to the conduct of contemporary life. As a result, American historical studies in communications developed without a vital relationship to the social sciences. More unfortunately, they developed along a particular model which I, stealing a memorable phrase from Herbert Butterfield, have chosen to call a "Whig interpretation of communications history."[10] Butterfield used the notion of the Whig interpretation to describe the marriage of the doctrine of progress with the idea of history. The Whig interpretation of communications history, to put it all too briefly, views the history of the press as the slow steady expansion of freedom and knowledge from the political press to the commercial press, the setbacks into sensationalism and yellow journalism, the forward thrust into muckraking and social responsibility. History is seen as the rise and expansion of freedom and responsibility.[11] When communication technology is the subject for historical study, pretty much the same story emerges. The history of communications technology is the story of the expansion of the powers of human knowledge, the steady democratization of culture, the enlargement of freedom, and the erosion of monpolies of knowledge through more democratic sharing. From the onset of literacy through the latest in computational hardware, it is the story of the progressive liberation of the human spirit. More information is made available and is made to move further and faster, ignorance is ended, civil strife brought under control. In this version of the rhetoric of the technological sublime it is the machines that possess teleological insight.[12]

THE INNIS ACHIEVEMENT

This was the situation, admittedly reduced to a sketch, that pertained when Harold Innis died in the early 1950s. It is against this background that the achievement of Innis should be assessed, at least for those of us working in an American context. Let me briefly summarize that achievement: Innis produced a body of historical and theoretical speculation that sets out the major dimensions of communications history and the critical propositions and problems of communication theory, and he did so with maximal pertinance to the circumstances of North America. Much remains to be done with his work, both in moving outward to a more systematic cultural analysis, and in altering the entire framework to fit subsequent advances in the social sciences. However, while recognizing Innis' achievements, it is best to avoid excessive piety before it. Innis' books are not sacred texts to be exegetically struggled over. They are examples of what can be done and without his work we would lack a powerful place to begin.[13]

Let me briefly outline what it is that constitutes part of Innis' achievement when set against the background of the American scholarship I have mentioned.

First, and most obvious, Innis pursued communications in a genuinely interdisciplinary way. He was simultaneously geographer, historian, economist, and political scientist, and he located communications study at the point where these fields intersected. Like the Chicago School, he shared in the revolt against formalism and not only ransacked experience without regard to discipline but restored communications study to an historical foundation. For myself, what was most critical was that he rescued communications from a branch of social psychology and freed it from a reliance on natural science models. This seems to me to be the critical intervention. Innis recognized that all scholarship must be grounded in the analysis of the radical particularities of time and place, history and geography. However, scholars that adopted natural science models suggested they were expounding, like physical scientists, laws that were universal, that held without regard to time, place, and circumstance. He saw up close the consequence of adopting this view in his analysis of the applicability of Manchester economics to economies such as Canada's. To avoid intellectual colonization he felt Canada must, in scholarship as in other matters, turn to an analysis of the radical particularities of Canadian experience and reach out from them to the experience of others. As he said late in his life in an essay entitled, "Great Britain, the United States, and Canada," and here he was thinking of more than scholarship, "Whatever hope of continued autonomy Canada may have in the future must depend on her success in withstanding American influence and in assisting the development of a third bloc designed to withstand the pressure of the United States and Russia."[14]

He was committed to the notion of pluralistic centers of scholarship as essential to cultural stability. To this end he attempted to restore to economics and communications an historical model of analysis. The central terms that he brought to the study of communications—the limitations of technology, the spatial and temporal bias inherent in technology, the monopolies of knowledge toward which they tend and which they support, the analysis of social change, selective advantage, cultural stability and collapse, legitimacy, the dialetical method—were not the terms of a verification model. They were, instead, a made in the kitchen group of concepts with which to examine the actual historical record. As I suggested in a recent essay, rather too much time has been spent analyzing the dictionary meaning of these terms, as if they were designed to enter a deductive model or formal theory. What I tried to emphasize, and Ian Parker suggested that I did not emphasize it strongly enough, was that they were terms with which to examine the historical record, precisely to cut down and limit the legitimacy of formal and universal theories. And, if anything, in following out his work we have not been empirical enough, have not followed out the concrete historical investigations that would, utilizing many of his concepts, set this record straight.

In short, Innis provided in communication studies, at a moment when no one else in the United States was dong so, a model of scholarly investigation that was historical, empirical, interpretive, and critical. His work was historical, as I have said, in the precise sense that he wanted to test the limits of theoretical work, to show the actual variations in time and space that rendered transparent the dangerous claim of universal theory. The historical imagination checked off the bias of the theoretical one. It was empirical in that he attempted to exhume the actual historical record and not those ironclad laws of development with which we have been plagued from Hegel forward. His work was interpretive in that it sought the definitions, the varying definitions, people placed upon experience in relation to technology, law, religion, and politics.

Finally, his work was critical in the contemporary sense in that he was not proposing some natural value free study, but a standpoint from which to critique society and theories of it in light of humane and civilized values.

Second, Innis reformulated the idea of the Chicago School often in a quite explicit way and attacked, albeit indirectly, the notions of communications that had gained currency in American historical and scientific scholarship. In particular, from his earliest work, he argued against the major versions of the frontier hypothesis "so gratifyingly isolationist that the source of inspiration and action was not at the center but at the periphery of Western culture." Every frontier, in short, has a back tier. The "back tier" interest was determined by the extent to which the frontier products strengthened its economy, supplemented rather than competed with its products and enhanced its strategic position.[15] That first back tier was Europe and to that extent North American economic and communications development was part of the trajectory of European history. The development of this continent was decisively determined by the policies and struggles of European capitals. The consequences of those policies and struggles were outlined in his studies of staples: fur, fish, timber, etc. With the gradual decline of the influence of Europe, the back tier shifted to the North American metropolitan centers, both Canadian and American, but effective control shifted toward New York and Washington, relative to both the Canadian and American frontiers. The studies of paper and pulp brought that home and also led to the realization that in mechanized forms of communications new types of empire and back-tier/frontier relations were elaborated: "The United States, with systems of mechanized communication and organized force, has sponsored a new type of imperialism imposed on common law in which sovereignty is preserved de jure and used to expand imperialism de facto."[16]

In this observation, he founded the modern studies that now exist under the banner of media imperialism but his sense of the complexity of that relationship was considerably more subtle than that of most contemporary scholars. In particular, Innis knew something of the tensions, contradictions, and accommodations that existed between trading and communications partners. This allowed him, from the beginning, to pierce the organic metaphors that so often led the Chicago scholars astray and masked the facts of history, geography, and power in a veil of metaphysics. Even if society were like an organism, there would be some controlling element, some centralized brain in the body, some region and group that would collect the power necessary to direct the nerves of communication and the arteries of transportation. There would be no transformation of the great society into the great community by way of disinterested technology but only in terms of the ways in which knowledge and culture were monopolized by particular groups.

He saw in the growth of communication in the late eighteenth and nineteenth centuries a continual process of decentralization and recentralization that moved forward in a dialectical way as small hinterland communities attempted to outrun metropolitan influence, only later to be absorbed back into it. The prevailing pattern of communication prior to the American Revolution was a classically imperial one. Messages moved on an east–west axis between London and the Colonies. Communication between the Colonies moved slowly and erratically and in general the Colonies communicated with one another via London. Following the Revolution this same pattern prevailed for a time. News in early American newspapers was almost exclusively European in origin and communication was stronger between the port cities and England than between the cities and their own American hinterland. Internal communication was slow and problematic, good only on the Atlantic sea corridor and only then when not adversely affected by weather. American towns and cities were relatively isolated from one another and connected only by common port cities or European capitals.

Following the War of 1812, the country embarked on a vigorous campaign for what were benignly called "internal improvements," the object of which, again benignly expressed, was an attempt to bind the nation together or connect the east with the west. In fact, what developed was the same pattern of communication of the Colonial period but now with New York replacing London as the central element in the system. As Arthur Schlesinger, Sr., emphasized, what grew up over the first half of the eighteenth century was a pattern of city–state imperialism.[17] The major cities of the East vigorously competed with one another to replace London as the geographic center of trade and communications. By the early 1800s, New York was firmly established as the center of American communication and controlled the routes of trade and communication with the interior, a position it has never relinquished. It maintained first contacts with Europe through shipping and therefore information passed between American cities by being routed through New York. But every major city on the East coast made its bid for control of the interior. New York's hegemony was secured by the Hudson River, the Erie Canal, and the resultant access to the Great Lakes, and by Chicago allowing New York to service and drain the Mississippi Valley. Philadelphia also attempted to control the West through an elaborate series of canals whose failure brought Pennsylvania to the verge of bankruptcy. Baltimore attempted through the first national highway, from Cumberland, Maryland, to connect into the Ohio River and terminate in St. Louis at the headwaters of the Missouri. Baltimore later tried with the Baltimore and Ohio Railroad, the first national railroad, to build this connection surer and faster, and even Boston, although blocked from the West by New York, attempted to become a railroad center and create access independent of the Erie Canal. As Alan Pred's studies have documented most thoroughly, the effect of the hegemony of New York was to draw the hinterland cities within its information field and to isolate other East Coast cities. Even Columbus, Ohio, was being served by New York with both goods and information in the 1840s.[18] New York's hegemony was in turn strengthened by the construction of the Illinois Central Railroad from Chicago to New Orleans. At the time of its building it was popularly called the "great St. Louis cut-off" because it was designed to isolate St. Louis from its natural trading partner, Baltimore. When the first transcontinental railroad was placed along the northern route, this again strengthened the centrality of New York. When this was tied to the increasing access of New York and Washington along the Atlantic trade and information corridor, the basic pattern was complete. New York, and therefore its merchants, firms, and elites controlled an increasingly centralized system of information which tied the northern tier together and even acted as a source of supply from many Canadian Cities. It just as effectively isolated the South. By every measure of communication the South, with the exception of New Orleans, was isolated from the rest of the country. There were poor interconnections between southern cities, and southern cities dealt with one another and the rest of the North only by first channeling communication through New York.[19]

Although this pattern of information movement has been importantly altered since the 1840s, its persistence, at least in outline, is even more striking. The trade routes of culture laid down by the canal and railroad have been altered by the telegraph, wire services, magazines, films, telephone, broadcasting, and jet aircraft to be sure. But the centrality of New York in the flow of communications and culture, the importance of the New York–Washington corridor, and the metropole–hinterland connections that flow east and west are still there to be observed. In other words, despite the enormous size of the United States, a particular pattern of geographic concentration developed that gave inordinate power to certain urban centers. This development undercut local and regional culture. Although it aided in forming a national culture, it disguised how local, even provincial, this national culture was: A national and even international culture was defined increasingly by how the world was seen from a couple of distinctively local places. The point is that since 1800 we have lived with essentially a dominant eastern corridor of American communication that has created an effective monopoly of knowledge in news and entertainment. This can be shown most graphically in the growth of the star system. Concretely, this means that today a few national figures and themes are pretty much exclusively focused on in politics and entertainment, that local issues are of interest only when they can be alchemized into national issues of concern in a few urban centers, and that the drama of news and entertainment must be made increasingly slick and abstract to appeal to national and, increasingly, international audiences.

That is only one-third of the story. Innis was also sensitive to the means by which the hinterland was in a continual struggle both to escape and accept metropolitan dominance. There was an important truth in the Chicago School's notion of the importance of local community building as a formative democratic experience. In his essay on "Technology and Public Opinion in the United States" Innis attempted to show how localities and regions resisted the spread of communication, how the issue was only decided by struggle over a protracted series of conflicts: the spread of standard time, of the mail order house, parcel post and rural free delivery, of the department store and regionalized corporation. Moreover, he was concerned to point out how the Western newspaper was an instrument for resisting metropolitan dominance, how the telegraph initially strengthened the local and regional press until that too was undercut by the power of the wire services and chain papers. That is, the spread of a spatially biased system of communication was not even and uniform but resulted in a complicated interplay of resistance and acceptance that we have yet to adequately lay out in detail.[20]

Moreover, the pattern of national spatial oraganization was reproduced in the organization of city after city and county after county. Seymour Mandelbaum's *Boss Tweed's New York* is a marvelous though complacent study of the reorganization of New York City essentially on a metropole–hinterland model.[21] My own studies suggest that same model of development holds true at the regional and county level.

The United States, then, at all levels of social structure pursued what I call high communications policy, one aimed solely at spreading messages further in space and reducing the cost of transmission. That is what Innis meant by exploiting the spatial bias of modern communication. Communication was seen, in other words, solely in the envelope of space and power. That communication might be seen as something else, as a container of human interaction that allows for the persistence and growth of culture, is a view that never entered United States policy. The distinction between power and container technology parallels Innis' distinction between space and time.[22] But what Innis saw more clearly than most was how modern institutions were thoroughly infected by the idea of space. The universities were not exempt. Economics, political science, urban planning, sociology, and the physical sciences charted the problems and challenges of society in space. Even time was converted to space as the social sciences, enamored by prediction, characterized the future as a frontier to be conquered. Even history had caught the bug for historical writing merely used time as a container to tell the narrative of progress: politics, power, empire, and rule.

In summary, as the United States pursued an almost exclusive policy of improving communication over long distance, as it saw communication as a form of power and transmission, the effective units of culture and social organization underwent major changes. There was a progressive shift from local and regional units to national and international ones, though not without considerable struggle and conflict. Individuals were linked into larger units of social organization without the necessity of appealing to them through local and proximate structures. Communication within these local units became less critical for the operation of society and less relevant to the solutions of personal problems. Finally, the growth of long distance communication cultivated new structures in which thought occurred—national classes and professions—new things thought about—speed, space, movement, mobility—and new things to think with—increasingly abstract, analytic, and manipulative symbols.

FREEDOM OF THE PRESS AND THE ORAL TRADITION

The third and final argument I want to make before concluding is that Innis also attacked the Whig interpretation of communications history. He did this by demonstrating at every point the paradoxical nature of changes in the technology of communication, and by disputing certain implicit notions concerning the nature of freedom and freedom of the press. I think this is the context of his long interest in Greek life and the nature of the oral tradition. That interest is to be understood, in other words, in terms of the relationship of democratic life to oral discourse and the public sphere.

As is well known, Innis argued that the first amendment to the United States Constitution did not so much grant freedom of speech and press as it gave constitutional protection to technology, and in this sense, restricted rather than expanded freedom:

> Freedom of the press has been given constitutional guarantees as in the United States [and] . . . has provided bulwarks for monopolies which have emphasized control over space. Under these conditions the problem of duration or monopoly over time has been neglected, indeed obliterated. Time has been cut into pieces the length of a day's newspaper.[23]

The free press clause served largely to consolidate the position of the newspaper's monopoly of knowledge and eventually, through the paper's dependence on advertising and news, was instrumental in telescoping time into a one-day world, in spreading the values of commercialism and industrialism and furthering the spatial bias of print. In granting freedom of the press, the constitution sacrificed, despite the qualifying clause, the right of people to speak to one another and to inform themselves. For such rights the Constitution substituted the more abstract right to be spoken to and to be informed by others, especially specialist, professional classes:

> The full impact of printing did not become possible until the adoption of the Bill of Rights in the United States with its guarantee of freedom of the press. A guarantee of freedom of the press in print was intended to further sanctify the printed word and to provide a rigid bulwark for the shelter of vested interests.[24]

He refused to yield to the modern notion that the level of democratic process correlates with the amount of capital invested in communication, capital that can do our knowing for us.

There certainly was something romantic in Innis' affection for the oral tradition but there was much more, a concern with the very possibility of public life. He identified the oral tradition with the Greeks and with Plato's attack on writing in the *Phaedrus:*

> If men learn this writing it will implant forgetfulness in their souls; they will cease to exercise memory because they rely on what is written, calling things to remembrance no longer from within themselves but by means of external marks; what you have discovered is a recipe not for memory but for reminder. And it is not true wisdom that you offer your disciples, but only its semblance. . . .[25]

The objections to writing here are twofold: It is inherently shallow in its effects, and essential principles of truth can only be arrived at dialectically. Writing is shallow in its effects because reading books may give a specious sense of knowledge, which in reality can only be attained by oral question and answer; and such knowledge in any case only goes deep when "it is written in the soul of the learner."[26]

We associate democracy with widespread literacy and a world of knowledge as transcending political units. Yet even though literacy can give rise to a form of democracy, it also makes impossible demands. Literacy produces instability and inconsistency because the written tradition is participated in so unevenly:

> Improvements in communication . . . make for increased difficulties of understanding. The cable compelled contraction of language and facilitated a rapid widening between the English and American languages. In the vast realm of fiction in the Anglo-Saxon world, the influence of the cinema and the radio has been evident in the best seller and the creation of special classes of readers with little prospect of communication between them. . . . The large-scale mechanization of knowledge is characterized by imperfect competition and the active creation of monopolies of language which prevent understanding. . . .[27]

That is, modern technology actually makes communication much more difficult. Rational agreement and democratic coherence become problematic when so little background is shared in common. As Bertha Phillpotts argued in 1931:

> Printing so obviously makes knowledge accessible to all that we are inclined to forget that it also makes knowledge easy to avoid. A shepherd in an Icelandic homestead . . . could not avoid spending his evenings listening to the kind of literature which interested the farmer. The result was a degree of really national culture, such as no nation of today has been able to achieve.[28]

Literate culture is much more easily avoided than an oral one and even when it is not avoided its actual effects may be relatively shallow. Lacking an oral culture one may easily fall prey to experts in knowledge who do our knowing for us, who inform us but whose knowledge does not easily connect to our actual experience and to the basic transactions of life.

In short, Innis believed that the unstated presupposition of democratic life was the existence of a public sphere, of an oral tradition, or of a tradition of public discourse as a necessary counterweight to printing. In the more telegraphic prose of his notebooks Innis observed that:

> Commercialism tends to make for imperfect competition between levels of reading public and to fix various groups within level. Average man cut off from literature. Problem of making fiction a channel of communication between publics . . . reading public disintegrated by imperfect competition in publishing industry.[29]

The first amendment did not secure the permanence of public life; in fact, it acted against it because it finally placed the weight of education on the written tradition. Modern media of communication, largely for commercial purposes, created a system of communication that was essentially private. Private reading and the reading audience replaced the reading public and the public of discussion and argument. The system of communication that actually evolved was grounded, therefore, not merely in a spatial bias but in a privatized one as well. It was the privatization more than the Bill of Rights that led to the decline of censorship:

"Decline in the practice of reading aloud led to a decline in the importance of censorship. The individual was taken over by the printing industry and his interest developed in material not suited to general conversation."[30] Under such conditions the public becomes a mere statistical artifact, public taste a measure of private opinion that has been both cultivated and objectified but not realized in discourse. With that, the public sphere goes into eclipse.

I think the breakdown in oral discourse is the key to Innis' thought and politics. The public he took to be grounded in the capacity through speech of rational discourse. He understood, of course, the difficulty of attaining these habits and realized the degree to which privatized existence inhibits the growth of such discourse. The strength of the oral tradition in his view was that it could not be easily monopolized. Once the habits of discourse were widespread, the public could take on an autonomous existence and not be subject to the easy control of the state or commerce. Therefore, the major intellectual project of Innis' later life, a project of importance to both politics and the university, was the restoration of the oral tradition—by which he meant a set of talents at memory, speech, and argument; and a sphere, a place of institutional home in which such a tradition might flourish. "Mass production and standardization are the enemies of the West. The limitations of the mechanization of the printed and the spoken word must be emphasized and determined efforts to recapture the vitality of the oral tradition must be made."[31] Here he agreed with John Dewey.[32] Speech is the agency of creative thought; printing of dissemination. It was precisely the imbalance between the processes of creativity and dissemination that Innis sought to correct. Mechanical communication transformed the reading and listening public into a reading and listening audience with disastrous consequences for democracy. Correcting the situation turned upon demonstrating that freedom of the press could ultimately stand as an enemy to freedom of expression.

Innis' attachment to the oral tradition finally, then, had a modern purpose: to demonstrate that the belief that the growth of mechanical communication necessarily expanded freedom and knowledge was both simplistic and misleading. For that to happen there would have to be a parallel and dialectical growth of public sphere, grounded in an oral tradition, where knowledge might be "written in the soul of the learner."

THE INVASION OF TIME

Let me emphasize, again, in conclusion, that the great challenge of Innis' work is not to attempt to figure out what he really meant. Rather, it is the attempt to apply and extend some of his major ideas by interpreting them within the context of concrete episodes. As one direction to take these interpretations, let me offer a closing observation on the relation of time, space, and communications.

The growth of communications in the nineteenth century had the practical effect of diminishing space as a differentiating criterion in human affairs. What Innis called the "penetrative powers of the price system"[33] was in effect the spread of a uniform price system throughout space so that for purposes of trade everyone was in the same place. In commerce this meant the decontextualization of markets such that local prices no longer depended on local factors of supply and demand but responded to national and international forces. The spread of the price system was part of the attempt to colonize space. The correlative to the penetration of the price system was what the late composer Igor Stravinsky called the "statisticalization of mind": the transformation of the entire mental world into quantity, and the distribution of quantities in space such that the relationship between things and people becomes solely one of numbers. Statistics widens and makes the market for everything more uniform and interdependent.

My interest is in that moment when the ecological niche of space was filled, so to speak, filled as an arena of commerce and control. Then, attention was shifted to filling time, now defined as an aspect of space, a continuation of space in another dimension. As the spatial frontier was filled, time became the new frontier. This is easiest to see in terms of trade. When the prices of commodities were equalized in space, largely as a result of the telegraph, speculation moved from a spatial to a temporal dimension. That is, the exhaustion of space as an arena of arbitrage gave rise to the futures market: a shifting of market activity from certain space to uncertain time. My suspicion is that this was the first practical attempt to make time a new frontier, a newly defined zone of uncertainty, and to penetrate it by the price system.

There are two other dimensions of time I want to mention briefly. I think the second time to be penetrated once space was exhausted, was sacred time, in particular the sabbath. I believe that the greatest invention of the ancient Hebrews was the idea of the sabbath, though I am using this word in a fully secular sense: the invention of a region free from control of the state and commerce where another dimension of life could be experienced and where altered forms of social relationship could occur. As such, the sabbath has always been a major resistance to state and market power. For purposes of communication, the effective penetration of the sabbath came in the 1880s with the invention of the Sunday newspaper. It was Hearst with his New York Sunday *World* that popularized the idea of Sunday newspaper reading and created, in fact, a market where none had existed before—a sabbath market. Since then the penetration of the sabbath has been one of the "frontiers" of commercial activity. Finally, when the frontier in space was officially closed in 1893, the "new frontier" became the night, and since then there has been a continous spreading upward of commercial activity. In a recent and suggestive paper in the *American Sociological Review*, Murray Melbin of Boston University has attempted to characterize "night as a frontier."[34] In terms of communication, the steady expansion of commercial broadcasting into the night is one of the best examples. There were no twenty-four-hour radio stations in Boston, for example, from 1918 through 1954; now half of the stations in Boston operate all night. Television has slowly expanded into the night at one end and at the other initiated operations earlier and earlier. Now, indeed, there are twenty-four-hour television stations in major markets.[35]

The notion of night as frontier, a new frontier of time that opens once space is filled, is a metaphor but it is more than that. Melbin details some of the features common to the spatial and temporal frontiers: They both advance in stages, the population is more sparsely settled and homogenous, there is solitude, an absence of social constraints and less persecution, settlements are isolated, government is decentralized, lawlessness and violence as well as friendliness and helpfulness increase, new behavioral styles emerge.[36] That is, the same dialectic between centralization and decentralization occurs on the temporal frontier as on the spatial frontier. On the one hand, communication is even more privatized at night. On the other hand, people are less controlled by communication because of the absence of authority.

My point here is merely a suggestive one. The end of space led to the invasion of time by the forces of commerce and politics and with something of the same dialectic of decentralization and recentralization that was found in space. The way in which time was redefined as an ecological niche to be filled and the actual way it has been progressively filled since the closing of the spatial frontier in the nineteenth century is, I think, among the many practical research tasks that the work of Harold Innis left to us.

NOTES

[1]The phrase comes from notes taken by Charles Cooley on a Dewey lecture in Ann Arbor. Quoted in Fred H. Mathews, *Quest for an American Sociology: Robert E. Park and the Chicago School*. Montreal, McGill–Queen's University Press, 1977, p. 18.

[2]Marx, Leo. *The Machine in the Garden*. New York, Oxford University Press, 1964.

[3]White, Morton. *Social Thought in America: The Revolt Against Formalism*. Boston, Beacon Press, 1957.

[4]Gouldner, Alvin. *The Dialectic of Ideology and Technology*. New York, The Seabury Press, 1977, Chs. 4 and 5.

[5]See, in particular, John Dewey. *The Public and Its Problems*. New York, Henry Holt and Company, 1927.

[6]Quandt, Jean. *From the Small Town to the Great Community*. New Brunswick, New Jersey, Rutgers University Press, 1970.

[7]McLuhan, Marshall "Introduction," to *The Bias of Communication*, by Harold A. Innis. Toronto, University of Toronto Press, 1964, p. xvi.

[8]The Registrar of the University of Chicago was kind enough to send me a copy of Innis' transcript with grades appropriately and delicately blanked out.

[9]I have taken these matters up at greater length in "A Cultural Approach to Communication." In *Communication*, Vol. 2, No. 2, 1975, pp. 1–22.

[10]Butterfield, Herbert. *The Whig Interpretation of History* (1931). Harmondsworth, England, Penguin Books, 1973.

[11]Carey, James W. "The Problem of Journalism History." In *Journalism History*, Vol. 1, No. 1, Spring 1974, pp. 3–5, 27.

[12]For a more extended argument on these matters, particularly as they relate to Innis and McLuhan, see James W. Carey and John J. Quirk. "The Myths of the Electronic Revolution." In *American Scholar*, Vol. 39, Nos. 2 and 3, Spring, Summer 1970, pp. 219–241, 395–424.

[13]Carey, James W. "Canadian Communication Theory: Extensions and Interpretations of Harold Innis." In *Studies in Canadian Communications*, edited by Gertrude Joch Robinson and Donald F. Theall. Montreal, McGill Programme in Communications, 1975, pp. 27–59.

[14]Innis, H. A. *Essay in Canadian Economic History*. Toronto, University of Toronto Press, 1956, p. 411.

[15]Heaton, Herbert. *The Economics of Empire*, The James Ford Bell Lecture, No. 3, University of Minnesota, 1966.

[16]Innis H. A. *Empire and Communications*. Oxford, Oxford University Press, 1950, p. 215.

[17]Schlesinger, Sr., Arthur. *The Rise of the City 1878–1898*. New York, Macmillan, 1933, p. 86.

[18]This argument is based, specifically, on the work of Alan Pred. See: *Urban Growth and the Circulation of Information*. Cambridge, Harvard University Press, 1973. Pred, in turn, relies upon Innis' analysis.

[19]Again, the analysis relies on Pred's work but the outlines of the argument are presented in Innis' early work, particularly as it concerns the relations between the American South, the American North, and Canada. See: Innis, H. A. *The Fur Trade in Canada* (1930). Toronto, University of Toronto Press, 1956, particularly the concluding chapter.

[20]Innis, *Bias of Communication*, p. 156ff.

[21]Mandelbaum, Seymour J. *Boss Tweed's New York*. New York, John Wiley and Company, 1965.

[22]The distinction between power and container technology is taken from Lewis Mumford. *The Pentagon of Power*. New York, Harcourt, Brace, Javonovich, Inc., 1970, Ch. 6.

[23]Innis, H. A. "Concept of Monopoly and Civilization." In *Explorations*, No. 3, August 1954, pp. 89–95.

[24]Innis, *Bias of Communication*, p. 138.

[25]Hackworth, R. (Ed). *Plato's Phaedrus*. Cambridge, Cambridge University Press, 1972, p. 157.

[26]Hackworth, *Plato's Phaedrus*, p. 159.

[27]Innis, *Bias of Communication*, pp. 28–29.

[28]Quoted in Jack Good, (Ed). *Literacy in Traditional Societies*. Cambridge, Cambridge University Press, 1968, p. 60. This section borrows from and paraphrases Goody's work.

[29]Innis, H. A. *The Idea File*. In the collection of Thomas Fisher Library, University of Toronto, p. 30.

[30]Innis, H. A. *Changing Concepts of Time*. Toronto, University of Toronto Press, 1952, p. 10.

[31]Innis, *Empire and Communications*, p. 215.

[32]Dewey, John. *The Public and Its Problems*, Chicago, Swallow Press, 1927, Ch. 6.

[33]Innis, *Essays*, pp. 252–272.

[34]Melbin, Murray. "Night as Frontier." In *American Sociological Review*, Vol. 43, No. 1, February 1978, pp. 3–22.

[35]Melbin, "Night as Frontier," p. 4.

[36]Melbin, "Night as Frontier," pp. 6–18.

II
INSTITUTIONS AND DEVELOPMENT: A FOCUS ON POLITICAL ECONOMY

> ... the economic history of Canada has been dominated by the discrepency between the centre and the margin of Western civilization.
>
> —Innis

> The study of Canadian economy becomes of crucial significance to an understanding of cyclical and secular disturbances not only within Canada but without. In a sense the economies of frontier countries are storm centres to the modern international economy.
>
> —Innis

As an economist, Innis was an institutionalist. He directed his attention to the realities of development, and found abstract theorizing a barren exercise. The papers in this section follow in the Innis tradition of institutional analysis.

Horace Gray's review of the development of institutional economies in the United States captures both the spirit and the difficulties of the institutionalists. Institutional economics grew from the work of Veblen and built on that of John R. Commons, Wesley Mitchell, J. M. Clark and others. It places the study of institutions at the center of research on economic problems and is critical of theorizing that ignores institutions, power relationships, and historical patterns. Institutionalists have never been bashful about foraging in other disciplines, particularly law, history, politics and sociology. The scope of institutional economics is defined by the problems that are addressed, not by the limitations of a specialist profession.

Gray's paper demonstrates the concern of institutional economics with critical analysis of existing institutions, the elimination of monopoly power and special privilege, and the implementation of reform by the revision of public policy. For most institutional economists, research is incomplete if one does not follow through with recommendations to improve circumstances in the areas under study. The ultimate goal in studying society's problems is to improve the situation in the real world. And that involves participation in the policy-making process.

We must recognize, however, that Innis is classified as an institutional economist largely because he did not fit into any of the other schools of economic thought. He was not a neoclassical theorist, a Keynesian, an econometrician, or a Marxist. He was a classical scholar, an unorthodox economic historian with a focus on institutions and their relationships. Although the nature of Innis' work meant that he had much in common with other institutional economists, his approach and his perspective were unique.

The papers by Smythe and Parker provide new insights into the relationships between economics and communication. Smythe shows how traditional economic analysis has ignored, or assumed away, essential characteristics of communication, and argues that this failure has been a major deficiency. His critique is one with which Innis would have sympathized.

Parker outlines a common line of inquiry between Innis and Marx on the economics of communication, showing some interesting parallels. Parker's paper raises an interesting question. Was Innis really applying Marxian analysis? Innis and Marx addressed many similar issues, each with rare insight into the historical pattern of development and a unique appreciation for the role of institutions. Both Innis and Marx had materialist conceptions of history.

Parker labels Innis' approach "dialetic materialist." But Innis' dialectics were very different from Marx's. For Innis, the term simply refers to the coexistence of opposing tendencies in the same historical circumstances. Although the dialectic pressures in any period might act as propulsion for change, for Innis dialectics were not central to understanding the nature of capitalism. From his perspective, therefore, Innis had no difficulty exploring in great detail the characteristics of coexistent Canadian metropolitan expansion and colonial status. Although Innis is clearly much closer to Veblen than to Marx, and the differences between Innis and Marx are substantial, Parker shows that Innis has more in common with Marx than previously was thought.

Robin Neill's analysis leads him to modify drastically the traditional explanation that the economics of staple exports has been the primary determinant of Canada's political structure. He concludes that "in reality, the causation runs the other way. Reliance on staple exports has been the result of political circumstances." "Reliance on staples has not caused regionalization. Regionalization has caused reliance on staples."

Neill's paper forces a recognition that what Innis showed was an association of staple exports and political structure, not necessarily a cause and effect relationship. But by showing that government policies were directed to facilitate staple exports, one might question whether he also demonstrates association, not causation. In any event, the association of economic and political factors should not be surprising. Powerful economic forces generally are able to use political structures to facilitate their development. And powerful political forces often are able to direct economic development to secure their ends.

Irene Spry's review and updating of the significance of overhead costs in Innis' analysis of economic development demonstrates how the characteristics of large economic systems can be determined by seemingly narrow, technical factors. At first blush, it is difficult to perceive that something as apparently mundane as the structure of costs could play a major role in determining economic development. One of Innis' teachers at the University of Chicago, J. M. Clark, developed the classical work on *The Economics of Overhead Costs* (Chicago, 1923). Innis extended Clark's work and applied it in the Canadian context. It is the nature of overhead costs that represents a key factor in explaining important aspects of the instability and dependency associated with staple resource development.

It is disappointing that Spry's review shows that there has been extremely little substantive contribution to the study of overhead costs over the past 25 years. This is doubly unfortunate, because the significance of overhead cost in modern economics has increased in major ways over the past quarter century. It is a key factor in the continuing decline in competitive forces in the economy, as well as the fundamental changing relationship between government and private industry.

The papers by Tussing and Usher provide differing views of the implications of current staple resource development in Alaska and Northern Canada. As context for interpreting these papers, we should note some contrasts. Alaska is not only a hinterland and a metropolis, as Tussing observes, it is also a state within a metropolitan economy. The Northwest Territories (NWT) and Yukon are both hinterland territories in a country with an economy characterized by the export of staples. Alaska can claim ownership to natural resources and receives massive royalty payments from oil and gas development. Neither the NWT nor the Yukon have provincial status; even if some form of self-government is obtained, royalty revenue derived from natural resource development belongs to the Federal Government of Canada. Moreover, in the Canadian North, most oil and gas permits have been let on long-term leases to private corporations. Thus, even the federal government may have limited room to negotiate an alternative allocation of development of natural resources.

The Alaska native claims settlement was generated or facilitated by the pressure that oil and gas discoveries created. The social and political upheaval following from the Berger Inquiry in the NWT and the Foothills application in Yukon grows from the possibility of a transmission line *across* either of these territories. Finally, the Alaskan native bourgeoisie was strong prior to and strengthened by the claims settlement. In the NWT, where there is a predominantly native population, there is only a small (mainly Metis) bourgeoisie, one experienced primarily in small business and service occupations. Were Canadian native people to opt for a settlement that guaranteed their initial participation in a corporate or industrial economy, their skills as hunters or craftspeople would be of little assistance.

Another interesting comparison might be drawn between Alaska and Alberta. In Alaska, as in Alberta, royalty revenues contribute to a giant fund of public capital held in reserve to sponsor or support economic development. Little is known yet about the potential effects of the injection of massive amount of public capital into an economy characterized by private development. Innis commented extensively on the subject, but few scholars have developed this theme from his work. This is yet another area where important current issues require research in the Innis tradition.

7

REFLECTIONS ON INNIS
AND INSTITUTIONAL ECONOMICS

HORACE M. GRAY
University of Illinois

It is a much appreciated honor for one of the last survivors of the school "institutional economics" in the United States to pay tribute to Canada's greatest exponent of that mystery. I use the word "mystery" in the enigmatic sense of Butler's classic portrayal of the Bank of England. All really important and complicated arrangements—institutional economics among them—are mysteries.

Harold A. Innis and I were near contemporaries. He was born in 1894, and I in 1898. He served his country in World War I in the Canadian Artillery, was wounded at Vimy Ridge and invalided home; I served my country in the U. S. Navy, survived the hazards of the North Atlantic and got home in time to enter college in the fall of 1919. Professor Innis qualified for his doctoral degree in Economics from the University of Chicago in 1920; I received mine from the University of Illinois in 1926. He died in 1952 at the age of fifty-eight; I have attained the age of eighty and am still active.

Our academic careers were generally similar, being a combination of teaching, research, administration, and public service, but the distribution of our labors was different. Innis found more time for research and writing than I did. In the United States, conditions at that time were so unstable and controversial that most institutional economists devoted a large portion of their time to reform efforts, to protecting the public interest against aggression by private monopolists and to administration of the regulatory system. They did a great deal of research, but it was largely of a practical rather than a scholarly character, as was that of

Innis. Ideally, this was an improper use of scarce resources, but an emergency situation seemed to require it.

Innis was closely associated with American economists from the time of his graduate study at Chicago (1919–20) until the time of his death in 1952. Thus, he knew us intimately—our history, our institutions, our leaders, our faults, our virtues. Whether from modesty or for diplomatic reasons, he carefully avoided becoming involved in our violent controversies. Some of my generation resented this—they still voiced the old cry: "Come over into Macedonia and help us!"—but he did not come. He saw clearly that we had to solve our own institutional problems. He did defend Thorstein Veblen's basic ideas in a brilliant review, thus removing the curse of radicalism from institutional economics.

As an institutional economist, reared in the Jeffersonian tradition and a practical reformer of democratic bent, I always felt challenged by the doctrine of determinism. If it were true, then man, to that extent, was unfree, but still free in respect to other aspects of life not bound by the chains of determinism. It was this margin of freedom that gave us hope for survival; if man were only partially free, might he not expand this area of freedom? The institutional economists of my generation had to be optimists to survive. We were in the predicament of Robert Burns when told by a fundamentalist preacher that the Devil would surely get him on account of his wayward conduct. Burns, the eternal optimist, replied smartly that he would "turn a corner and cheat him yet." This optimism proved correct for the people laughed the preacher out of town, and they got another—a kindly amiable gentleman who sympathized with sinners like Burns while trying to convert them to a better way of life.

My first insight to the thought of Innis on this crucial issue was derived from his staples studies, particularly on the fur trade. It started off like the Book of Genesis: In the beginning the earth was without form and void—darkness was upon the face of the deep! How deterministic can a situation be? Then came Man—three categories of them: the Natives, the merchant adventurers, the wealthy buyers of fine furs. These men created a "going concern," a functional operating entity called "the fur trade," which flourished for years to come. It, like the Bank of England, was a mystery.

Now this "going concern," this fur trade, was the product of powerful material forces—land, weather, animal population, techniques, navigation, processing, marketing, finance. Some of these were dictated by nature, and were thus beyond human control, but others were neither fish nor fowl; rather, it was an admixture of the material and immaterial, the natural and the human elements, put together by human ingenuity into a "going concern" to maximize human welfare.

The great merit of Innis was that he saw this distinction clearly and used it precisely to explain economic development. Some things were determined by nature, others by man. Thus, in his view, the scope of determinism was limited and, hence, no situation was ever wholy deterministic. It was the role of rational man to make decisions and thus, as Adam Smith said, "to labour along with nature," In this way, man could be free, in a broad humanistic sense, while recognizing and conforming to the constraints imposed by nature. It was this wisdom and insight that set Innis apart from our modern determinists. This insight would stand him in good stead when he had to deal with Marx, Veblen, the technological determinists and, later, the psychological and cultural determinants.

Innis was from first to last an economic historian and a humanist. Thus, he could not accept the blind determinism of Darwin in biology, Marx in social structure, Veblen in technology, Freud in psychology, or the modern anthropologists in their study of cultures. He always found in his analysis evidence of the free, uninhibited human spirit and intellect working effectively against total determinism. In a state of nature determinism might prevail but in a vital human society it never could, over time, dictate the course of institutional development. It was, I think, his strong feeling on this issue that led Innis to disapprove of Veblen's extreme determinism, especially in the areas of technology and industrial organization.

INNIS ON VEBLEN

Critics probably never will agree on the exact relationship between these two great figures in the development of institutional economics. Veblen was some thirty-five years older than Innis and had achieved world-wide recognition by the time Innis became well known. What the older man thought of his young admirer we do not know. But Innis, in a carefully written and diplomatic article, published in 1929, provides an excellent review of Veblen's background, principal writings, and basic philosophy.[1] This review is a work of art, both as scholarship and as diplomacy. Innis dismisses with contempt the wild charges of immorality and anarchism made by Veblen's enemies and pleads for a fair hearing for his basic economic and philosophic views. In a classic summation he says of Veblen: "If modern economic theorists were taxonomists [i.e., mere describers], Veblen attempted the study of embryology, morphology, physiology, ecology, and aetiology of economics [i.e., all the dynamics of living organisms]. Like Professor MacIver and Professor Unwin [the two English economic historians Innis admired] he insisted upon the existence of laws of growth and decay of institutions and associations. His life work has been primarily the study of processes of growth and decay."[2]

Innis then supplies some background material not too widely known. Veblen came into economics with a strong background in philosophy, particularly Kant, Hume, Locke, Comte, Spencer, and the post Darwinians. Innis states categorically that Veblen's philosophy was not derived from Hegel and Marx, as alleged by some of his enemies. He was working at Johns Hopkins for a doctorate in philosophy when he suffered a breakdown; subsequently he shifted to economics and took his doctorate at Yale.

He was interested from the beginning in dynamics and in the process of industrial change and in this connection studied both German and American industrialism, as of 1870 and subsequently. In these studies, he followed Schmoller and the German Historical School.

From 1895 to 1905, he was editor of the *Journal of Political Economy* at Chicago and, as such, favored articles on descriptive rather than theoretical economics. In 1899 he published his famous *Theory of the Leisure Class*. Innis regarded this as good popular satire but bad economics, a general verdict from which Veblen's reputation as a scholar never quite recovered. It was a direct attack on classical economics, from both the production and consumption point of view. He attempted to destroy the hedonistic calculus of Jeremy Bentham.

In 1908–09 he launched his heaviest criticism against the orthodox classical economists, such as J. M. Clark, Irving Fisher, and Alfred Marshall, in a series of scathing reviews of their work. They were, he said, merely taxonomists describing the status quo, without regard to the dynamic forces at work in the society. By this time the break between classical and evolutionary economics had become so sharp and general that reconciliation of the divergent groups became increasingly difficult. Innis praises Veblen for his dedication to the study of growth and decay, but thinks he spread his efforts over too broad a field for one man to master. This was a minor fault; it was the method that was important, not the conclusions. Innis concludes this paragraph with a caustic reference to the critics of Veblen: "It has been unfortunate that the slight character of the work in criticism has been responsible for the violence of modern controversy and that, in consequence, the main constructive work has been forgotten."[3]

Having disposed of the critics, Innis then summarizes his judgment of Veblen. The net results are difficult to estimate. The best of the young economists have been strongly influenced by Veblen, as evidenced by the increase of descriptive studies in the United States. Veblen's work has split American economics into two warring camps. The British Labour Party economists have praised his work. Innis regards Veblen as the leading figure in the American industrial revolution just as Adam Smith was in the machine revolution of his day. He regards Veblen, along with Unwin, MacIver, Fay, and Tawney, as continuing the work of Adam Smith on behalf of the individual and the common man. He restates one of Veblen's favorite quips, that England was the first to feel the effects of the industrial revolution but was never conquered by it; America and the new continental countries have been less fortunate. That is, America lacked the cultural strength to resist the raw materialism of industrial development.

In a final two-paragraph summation, Innis pays high tribute to Veblen: "His work is a consistent whole and springs essentially from a post-Civil War environment. . . . It stands as a monument to the importance of an unbiased approach to economics. . . . Any substantial progress in economic theory must come from a closer synthesis between economic history and economic theory. . . . It is to be hoped . . . that Veblen's attempts at synthesis may be revived and steadily improved."[4]

This was in 1929—nearly fifty years ago, when Innis was thirty-five years old. It was before the Great Depression, before Roosevelt Reforms, before World War II, before the great upsurge of deterministic thought in all branches of social science after 1945. In the light of all that has transpired since 1929, how may one evaluate the judgment of Innis today? His positive assertions still hold: Veblen's work was "a consistent whole." It did spring from the post Civil War environment in the United States; Veblen did wage a war of emancipation against static economics. These may be conceded, as self-evident truths. But what then? Innis merely restates his favorite theme—there must be a closer synthesis between economic history and economic theory—and he expresses the hope that Veblen's attempts at synthesis may be revived and steadily improved. He does not meet head on the basic issue raised by Veblen of economic determinism in an advanced, high technology, monopolistic system of capitalism. Neither does he explore the related political question of whether democracy can be preserved in such a society. These two related questions are still undecided and will remain so until the Keynesian folly subsides; then, perhaps we can get back to the basic issue of institutional reform.

THE GHOST OF VEBLEN IN THE UNITED STATES

Since 1892, when Veblen published his first economic article, and was appointed Reader in economics at the University of Chicago, institutional economics has been haunted by his ghost. Canada, thanks largely to the good offices of Innis, has withstood this shock with calm equanimity; it has been otherwise in the United States.

In the United States, reactionary capitalistic interests, to protect their economic power, launched a vicious propaganda attack against Veblen. They elevated him to the godhead of all devils; not since Milton and Goethe created their magnificent devils had such a fearful and malignant apparition appeared. Veblen was a wild man, a primitive, uncivilized creature, a libertine, an anarchist, a communist, a revolutionary conspirator bent on the destruction of our glorious Republic and the creation of a socialistic dictatorship. His disciples and secret agents, it was said, were quietly invading and taking over our institutions of higher learning with the intent to subvert them to the service of revolution. These conspirators concealed their malignant purpose under the mysterious title of "institutional economics," which no one seemed able to define clearly. It seemed self-evident to these embattled business interests that such traitors and anarchists ought to be excluded from our colleges and universities lest they corrupt the minds of the young and prepare the way for revolution.

This frenzied propaganda against Veblen and Institutionalism might have been laughed out of court as low comedy, except that the charges against the existing system were generally true. The economy was in a state of disorderly transition from individualistic free enterprise to corporative, monopoly capitalism. The plight of workers and displaced yeomen farmers was desperate. Immigrants were pouring into congested urban areas, but could find no employment. The monopoly and finance capitalists had acquired significant, but not yet total, control over the industrial economy and over the national government. These harsh realities had called up from the educated class a brilliant group of writers and social critics who wrote scathing denunciations of the ruling hierarchy and of the economic system. To these critics—popularly termed muckrackers—Veblen and his coherts were a gift from heaven. They dug up the lurid facts about the system, supplied the framework for criticism, suggested reforms and, not the least, invented a sparkling new vocabulary of name calling and smear words with which to blast the ruling economic overlords. It was the first time in American industrial history that the literary avant garde had joined the workers on the barricade. Thus was battled joined.

This anti-Veblen campaign plagued American universities for a quarter of a century, say from 1900–1924, and left many scars in its wake. Some faculty men lost their posts for suspected Veblenism, others were denied appointments and promotions. Many institutions avoided the conflict by the simple device of excluding institutions studies from their programs. This hostility to Veblenism had a serious effect on economics in the United States for the next generation, 1925–50. Instead of following the wise advice of Innis, to investigate some of the basic humanistic questions suggested by Veblen, we abandoned Veblenian studies altogether, and sought peace and quiet in Marshallian statics. A small group of extreme technological determinists continued to exploit Veblen's interest in technology and were termed "technological fascists" by all liberal groups. Ultimately, this splinter group was absorbed by the much larger group of general determinists. Eventually, the Marshallians, having nothing better to do, joined the "Keynesian folly," as Innis termed it.

INSTITUTIONALISM IN THE U. S. TO 1933

In the late nineteenth and early twentieth centuries, the concept of institutionalism, as developed by Veblen, the Chicago economists and Innis, and publicized by their students and the muckrakers, took root but did not flourish; like the parable of the sower, most of the seed fell on infertile soil. The very name of the new doctrine was suspect— institutionalism implied collectivism, and this was synonymous with communism when applied to economic activity. It was readily conceded that institutionalism might have merit and serve a useful purpose if applied to noneconomic areas, where collective group action was necessary and long established, such as politics, government, religion, education, welfare, culture, and military operations. In respect to these activities man was a social animal and his well-being required close association with his fellow men in all these group activities.

This reasoning did not apply to private, profit-seeking enterprises. These were not collective or communal enterprises carried on for the good of the community; rather they were individual undertakings for the sole benefit of the owner. The capitalist conceived the project, procured the capital and raw material, hired and trained the workers, developed a market, and accepted all the risks of failure. A capitalist had to meet the competition, in respect to quality and price, in order to survive. In return for this commitment society protects the capitalist in respect to property, freedom of action, and profits.

This bland, simplistic rationalization of capitalism may have been acceptable for a small, local, metal-working shop in Adam Smith's day, but it is totally inappropriate for our modern large-scale, monopolistic, subsidized industry. It begs all the basic social questions raised by institutionalists of the stature of Veblen and Innis. They were not complaining about competive profits, of unearned increments accruing from technological and social changes, and of illicit gains derived from exploitation of workers, corruption of government, evasion of taxes, subsidies, noncompetitive procurement contracts, or appropriation of social gains accruing from social cooperation in production. The capitalist simply capitalized income from every source, both legitimate and illegitimate, and claimed title to the whole, thus appropriating the social gains along with the legitimate private gains. The socialists, of all schools, had long condemned this *appropriation of the social surplus by monopoly capitalists.* The institutionalists, however, were hopeful that by study of dynamics and technical changes and social inventiveness they might fix responsibility for improvements more equitably and thus reduce the social tension in society by peaceful adjustment rather than by blind revolution. "Those whom the gods would destroy they first make mad!"

But the Lords of Creation, who then dominated the economic and political life of the nation, were in no mood to tolerate such folly. Veblen, they said, was a communist or an anarchist—they were not quite sure which —and Innis, though civilized enough, was suspected of entertaining socialistic ideas. The students and disciples of these men had infiltrated the universities, the press, civic organizations, labor unions, and agencies of government preparatory to seizure of political power and the establishment of a socialistic system. Institutionalism was just a fancy word to conceal their real purpose—the creation of a socialist society. Not even the timely intervention of Franklin D. Roosevelt in 1933—to save capitalism from the follies of the capitalists—could abate their hostility to governmental intervention in economic affairs.

COMMONS, HAMILTON, AND THE "LAW OF THE LAND"

In 1924, when it appeared that institutional economics was dead for lack of support, leadership, and a sense of direction, that it could not be revitalized on the basis of Veblin–Innis abstractions, John R. Commons of Wisconsin published his masterpiece—*The Legal Foundations of Capitalism.*[5] This book did not challenge the idealism of the Veblen–Innis version of institutional economics but it did put the American problem in a new perspective and it did point the way toward institutional reform in the United States on a narrower front than that contemplated by Innis and Veblen in their general theory. Commons was an idealist, but also a master of the pragmatic sanction.

He started with the basic assumption that in the American tradition law was the controlling institution; the Constitution, as construed by the Supreme Court, was the "law of the land," and all statutory and police regulations had to conform. Nothing could be done, or undone, except by law. The evil in our system resulted from bad laws; the good derived from wise and beneficient laws that were consistent with the Constitution; where there was no law, anarchy and injustice prevailed. Law was a dynamic force in our society, either for good or evil, as we might use it. Commons, like Thomas Jefferson, was an ardent Democrat and believed in simplicity and directness when drafting laws and applying them to human affairs. He was fond of telling Jefferson's story about the boy who had outgrown his coat: The kindly neighbors offered a variety of suggestions as how best to relieve the boy's distress, most of them impracticable. Finally, his father solved the problem by taking the boy to a tailor and having him measured for a new coat. Franklin Roosevelt, a kindred spirit, enjoyed this story so much he had it engraved on Jefferson's monument in Washington.

This was the secret of Common's success in institutional reform. If some institution doesn't work properly, repair it—by better administration, if possible; by changing the law, if necessary. Since all formal institutions exist by law, they should be changed by amending the law. If it can be done by consensus, so much the better, for this is quicker and easier. Don't bite off more than you can chew! Don't try to solve all of society's problems in one fell swoop; you will solve nothing and create more problems. Don't insist on imposing decisions on others, to demonstrate your power; help them find solutions themselves. These homely counsels, over time, made him a successful economic reformer—in the American tradition of gradualism by due process of law. If, at times, he thought, with Dr. Johnson, "The law is an ass!" he didn't say so, but rather suggested remedial steps that would improve it.

My generation, from 1925 onward, tended to follow the pragmatic counsel of Commons, rather than the idealized social visions of Veblen and Innis. We studied the latter, admired their vision and idealism, but despaired of general industrial reoganization as their analysis seemed to require. This would never be accomplished in our lifetime and if we attempted it we would only end up in frustration and failure. Thus, we elected the difficult and exasperating road of gradual reform of particular institutions, by due process of law, in the hope that by a slow process of accretion we might eventually affect some improvements in our society.

It pained many of us, I am sure, to forsake a humanistic philosopher like Innis and a mad prophet like Veblen to bargain and traffic with wretched politicians and lawyers for minor reforms of existing institutions that might better the human condition in some slight degree. The law may be an ass, but to live without it would be anarchy, which is far worse. Thus, we must do the best we can with the institutions we have, while trying to devise new and better ones. Thus, the justification of my generation was like that of the poor widow: "She hath done what she could."

Another noble spirit, who like Commons emphasized the place of law in the American political system, was Walton Hamilton, professor of law at Yale.[6] He saw clearly that American law relating to property was derived from ancient English law, and that some of the latter was bad for a democracy, being derived from feudal and crown law not common law. He discovered that American courts had adapted many of these feudal and mercantilist precedents and embodied them in our "law of the land." These residues from the feudal and crown law had to do with royal grants of privilege, engrossment of the public domain, royal charters, hereditary rights, enfiefments, patents, forfeitures, royal benefices, royal fees and rents, grants of monopoly, exclusive and perpetual rights in the public domain, immunity from taxation—all forms of special privilege, all repugnant to democracy.

These residues from feudal and crown law did not, as commonly supposed, vanish with the advent of democracy. On the contrary, they survived, in attenuated form to be sure, to plague modern democratic law and government. Though obsolete in practice they still influenced "the spirit of the law" toward conservatism and against democracy. As a consequence, exclusive grants of privilege, based upon some ancient precedent, were beyond the effective reach of democratic legislation. Only in extreme circumstances would the courts permit these time-honored privileges to be modified.

From his studies in this no-man's land between democracy and absolutism, Hamilton came to the conclusion that *privilege is sanction.* That is, the one who possesses privilege issues orders; the one who lacks privilege obeys! The privileged, therefore, become progressively richer and more powerful; and the unprivileged become progressively poorer and more degraded. This was only the *logic* of Hamilton, not his *faith;* his faith called him to the barricades! The enemy was not sinful men, as such, but rather evil institutions (i.e., monopoly), which enabled a few men to oppress and rob the many. The obvious remedy was to eliminate special privilege—the source of all monopoly power.

THE DARK SHADOW OF PRIVILEGE

I have indicated previously that American institutionalism, after 1920, for legal, constitutional, and cultural reasons, rejected the materialistic radicalism of Veblen in favor of the idealistic institutional reforms of Commons. This meant, in practice, that we would try to maintain free competition wherever possible, impose strict public regulation where competition was not feasible and move to public ownership where neither of the first two systems was practicable. This program assumed that government would break up existing monopolies, by vigorous enforcement of the Sherman Act, and that free competition would then compel private business to operate efficiently.

This was a modest, cautious program, which promised benefits to all and injury to none, except recalcitrant monopolists. Furthermore, and this appeared compelling to the reformers, it appeared to be consistent with our legal and constitutional system. There ensued, between 1920 and the beginning of World War II, a great stir of regulatory activity at both state and federal levels. New regulatory commissions were created and additional industries were brought under control—water power, trucking, avaiation, natural gas, communications. A new branch of law—administrative law—was developed and leading schools began to train young men for this branch of the legal profession.

There was, however, a fatal flaw in this system. It prohibited monopolistic practices, but it did not touch the tap root of monopoly power—*grants of special privilege*. Both state and federal governments were constitutionally free to grant special privileges to private individuals and corporations for the furtherance of some alleged public purpose. The courts, both state and federal, were disposed to uphold the constitutionality of such grants, barring evidence of fraud or violation of some constitutional provision.

During our two hundred years of national existence, both state and federal governments have spawned millions of these grants of special privilege in furtherance of trade and commerce, both domestic and foreign. The federal government has done so in connection with its disposal of the public domain, its control of interstate and foreign commerce, its chartering of national banks, its fiscal, tax, and procurement policies. The states have done so in the chartering of corporations. Their tax policies, their licensing activities, their letting of contracts, their regulation of banks, insurance companies, and public utilities. As one of our least qualified presidents, Calvin Coolidge, said: "The business of this country is Business!" Given this philosophy, grants of special privilege are nothing more than customary devices for getting necessary and profitable things done expeditiously. In short, they are a necessary and useful expedient in a system of monopoly capitalism.

Thus privilege has become sanction, in the United States, as Hamilton predicted it would. Let those who doubt the truth of this general indictment consider who controls our natural resources, our technology, our money and credit system, our investment capital, our communications system, our foreign and military policies, our tax system, our industrial organization, our politics, even our educational, social welfare, and cultural values. We became a free nation under the stirring slogan of "freedom for all, privilege for none." Now, two hundred years later, we have forfeited our birthright and become abject subjects of our Big Finance–Big Business–Big Military overlords. The principal means by which this subversion has been accomplished is grants of special privilege. They have debauched both the giver and the receiver; government has become a corrupt tyranny and big business has forfeited its only excuse for being—economic efficiency. Innis, in one of his last papers, entitled, "Great Britain, the United States and Canada," recognizes the imperialistic potential of the American system and expresses the hope that Britain and Canada may find means to avert it.[7] This appears to be a faint hope unless we muster the courage and intelligence to discard our corrupt system of special privileges for the favored few.

NOTES

[1]Innis, H. A. "The Work of Thorstein Veblen" (1929). In *Essays in Canadian Economic History,* edited by Mary Q. Innis. Toronto: University of Toronto Press, 1973, pp. 17–26.

[2]Innis, *Essays,* p. 24.

[3]Innis, *Essays,* p. 24.

[4]Innis, *Essays,* p. 26.

[5]Commons, John R. *The Legal Foundations of Capitalism,* 1924 (out of print). Republished in 1957 by the University of Wisconsin Press, Madison, Wisconsin, p. 894.

[6]Hamilton, Walton Hale. *Anti-trust in Action,* Monograph No. 16, 1940, Temporary National Economic Committee, Government Printing Office, Washington, D. C.; *Patents and Free Enterprise,* Temporary National Economic Committee Monograph No. 31, 1941, Government Printing Office, Washington, D. C.; *The Politics of Industry,* Knopp, 1957, New York. 100 pp; Five lectures delivered at the University of Michigan, February–March, 1955; *The Power to Govern; the Constitution Then and Now,* Da Capo Press, New York, 1972, 254 pp.; *Price and Price Problems* (with Mark Adams), 1st Edition, 1938, 505 pp., McGraw–Hill Book Co. Inc., New York and London.

[7]Innis, H. A. "Great Britain, the United States and Canada" (1948). In *Essays in Canadian Economic History,* edited by Mary Q. Innis. Toronto: University of Toronto Press, 1973, pp. 394–412.

8

COMMUNICATIONS:
BLINDSPOT OF ECONOMICS*

DALLAS W. SMYTHE
Simon Fraser University

The mass media of communications (principally television, radio, and the press) were a systemic invention of capitalism, developed since the last quarter of the nineteenth century. They were innovated to aid in the mass marketing of consumer goods and services produced by giant oligopolistic corporations using science both in managing production and marketing. Their principal product is audiences, which are sold to advertisers. Thereafter "audience-power" is exercised by the population mass-marketing consumer goods and services to themselves at no further cost to producing firms.

The mass media first appeared in the United States and England in the 1890s. Since World War II they have been the leading formation among the transnational corporations which have substituted cultural imperialism around the world in the interest of the capitalist core for earlier formal empire. That giant corporations manage demand has been observed by a few institutional and Marxist economists, although not by the dominant neoclassical economists. But the role of the market for audiences, produced by mass media and bought by advertisers, has been totally ignored. Economists have omitted to take account of a building block in economic reality which is crucially important to the functioning on monpoly (or corporate) capitalism.

Not surprisingly, the distance from recognition of the reality of mass communications in economic life differs according to the methodological/ideological stance of economists. In general, neoclassical theorists ignore the existence of mass communications, advertising, the conditions and ultimate consequences of the production and consumption of audience-power, and the fact of demand management by what is coming to be recognized as Consciousness Industry (the cluster of institutions most directly concerned in the design of consumer goods and services, their packaging, audience production, advertising, and marketing). Keynesians, despite their focus on aggregate demand management in the economy using tax, public expenditure, interest rate and money supply policies, have paid scarce attention to the implications of mass communication. A few institutional economists, for example, Galbraith[1] and Boulding,[2] do recognize the existence of the mass media, the reality of demand management by giant corporations through advertising, market research, product and package design, but stop short of recognizing the audience commodity. Marxist economists, like their bourgeois contemporaries, either ignore mass communications, demand management, and the audience commodity (such as Lenin) or they recognize mass communications and demand management but fail to see the significance of the market for audiences and audience-power (Baran & Sweezy[3]). Harold Innis also did not address the significance of mass communication in either his economic or his communication writings.

NEOCLASSICAL ECONOMICS

Advertising is the unexplored frontier which has been an embarrassment to economic theorists since Alfred Marshall noticed it and naively distinguished between "combative" and "constructive" advertising.[4] At that point economic theory leapt into a psychological conception of advertising, one of manipulation, influence, persuasion, and so on, and stopped viewing it as an economic process. E. H. Chamberlin's comments to the effect that the objective is to establish "control of the buyer's consciousness" have been acquiesced in ever since by economic theorists.[5]

The "ostrich head in the sand" effect that economic theory exhibits regarding mass communications and advertising is traceable methodologically to its essentially idealistic perspective which substitutes for institutional analysis of oliogopolistic reality the projection of competitive models that now correspond to nothing significant in the real world. What do advertisers buy? Stigler defines "selling media" as the object purchased with advertising expenditures.[6] In fact, of course, the object purchased is *audiences produced* by "selling media." Kaldor defines the function of advertising as ". . . undoubtedly the provision of information concerning the prices and qualities of goods and services available in the markets."[7] The list of supposed objects of advertising expenditures could be extended lengthily and would yield a variety of idealistic, subjective entities: information, messages, images, meaning, manipulation, education. The consequence is that economic theorists get diverted from real products and real markets in which advertisers deal— audience-power and audience-markets—into innumerable cul-de-sacs. For example, Kaldor, regarding advertising "information" as the object of the exercise, treats *it* as a commodity, produced under joint-supply conditions with the product being advertised, and thus finds himself with a market for "advertising service" between advertising producers and advertising "buyers," for whom its price is always zero.[8] His logic is inescapable, given his wrong conception of the advertising process: The buyer of advertised goods is being subsidized by the advertiser by getting the advertisements at no price. What a bonus for the consumer, who of course is assumed to have sufficient information to exercise his/her consumer " sovereignty"! It is some kind of indoor sport for economic theorists and we find, inter alia, Lester G. Telser elaborating a model of "Supply and Demand for Advertising Messages"[9] untroubled by the fact that in the real world there is no such market but there is a market in which advertisers buy audiences produced by the communications mass media which somehow escapes his attention.

An amazing metaphysical tour de force of similar character is that of Stigler and Becker, concerning theory of taste.[10] Neoclassical economic theory eschewed applying marginal theory to phenomena outside the markets in which firms seek profits ("externalities" if they took the form of constraints on market behavior). Stigler and Becker violate this self-imposed restraint by projecting "a generalized calculus of utility-maximizing behavior" into nonmarket phenomena, specifically a taste for musical appreciation, for addictive commodities, and for fashion (including the role of advertising). They invent a subsequent generation of "commodities," which are produced by consumers who ". . . maximize a utility function of objects of choice, called commodities, that they produce with market goods, their own time, their skills, training, and other human capital and other inputs."[11] Thus the factors used by the consumer to produce the commodity (for self consumption, presumably) "music appreciation" include music lessons, attendance at musical performances, time spent on both, and so on. The "commodity" produced by addictions is "euphoria"; that from styled products bought in the real market for real prices, "social distinction." Economic concepts such as capital, investment, division of labor, price are all applied in this purely subjective fantasy without the quotation marks that might warn readers they were being used metaphorically and without rigor. Thus in one paragraph the terms "human capital conducive to music appreciation," "music capital," and "music human capital" slither around, undefined.[12]

The authors take seriously Galbraith's charge that corporate capitalism manages demand through advertising and creates desires among consumers. Predictably, given the authors' ideological presuppositions, they argue "it is neither necessary nor useful to attribute to advertising the function of changing tastes."[13] By a definitional sleight-of-hand concerning the information content of advertising, and by integrating end-product advertising expenditures in the real world with their imaginary market in second-generation "commodities" produced by consumers for their own consumption, they use their marginal utility formulas to refute Galbraith. Lo and behold, the by-gone days when people did produce a substantial portion of their own consumption goods, such as baking meat pies, have been reproduced, only now the purchased ingredients are frozen foods and microwave ovens, and the "commodity" produced and consumed in the home is not edible food, but the "social distinction" resulting from popping the frozen meat pie into the microwave oven for a minute and then whisking it onto the damask-covered table for the happy family to greet ecstatically—just as in the television commercials.

Harvey Leibenstein in *Beyond Economic Man*[14] has been seen by many as offering significant improvements over the neoclassical marginalists. Arguing that the latter, with their idée fixe about allocative efficiency, have a useless tool, he analyzes what he calls "X-efficiency" by which he refers to all manner of motivational devices available to management which significantly affect the firm's profit performance. In several chapters he attempts to provide an "atomistic theory of consumers' behavior." Here he departs from the neoclassical assumption of consumer rationality by introducing what he calls "the snob effect," "the Veblen effect" (conspicuous consumption), and game theory as applied to intrahousehold allocation of spendable income. It is understandable that such innovations would cheer up academic economists, even if the cultural lag is remarkable. (Snobbery has been a conspicuous feature of capitalism, since the thirteenth century[15] and Veblen's Theory of the Leisure Class appeared some eighty years ago, game theory about thirty-five years ago.) Such anecdotal excursions lend a tinge of realism to the economists' indoor game. The fact remains, however, that Leibenstein does not recognize the role of demand management by monopoly corporations by means, inter alia, of advertising to get audience members to do their marketing for them, unpaid. Although he divides utility in unconventional ways (empathy utility, nonfunctional utility, and frustration utility), he never seems to escape the basic and naive notion that utility as a pleasure–pain calculus is the psychological footing of neoclassical economics. Moreover, in pursuit of his

X-efficiency factor, he completely ignores the role of imagination and motivation in what we now call Consciousness Industry even from the standpoint of profits-for-the-firm. That the role of Consciousness Industry may produce fatal contradictions for the monopoly capitalist system is a systemic X factor which any exercise such as his, based on the capitalist firm as solidly as any neoclassical economist, could not be expected to envisage. I refer here merely to the tendency of capitalist industry to generate ever more trivial product and style changes which contribute, for example, to the present evidence of rigidity in the face of the energy crisis in the capitalist core. More dramatic contradictions abound in the real world.

Apart from the stultified area of neoclassical marginal theory proper, it should be noted that efforts have been made to apply conventional theory to advertising on several overlapping fronts.[16] Joseph Bain and others have analyzed its relation to the growth of monopoly with an eye to the problems faced by the Antitrust Division and Federal Trade Commission in the United States, while Kaldor, Else, and Taplin considered similar and related issues in Britain. Two economists have tried to synthesize a long list of studies, which apply traditional microtheory with statistical techniques to advertising.[17 18] Because the methods used failed to cope with the material historical processes by which monopoly capital achieved hegemony, their books are inconclusive except negatively. For example, Schmalensee concludes, "There is no evidence to suggest that advertising outlays have permitted some firms to create barriers to entry. . . . So far it, along with many other problems involving advertising's effects, has not been solved."[19]

Economists increasingly since the early 1960s have shown interest in developing theories of taste and buying behavior, joining in the interest of major firms in market research. For example, the authors of two short articles in 1978 cautiously recognize some of the large volume of evidence from psychology and sociology concerning consumer behavior while seeming to glance fearfully over their shoulders at the dogma of marginal theory.[20] A third, T. A. Marschak, reveals the deep contradiction between the conservative tradition of marginal neoclassicism and reality, boldly asserting that the former ". . . risks turning Economic Man into a complex monster of calculated schizophrenia. . . ."[21] In the "long-forbidden territory" of tastes in real life, Marschak identifies (but does not analyze) three relevant issues: (1) nonrenewable resource exhaustion and consumer taste; (2) the relation of advertising, education, and the mass media to taste formation; and (3) disenchantment with purchased goods as the measure of welfare. None of these exercises in economic theory involve recognition of demand management by monopoly capitalism, and the role of the mass media in producing the marketing agent for it (the audience). Among bourgeois economists that leaves institutional economists to be considered.

INSTITUTIONAL ANALYSIS

As noted above, Galbraith, prominent among institutional economists, comes close to confronting the audience market but stops short at the traditional psychological curtain drawn by Chamberlin. He realistically identifies the dependence of corporate capitalism on the regular creation of wants through advertising, model changes, and so on. He properly criticizes the fixation on durable goods production, inherited from the classical economists, and at the root of the theory of F. H. Knight and his disciples. He also summarizes the rationale with which economists conceal their blindness to the audience commodity:

> The theory of consumer demand, as it is now widely accepted—is based on two broad propositions. . . . The first is that the urgency of wants does not diminish appreciably as more of them are satisfied, or . . . to the extent that this happens it is not demonstrable and not a matter of any interest to economists or for economic policy. When man has satisfied his physical needs, then psychologically grounded desires take over. These can never be satisfied, or in any case no progress can be proved. . . . The second proposition is that wants originate in the personality of the consumer or in any case that they are *given data* for the economist. The latter's task is merely to seek their satisfaction. He has no need to enquire how these wants are formed.[22]

In his later *The New Industrial State,* he sharpens the analysis of demand management, applying it both to the civilian and to the military sectors. He emphasizes the essential function that advertising and related activities perform in creating demand for commodities in particular and in general, including the practice of going into debt to buy them: "Advertising and salesmanship—the management of consumer demand—are vital for the planning in the industrial system. At the same time, the wants so created insure the services of the worker."[23] Indeed, he carries the argument to the brink of discovery of the audience market:

> The present disposition of conventional economic theory to write off annual outlays of tens of billions of dollars of advertising and similar sales costs by the industrial system as without purpose or consequence is, to say the least, drastic. No other legal economic activity is subject to similar rejection. The discovery that sales and advertising expenditures have an organic role in the system will not, accordingly, seem wholly implausible.[24]

He then draws back from the prospect of analyzing the "organic role" of the most essential market for the existence of modern monopoly capitalism: the audience. As will be argued below, the audience is now the unnoticed form which stands in contradiction to the domination by commodities in the capitalist core area. It just might be the organic agent that may act to transfer the system at its core. Short of this eventuality, analysis of its role could serve many needs of industry, government, and education.

MARXIST ECONOMICS

Have Marxist economists carried the theoretical analysis of monopoly capitalism any further than Galbraith? Marxists from Marx until about 1920, including Lenin, could hardly be expected to recognize and deal with the demand management function of advertising and mass communication on behalf of monopoly capitalism, the characteristics of which had not yet developed.[25] Accordingly, it is not surprising that those Marxists held a manipulative, idealist theory of communications. For Marx, "ideology" was considered to act as a sort of invisible glue that holds together the capitalist system. This subjective substance, divorced from concrete historical materiality, is similar to such concepts as "ether"; that is, the proof of its existence is found to be the necessity for it to exist so that certain other phenomena may be explained. It was thus an idealist, *pre*scientific rather than a nonscientific explanation. For Marxists after about 1920, the concrete material basis existed on which ideology could be approached scientifically, and the mass media of communications were central to that approach. The first question that historical materialists should ask about mass communication systems is what economic function for capital do they serve, attempting to understand their role in the reproduction of capitalist relations of production. What is surprising, given the methodological commitment of Marxists to historical material realism, is to find that Marxists writing since about 1920 hold a subjective and superficial view of the commodity produced by the mass media of communications under monopoly capitalism. For them, as for bourgeois economists, it is manipulation, information, images, and so on. This is conspicuously true for the Frankfurt School. It is also true for those who take a more or less Marxist view of communications (Nordenstreng, Enzensberger, Hamelink, Schiller, Murdock, Golding, and myself until recently). I am therefore suggesting that the literature of Marxism is conspicuously lacking in materialist analysis of *how* "Consciousness Industry" uses advertising and other mass media content to produce and reproduce a certain ideology. *Why* Marxists have had a blindspot about the relation of mass media, audiences, advertisers, the labor theory of value and ideology to each other it is not my present task to determine.[26]

Baran and Sweezy in *Monopoly Capital* recognize the demand management practices of monopoly capitalist corporations, but they, like Galbraith, draw back from the brink of recognizing the reality of the audiences as the principal product of the mass media, produced to sell to advertisers.

EXPLORING THE BLINDSPOT

Even a little analysis permits us to raise questions that may open up that blindspot for exploration:

1. What do advertisers buy with their advertising expenditures? As hard-nosed businessmen they are not paying for advertising for nothing, nor from altruism. I suggest that what they buy are the services of audiences with predictable specifications, who will pay attention in predictable numbers and at particular times to particular means of communication (television, radio, newspapers, magazines, billboards, and third-class mail).[27] As collectivities these audiences are commodities. As commodities, they are dealt with in markets by producers and buyers (the latter being advertisers). Such markets establish prices in the familiar mode of monopoly capitalism. Both these markets and the audience commodities traded in are specialized. The audience commodities bear specifications known in the business as "the demographics." The specifications for the audience commodities include age, sex, income level, family composition, urban or rural location, ethnic character, ownership of home, automobile, credit card status, social class, and, in the case of hobby and fan magazines, a dedication to photography, model electric trains, sports cars, philately, do-it-yourself crafts, foreign travel, kinky sex, and so on.

2. Are audiences homogenous? By no means, although all of them have the common features of being produced by mass media and priced and sold in oligopolistic markets to advertisers for whom they perform services which earn their keep, that is, keep advertisers advertising because the expenditure is productive from the advertisers' standpoint. Audiences produced for sale to advertisers fall into two groups: those produced in connection with marketing consumers' goods and those for producers' goods. The latter are typically produced by trade or business media (magazines, newspapers, or direct mail). The buyers of producers' goods are typically institutions (government in the case of the "Military Sales Effort" or private corporations) which presumably buy on specifications of objective qualities. Moreover, this latter type of advertising is a relatively small part of the total. For these reasons the following analysis will disregard this category of audience.

Strategically the most important class of audiences are produced for advertisers marketing consumers' goods. Again, these audiences fall into two classes. The first of these are for producers of what Julian L. Simin calls Homogenous Package Goods (HPG), which have certain common features: "(1) Slight or no objective physical difference between the brands; (2) Low unit cost; (3) Short time period between repeated purchases; (4) Large total dollar volume for each product industry; (5) Except for liquor, heavy use of television as an advertising medium; and (6) Large proportions of sales spent for advertising."[28] In the HPG category are soft drinks, gum, candy, soaps, cleaners, waxes, and other household cleaning products, tobacco products, beer, wine, liquor, gasoline, patent drugs, perfumes, cosmetics, deodorants, razor blades and other personal toiletry articles, as well as fast foods and restaurants. The second subclass of audiences for consumers' goods is that for durable consumer goods. Here are automobiles, snowmobiles, clothes, boats, shoes, hobby equipment (e.g., cameras, sports equipment, household tools), electric household appliances, and the like. Although objective qualitative characteristics are ascertainable, annual style changes dominate them. It is the consumer goods advertisers whose audiences are produced by the mass media to generate the "demand" that can increase GNP.

    3. How are advertisers assured that they are getting what they pay for when the buy audiences? A subindustry sector of the Consciousness Industry checks to determine. The socioeconomic characteristics of the delivered audience readership *and* its size are the business of A. C. Nielsen and a host of competitors who specialize in rapid assessment of the delivered audience commodity. The behavior of the members of the audience product under the impact of advertising and the "editorial" content is the object of market research by a large number of independent market research agencies as well as by similar staffs located in advertising agencies, in the advertising corporation and in media enterprises.

    4. What institutions produce the commodity which advertisers buy with their advertising expenditures? The owners of television and radio stations and networks, newspapers, magazines and enterprises which specialize in providing billboard and third class advertising are the principal producers. This array of producers is interlocked in many ways with advertising agencies, talent agencies, package program producers, film producers, news "services" (e.g., AP, UPI, Reuters, CP), "syndicators" of news "columns," writers' agents, book publishers, and motion picutre producers and distributors. Last, but by no means least, in the array of institutions that produce the audience commodity is the family. The most important *resource* employed in producing the audience commodity are the individuals and families in the nations that permit advertising.

    5. What is the purpose of the so-called entertainment, information, and educational material content? As well as the advertising material in the mass media, the "programs" themselves are advertisements. The content between the formal advertising material is a lure or inducement (or gift, bribe, or free lunch) to recruit potential members into the audience and to maintain their loyal attention to the advertisments. The analogy of such material to the free lunch in the old-time saloon, suggested by A. J. Liebling,[29] is appropriate: The free lunch consists of material to whet the prospective audience member's appetites and thus: (1) attract and keep them attending to the program, newspaper, or magazine; and (2) cultivate a mood conducive to favorable reaction to the explicit and implicit messages from the advertiser. In the policy of the mass media, the characteristics of the free lunch must always be subordinated to those of the formal advertisements, because the purpose of the mass media is to produce audiences to sell to the advertisers. Therefore a "program" that is more arousing than the adjacent advertisements will not survive, and it could only survive the preliminary screening because of faulty judgment on part of the media management. The cost per unit of time or space of producing an explicit advertisement is many times the cost per unit of time or space of producing the free lunch (in a ratio of 8 or 10 to 1 in television), which is a rough index of the relative attention paid to the qualities of the two. There is of course, a market for the free lunch, and this market spans not only the totally advertiser-dependent media (television and radio) but also cinema, magazines, newspapers, and book industries. A particular commodity in the free lunch market (*Roots,* for example) will appear in more than one of these media, sometimes simultaneously (as with the book and film *China Syndrome*) and often subsequently in other media, in each case being edited appropriately to fit the buyers' needs.

Under monopoly capitalism television-radio programs are provided "free" and newspapers and "consumer" magazines at prices that perhaps cover delivery (but not production) costs. In the case of newspapers and some magazines, some readers typically buy the media product *because* they want the advertisements rather than the free lunch. Such is the case with classified advertisements and display advertising of products and prices by local merchants in newspapers. Likewise, product information in advertisements in certain magazines (e.g., hobby magazines) may be the object of purchase by the consumer.

Of course, to call the traditional "news" content of the newspaper a free lunch does not denigrate the role of the mass media in daily setting an agenda for everyone's attention or of the prime significance of that role. On the contrary, it emphasizes an essential aspect of *how* some items get on the agenda, and with what priority, and how other agenda items are left off.

6. What is the nature of the service performed for the advertiser by the members of the purchased audiences? In economic terms, the audience commodity is a nondurable producers' good which is bought and used in the marketing of the advertiser's product. The work audience members perform for the advertiser to whom they have been sold is to learn to buy goods and to spend their income accordingly. Sometimes it is to buy any of the class of goods (for example, an aircraft manufacturer is selling air transport in general, or the dairy industry, all brands of milk), but most often it is a particular "brand" of consumer goods. In short, they work to create the demand for advertised goods that is the purpose of the monopoly capitalist advertisers. While doing this, audience members are simultaneously reproducing their own labor power. In this regard, it is appropriate to avoid the trap of manipulation explanation by noting that if such labor power is, in fact, loyally attached to the monopoly capitalist system, this would be welcome to the advertisers whose existence depends on the maintenance of that system. In reproducing their labor power, workers respond to other realistic conditions that may on occasion surprise and disappoint the advertisers. It seems, however, that when workers under monopoly capitalist conditions serve advertisers to complete the production process of consumer goods by performing the ultimate marketing service for them, these workers are making decisive material decisions that will affect how they will produce and reproduce their labor power. As the Chinese emphasized during the Cultural Revolution, if people are spending their time catering to their individual interests and sensitivities, they cannot be using the *same* time to overthrow capitalist influence and to build socialism.

7. How does demand management by monopoly capitalism by means of advertising relate to the labor theory of value, to "leisure" and to "free time"? As Bill Livant puts it, the power of the concept of surplus value ". . . rests wholly on the way Marx solved the great value problem of classical political economy, by *splitting the notion of labor in two,* into labor in productive use and labor power (the capacity to labor)."[30] Labor in productive use in the production of commodities-in-general was Marx's concern in the three volumes of *Capital,* except for Volume 1, Chapter 6 and scattered passages in the *Grundrisse.* It is clear from these passages that Marx assumed that labor power is produced by the laborer and by his or her immediate family *under the conditions* of handicraft production. In a word, labor power was "home-made" in the absence of dominant brand-name commodities, mass advertising and the mass media (which had not yet been invented by monopoly capitalism). In Marx's period and in his analysis, the principal aspect of capitalist production was the alienation of workers from the means of producing commodities-in-general. Now the principal aspect of capitalist production has become the alienation of workers from the means of producing and reproducing themselves. The prevailing western Marxist view today still holds the incorrect assumption that the laborer is an independent commodity producer of labor power which is his to sell. As Livant states it:

> What often escapes attention is that just because the laborer sells it (his or her labor power) does not mean that he or she produces it. We are misled by fixating on the true fact that a human must eat and sleep into thinking that therefore the seller of labour power must also be the producer. Again the error of two combines into one.[31]

In the original blindspot article I contended that work time included all but sleeping time. In the capitalist core area I now believe work time for most people is twenty-four hours a day. George Allen, famous professional football coach in the United States, may be closer to the mark than most economists, though typically conservative, when he tells his players, "Nobody should work all the time. Leisure time is the five or six hours you sleep at night. You can combine two good things at once, sleep and leisure."[32]

It should be clear that for at least several generations labor power in advanced monopoly capitalist countries has been produced primarily by institutions *other* than the individual and his/her family. The mass media of communications and advertising play a large and probably dominant role through the process of consumption (by guiding the making of the shopping list) as well as through the ideological teaching that permeates both the advertising and ostensibly nonadvertising material with which they produce the audience commodity.[33] When cosmetic counters in department stores display "Boxed Ego" (Vancouver, December, 1975), the dialectical relation of the material and consciousness aspects of the production of labor power should be evident.

If between 1850 and 1960 the average worker gained seven hours per week of apparent "nonwork" time, how much time does he now spend as part of the audience product of the mass media—time sold to the advertisers?[34] David Blank, economist for the Columbia Broadcasting System, in 1970 found that the average person watched television twenty-three hours per week on an annual basis, listened to the radio for eighteen hours per week and read newspapers and magazines seven hours per week.[35] If we look at the audience product in terms of families rather than individuals, we find that in 1973 advertisers in the United States purchased television audiences for an average of a little more than forty-three hours per home per week.[36] By industry usage, this lumps together specialized audience commodities sold independently as "housewives," "children," and "families." In the "prime time" evening hours (7:00 P.M. to 11:00 P.M.), the television audience commodity consisted of a daily average of 83.8 million people in the United States, with an average of two persons viewing per home. Women were a significantly larger proportion of this prime time audience than men (forty-two per cent as against thirty-two per cent, while children were sixteen per cent and teenagers, ten per cent).

We do not know even approximately how the worker's exposure to the mass media articulates with the other components in his/her use of time when not at the job front. It is relatively easy to determine how much radio listening and newspaper and magazine reading takes place while traveling to and from work. But much television and radio programing is attended to incidentally while people engage in other activities such as performing household chores, visiting with friends, reading, and now even while attending spectator sports.[37]

Audience members bear directly a heavy cost in dollars for the privilege of being in the audience and getting their daily work assignments from the advertisers. In Canada in 1975 the annual cost to audience members of providing their own broadcast receivers (and paying for cable television) consistent of depreciation, interest on investment, maintenance and electric power, amounted to slightly more than $1.8 billion, while the over-the-airbroadcasters (Canadian Broadcasting Corporation plus private broadcasters) and cable television operators' costs were about $631 million—a ratio of about three to one.

Constrained by the ideology of monopoly capitalism, the bourgeois notion of free time and leisure is only available to those who have no disposable income (and for whom it is, of course, a bitter mockery) and to those who are so rich that, as Linder says, for them, "the ultimate luxury is to be liberated from the hardships of having to do one's own buying."[38] For everyone else, "free time" and "leisure" belong only in the monopoly capitalist lexicon alongside "free world," "free enterprise," "free elections," "free speech," and "free flow of information."

What has happened to the time workers spend off-the-job is that enormous pressures on this time have been imposed by all consumer goods and service branches of monopoly capitalism. Individual, familial, and other associative needs must be dealt with, but in a real context of products and advertising which, taken together, make the task of the individual and family basically one of *coping* while being constantly on the verge of being overwhelmed by these pressures. In this context, the work of the audience members which advertisers find productive for them is one of learning the cues used when the audience member makes up his/her mental shopping list and spends his/her income.

8. Does the audience commodity perform an essential economic function? Baran and Sweezy state that "advertising constitutes as much an integral part of the system as the giant corporation itself"[39] and that "advertising has turned into an indispensable tool for a large sector of corporate business."[40] In this they go as far as Galbraith who said ". . . the marginal utility of present aggregate output, ex-advertising and salesmanship is zero."[41] When the president of the Revlon corporation says: "We manufacture lipsticks. But we sell hope," he is referring to the creation of products initially posited by it as objects in the form of a need felt by the consumers—similarly with Contac-C, the proprietary cold remedy, which so disturbed Baran and Sweezy.[42] The denial of the productivity of advertising is unnecessary and diversionary: a cul-de-sac derived from the premonopoly-capitalist state of development, a dutiful but unsuccessful and inappropriate attempt at reconciliation with *Capital*.

9. Why have economists been indifferent to the historical process by which advertising, brand-name merchandise, and the mass media of communications have developed in monopoly capitalism over the past century? Why do they continue to regard the press, television, and radio media as having the prime function of producing news, entertainment and editorial opinion and not audiences for sale to advertisers? My original "blindspot" paper offered a preliminary analysis of the dynamics of the process by which Consciousness Industry developed through the merger movement and created the mass media to produce audience power.

CONCLUSION

The mass media institutions in monopoly capitalism developed the equipment, workers, and organization to produce audiences for the purposes of the system between about 1875 and 1950. The prime purpose of the mass media complex is to produce people in audiences who work at learning the theory and practice of consumership for civilian goods and who support (with taxes and votes) the military demand management system. The second principal purpose is to produce audiences whose theory and practice confirms the ideology of monopoly capitalism (possessive individualism in an authoritarian political system). The third principal purpose is to produce public opinion supportive of the strategic and tactical policies of the state (e.g., presidential candidates, support of Indochinese military adventures, space race, detente with the Soviet Union, rapprochement with China, and ethnic and youth dissent). Necessarily in the monopoly capitalist system, the fourth purpose of the mass media complex is to operate itself so profitably as to ensure unrivaled respect for its economic importance in the system. It has been quite successful in achieving all four purposes.

If we recognize the reality of monopoly capitalism buying audiences to complete the mass marketing of mass produced consumer goods and services, we have begun to grapple with the contradiction between capital and labor in the period of monpoly capitalism when most people work *all the time;* not only when at the job front where they are paid for working but also in every other mode for which they are not paid.

It appears that in seeming to perfect its system for managing demand through producing and consuming audiences for the purpose of marketing its products, monopoly capital has produced its principal antagonist: people commodified in audience markets who are consciously seeking noncommodified group relations. A symptom is a downward trend in television viewing in 1977 and 1979 in the United States after thirty years of rising viewing.[43] It has long been noticed that all traditional social institutions (family, church, labor union, political party, and so on) have been stripped of much of their traditional purpose by the impact of mass produced communications. The mysticism attached to technique has incorrectly assumed that the medium basically defines the audience. As an historical analysis of the rise of the mass media will show, the opposite has been true: the availability and actions of the audience is the basic feature in the definition of the medium, singly and collectively. By placing the contradiction between advertisers/media on the one hand and audiences on the other on the level of social relations, we are on solid ground and can repudiate the mysticism of the "technological" trap by which audiences are tied to hardware, software, and technique (as in Innis, McLuhan, and others).

NOTES

*An earlier essay exposed the blindspot of western Marxist scholars to the reality of communications. Here the analysis is generalized to encompass all branches of the contemporary economic theory. The argument here builds on that in "Communications: Blindspot of Western Marxism." *Canadian Journal of Political and Social Theory*, Vol. 1, No. 3, Fall, 1977, pp. 1–27.

[1]Galbraith, J. K. *The New Industrial State.* Boston: Houghton Mifflin, 1967.

[2]Boulding, K. *Econoimc Analysis.* New York: Harper, 1955.

[3]Baran, P. A., and Sweezy, P. M. *Monopoly Capital.* New York: Monthly Review Press, 1966.

[4]Marshall, Alfred. *Industry and Trade.* London: Macmillan, 1922.

[5]Chamberlin, E. H. *The Theory of Monopolistic Competition.* Cambridge, Mass.: 1931, pp. 119, 133–134.

[6]Stigler, G. J. *The Theory of Price.* New York: Macmillan, 1961.

[7]Kaldor, N. "The Economic Aspects of Advertising." *Review of Economic Studies*, Vol. 18, 1950, p. 1.

[8]The buyer of advertised goods is charged no price for the advertising. *Sup. cit.*, p. 2.

[9]Tesler, Lester G. "Supply and Demand for Advertising Messages." *American Economic Review*, May, 1966, pp. 457–466.

[10]Stigler, George J., and Becker, Gary S. "DeGustibus non est Disputandum." *American Economic Review*, Vol. 67, No. 2, March, 1977, pp. 76–90.

[11]*Ibid.*, p. 77.

[12]*Ibid.*, p. 78.

[13]*Ibid.*, p. 84.

[14]Leibeutein, Harvey. *Beyond Economic Man.* Cambridge, Mass.: Harvard University Press, 1976.

[15]See, for example, Martines, Lauro. *Power and Imagination: City States in Renaissance Italy.* New York: Knopf, 1979, p. 85.

[16]See Doyle, Peter. "Economic Aspect of Advertising: A Survey." *Economic Journal*, Vol. 78, 1968, pp. 570–602.

[17]Simon, Julian L. *Issues in the Economics of Advertising.* Urbana: University of Illinois Press, 1970.

[18]Schmalensee, R. *The Economics of Advertising.* Amsterdam/London: North–Holland Publishing Company, 1972.

[19]*Ibid.*, p. 244.

[20]Pollack, Robert A. "Endogenous Tastes in Demand and Welfare Analysis" Pessemier, Edgar A. "Stochastic Properties of Changing Preferences." *American Economic Review*, May, 1978 pp. 374–379; 379–385.

[21]Marschak, T. A. "On the Study of Taste Changing Policies." *American Economic Review*, May, 1978, pp. 386–391.

[22]Galbraith, J. K. *The Affluent Society.* Boston: Houghton–Mifflin, 1958, pp. 143-144. Emphasis added.

[23]Galbraith, J. K. *The New Industrial State, sup. cit.,* p. 273.

[24]*Ibid.,* p. 205.

[25]Lenin had a manipulative theory of the mass media and admitted naiveté in this respect. "What was the fate of the decree establishing a state monopoly of private advertising issued in the first weeks of the Soviet government?. . . It is amusing to think now naive we were. . . The enemy, i.e., the capitalist class retaliated to this decree of the state power by completely repudiating that state power." "Report on the New Economic Policy," Seventh Moscow Gubernia Conference of the Russian Communist Party, October 21, 1921, in *Lenin About the Press.* Prague: International Organization of Journalists, 1972, p. 203. Lenin's *Imperialism* is devoid of recognition of the relation of advertising to monopoly capitalism and imperialism.

[26]The analysis here presented originally aimed to stimulate debate among Marxists over this issue. Following publication of the original "Blindspot" article, the *Canadian Journal of Political and Social Theory* published "Blindspots about Marxism: A Reply to Dallas Smythe" by Graham Murdock and my "Rejoinder to Graham Murdock" (Vol. 2, No. 2, 1978, pp. 109–119, and 120–127) and "The Audience Commodity: On the 'Blindspot' Debate," by Bill Livant (Vol. 3, No. 1, 1979, pp. 91–106).

[27]It is argued by one of my critics that a better term for what advertisers buy would be "attention." At our present naive stage concerning the matter, it does *seem* as if attention is indeed what is bought. But where people are paid for working on the job, should Marxists say that what the employer buys is "labor power" or "the manual dexterity and attention necessary for tending machines?" Where I refer to audiences as being produced, purchased, and used, let it be understood that I mean "audience-power," however it may turn out upon further realistic analysis to be exercised.

[28]Simon, Julian L. *Sup. Cit.,* p. 271.

[29]Liebling, A. *The Press.* New York: Ballantine, 1961.

[30]Livant, William. "Notes on the Development of the Production of Labour Power." 22 March, 1975 (dittoed).

[31]Livant, William. "More on the Production of Damaged Labour Power." 1 April, 1975 (dittoed).

[32]Quoted in Terkel, Louis. *Working.* New York: Pantheon, 1974, p. 389.

[33]For the present purposes I ignore the ancillary and interactive processes which contribute to the production of labor power involving also the educational institutions, the churches, labor unions, and a host of voluntary associations (for example, YMCA, Girl Scouts).

[34]In the "Blindspot" paper I contrasted the hours of work at the job front and the condition of reproducing labor power (including so-called leisure time between 1850 and 1960).

[35]Blank, David M. "Pleasurable Pursuits—The Changing Structure of Leisure-time Spectator Activities." National Association of Business Economists, Annual Meeting, September, 1970 (dittoed).

[36]*Broadcasting Yearbook,* 1974, p. 69.

[37]For many years patrons at professional baseball and football games have been listening to portable radios broadcasting the same game. By the mid-1970s patrons at professional football games were beginning to watch the same game on portable television sets for the "instant replays."

[38]Linder, Staffen B. *The Harried Leisure Class.* New York: Columbia University Press, 1970, p. 123.

[39]Baran, P. A., and Sweezy, P. M. *sup. cit.,* p. 122.

[40]*Ibid.,* p. 119.

[41]Galbraith, J. K. *The Affluent Society, sup. cit.,* p. 160.

[42]Referring to a reported $13 million advertising budget, which produced $16 million in drug store sales, expressed in wholesale prices, they say: "Allowing for a handsome profit margin, which of course is added to selling as well as production cost, it seems clear that the cost of production can hardly be more than a minute proportion of even the wholesale price." Baran, P. A., and Sweezy, P. M., *sup. cit.,* p. 119.

[43]*Time,* 12 March, 1979, p. 57.

9

INNIS, MARX, AND THE ECONOMICS OF COMMUNICATION: A THEORETICAL ASPECT OF CANADIAN POLITICAL ECONOMY

IAN PARKER
University of Toronto

Innis and Marx are the two most important historical figures in the resurgence of Canadian political economy. Despite significant differences between their styles and analytical approaches, their works manifest important conceptual affinities. These have been insufficiently acknowledged by many current writers who view themselves as articulating and extending Canadian political economy. The practical theoretical gap between those who view themselves as working principally in the "Innisian" tradition and those principally in the "Marxist" tradition is unnecessarily large and has hampered development of an integrated political–economic analysis of Canadian and global historical development. In particular, the gap has hindered recognition of some of the principal theoretical affinities between Innis and Marx: the dialectical materialist basis of their thought; their common ecological approach to the historical process; and their common awareness of the political–economic significance of communications phenomena. I have developed this argument elsewhere.[1]

This paper outlines in more detail the role of communication in the political–economic thought of both men and the significance of the similarities and differences between their analyses of communication for political economy in general and within a Canadian political–economic context. It emphasizes economic aspects of the political economy of communication and sets out evidence that warrants the following propositions. First, the economics of communication (as I define it below) is far more important, empirically and theoretically, than would be inferred

from the proportion of contemporary mainstream or neoclassical economic research being devoted to communication study; more strongly,
communication processes, viewed in their full extent, systematically
undercut the axiomatic foundations of contemporary neoclassical
theory. Second, a concern with the economics or political economy of
communication permeates the writings of both Innis and Marx precisely
because of their common awareness of the centrality of communications
phenomena as determinants of historical patterns of development in
open economic systems; moreover, the analytical frameworks or modes
of analysis they each developed largely transcend those problems encountered by neoclassical theory. Finally, the analyses of Innis and Marx
are fundamentally complementary, in the last instance, and both are
required to forge an adequate understanding of the political economy of
communication in contemporary Canadian and global systems.

To substantiate the foregoing propositions requires a clear definition of "the economics of communication" and of those economic activities that constitute the "communication" sector of historical
economies. It also requires evidence of the permeation of the work of
both Innis and Marx by a continuous concern with communications
phenomena as basic determinants of processes of political–economic
change. More particularly, in the case of Innis, it is necessary to illustrate
the fundamental analytical continuity that exists between the earlier
"staples" studies and the later "communication" studies. In the case of
Marx, it is necessary to highlight those aspects of his thought that demonstrate the extent to which his overall theoretical framework was pervaded by a recognition of the significance of communications phenomena in the analysis of historical processes of class struggle, surplus
extraction, and exploitation.

Finally, in assessing relationships between Innis and Marx, it is
necessary to distinguish between two different interdependent levels of
analysis to grasp them more certainly in their mutual interdependence:
the first is *pure theory of political–economic development*, and the second
could be termed *contradictions analysis*. Pure theory of political–economic
development is concerned with laws of motion of and within different
historical modes of production. It therefore necessarily largely abstracts
from the particular differences that characterize, for example, capitalist
production at different points in space and moments in time. Definition
of "the mode of production" as was resolved by Marx in relation to the
capitalist mode of production in terms of the categories, "commidity,"
"capital," "wage labour," and "surplus value," is therefore a necessary
precondition for the pure theory of political–economic development.
Contradictions analysis, on the other hand, is concerned with an identification of the determinants of the historical development of particular

social–economic systems or modes of production in specific historical situations. It is concerned, in particular, with locations during particular periods in relation to particular other systems and modes of production, separated spatially or temporally from the systems under study.

One feature of Innis' and Marx's work that needs to be acknowledged in developing an integrated understanding of the relations between their contribution is that Innis' work is principally grounded in contradictions analysis, or in detailed historical study of particular systems. As a result, notwithstanding some passages that appear to summarize aspects of his theoretical position, most of his analytical framework is *only* available in *implicit* form and can only be extracted and rendered *explicit* through an extended inductive process involving a period of intensive absorption in his works.

In contrast, Marx's major works, in particular the *Grundrisse* and the four volumes of *Capital*, are principally studies in pure theory of social development. Notwithstanding extensive historical detail, which is contained in and informs the argument of *Capital* for example, that work is fundamentally theoretical in nature. Moreover, Marx's explicitly historical studies, such as the *Eighteenth Brumaire* and his articles on the U. S. Civil War, were primarily journalistic in character. What is perhaps most impressive about them, given the circumstances of their composition, is the extent to which Marx's historical appraisals have in their essentials been confirmed by subsequent research, and the degree to which they articulated and extended the basic theoretical categories of *Capital* here to take account of the historical specificity of mid-nineteenth century France and of the United States in the 1860s. The reference to *Capital* is not anachronistic, despite the fact that Volume I was not published until 1867, since Marx's basic categories have been developed by the late 1840s, although not in the detail that they attained in *Capital* itself. In these terms, it can be suggested that Marx's own historical writings provide one of the strongest arguments against the "categorical dogmatism" which has infected some subsequent "Marxist" writings, and which Innis resisted in his own life and work. The preceding discussion primarily indicates that account must be taken of the different epistemological status of Innis' and Marx's major work in analyzing theoretical relations between them.

With the foregoing as background, it is possible to indicate the scope and significance of the economics of communication and to suggest why it provides intractable problems for neoclassical economic theory which can be largely overcome by recourse to the theoretical analyses of Innis and Marx. Abstractly conceived, the economics of communication may be defined as *the study of the determinants of the structure of spatial and temporal relations within and between open economic systems.*

"Open" economic systems are empirical or historical economic systems. They have five principal defining or determining characteristics: first, continuous interaction with the natural environment and with other economic systems; second, the operation of the entropy law in both system and environment, involving costs of system—maintenance, system reproduction, system expansion, and system transformation, all of which entail the prevention of an increase in entropy within the system (or in parts of the system) through an acceleration of the increase of entropy in the environment (or in other parts of the system) with a consequent potential for intersystem and intrasystem contradictions and conflict and resource-base exhaustion; third, processes of growth and of knowledge and capital accumulation (or, more generally, of accumulation of the means of production) within the system; fourth, technical change in both production and communication technology and organization; and fifth, uncertainty, insecurity, and instability of a more or less structured character.

In short, the fundamental characteristic of all "open" or historical economic systems is that they have an existence in space and in time and imply continuous mediated anti-entropic activity as a precondition for their extended survival or reproduction in space and time. Hence Marx, given his preoccupation with capital, observed: "Economy of time, to this all economy ultimately reduces itself."[2] Hence, Innis, following Hegel more closely than Marx did on this point (at the same time, transmuting Hegel's analysis into a dialectical materialist context), suggested: "History is not a seamless web but rather a web of which the warp and woof are space and time, woven in a very uneven fashion and producing distorted patterns."[3]

Communication activities are undertaken within open economic systems and are instrumental in determining feasible structures of spatial–temporal relations within them, just as their character is reciprocally determined by social, economic, and technical foundations of such systems. Five basic communication activities are central determinants of processes and patterns of system reproduction: first, transportation through time between spatially separated centers of material goods or commodities (including "trade flows"); second, as a special case of the first category, translation through time of material goods or commodities, without a change in spatial location (including "storage activities" and "inventory management"); third, transportation of persons between spatially separated locations (including "migration," temporary and permanent, as well as more specialized phenomena such as "troop movements" and "military-political occupation"); fourth, transmission of property claims to real resources (including "monetary transfers" and "capital flow"); and fifth, transmission of information and of power-based instructions over time and space (including processes of "education," "issuing of commands," "scientific exchange," "ideological and technical indoctrination," and "cultural and technological change and diffusion").

The empirical importance of these basic communication activities in technically advanced capitalist economies may be suggested by the fact that they represent roughly fifty percent of the Gross National Product as conventionally measured, in such economies.[4] The theoretical importance of the economics of communication is underlined by the fact that communications processes raise some of the most intractable problems faced by neoclassical economic theorists: problems related to the measurement of economic "output" (aside from standard "aggregation" and "index-number" problems); the theory of uncertainty; information and expectations; the political economy of power; and what might be described as "the economics of space and time" (as distinct from the question of allocation of resources *within* a *given* structure).[5]

Conventional neoclassical economic theory is singularly ill-equipped to deal with the above set of problems insofar as it relies on a model of the economic universe that presupposes the existence of a well-behaved price-system; deals with problems of uncertainty only within a context in which cardinal well-defined probability measures exist; incorporates the political economy of power only to the extent that it reflects the *effects* of narrowly *economic* monopoly power within a well-defined price system rather than the more general causes and effects of power differentials and power struggles; and typically ignores problems related to the structural determinants of the spatial–temporal relations within and between economic systems (as manifested in the neglect within advanced neoclassical theory of the elementary school formula, d = rt, distance = rate times time). Significantly, the analyses of both Innis and Marx involve considerations that directly address these aspects of the economics of communication with which neoclassical economics cannot adequately deal.

The remainder of this study is hence addressed to three principal issues: why Innis and Marx together provide a more practical and penetrating foundation for the political economy of communication than does conventional economic theory; the extent to which the studies of Innis and Marx are focused on communications and provide insight into communication media and processes; and the ways in which Innis' analysis of the economics of communication provides a necessary complement to Marx's analysis, just as Marx provides the basis for an exploration of issues incompletely dealt with by Innis.

Resolution of the first issue hinges on recognition of the fundamentally dialectical, ecological, or holistic, materialist and heuristic character of both Innis' and Marx's theoretical frameworks in the contradistinction to the nondialectical, logical–deductive, idealist, and ahistorical or (equivalently) transhistorical character of the axiomatic and categorical foundations of conventional economic and social theory. Indeed, there is a certain amount of redundancy (although redundancy is not necessarily unproductive) involved in drawing the distinction in the above terms.

In the mature works of both Innis and Marx, there is an epistemological acknowledgment of the difference between social–economic systems and the physical systems that provide an empirical analogue of the mathematical systems taken by neoclassical economic theory to represent the foundations of social–economic behavior. Both Innis and Marx, in contrast, demonstrate an awareness of the dialectical implications of changes in the spatial extent, temporal duration, and communication networks and processes of political–economic systems for changes in the structure of contradictions of such systems. Both in this way acknowledge the historical necessity of *categorical flexibility,* or of reflecting changes in the configurational referential character of logical categories (and even of the necessity of introducing new categories) in the historical analysis of economic change, on the basis of the emergence and discovery of significant and qualitatively "new" historical facts that require a change in understanding of the structure of qualitative relations in terms of which quantitative changes can be accurately analyzed. Both were sensitive to the interdependence of qualitative and quantitative historical change.

Both Innis and Marx, in short, relied on detailed historical knowledge in formulating their implicit and explicit general historical theses and in the historical categorical and empirical closure of their analyses at the level of contradictions analysis. Finally, and more concretely, both Innis and Marx recognized the signifiance of analyzing the socially mediated origins and impact of new technologies of production and communication as a way of gaining insight into historical political–economic transformation. Just as Innis distinguished in *The Cod Fisheries* and elsewhere between effects of commercial and industrial capitalism, for example, so Marx explored in *Capital* the differences between manufacture and machinofacture under capitalism in a way that underlined the different significance of each in the historical development of capitalism.

Innis' preoccupation with the political economy of communication is evident from the appearance of his first major published work, *A History of the Canadian Pacific Railway* (1923), although it only became fully apparent after the mid 1930s, in his increasingly systematic and explicit exploration of the economic history of communications media and processes, which resulted in the publication of *Political Economy and the Modern State* (1946), *Empire and Communications* (1950), *The Bias of Communication* (1951), and *Changing Concepts of Time* (1952), and in the compilation of his unpublished 300-page "Idea File" and his 1400-page "History of Communications" (both available in the Archives of the University of Toronto).

Yet many of the basic themes of the communication studies pervade his explorations into the history of the succession of staple exports, which acted as a fundamental determinant of the character of Canadian political–economic development, and many of the analytical tools he forged in his earlier economic-historical studies were instrumental in enabling his path-breaking advances in the political–economic theory and economic history of communications. The notion of two Innises, an "early" Innis preoccupied with the mundane details of Canadian staple exports and a "later" Innis, who (like Saul on the road to Damascus) either saw or was blinded by the light of communication phenomena (depending on one's disciplinary or political perspective), has gained some credence in academic circles. Notwithstanding the fact that Innis' work (like that of Marx) displays a growing theoretical sophistication and maturity over time, ignorance or neglect of the essential relationship between Innis' early works and his later studies of communication has been as misleading as the Althusserian dichotomization of Marx's work in similar fashion.

Like Marx, Innis placed considerable stress throughout his writings on the determinative influence of developments in technology (in the spheres of material production, transportation and information transmission and, in the general forces of production, on patterns of development that emerged in different political–economic systems. Like Marx, moreover, Innis did not equate the determinative influence of technological developments with a naive form of "technological determinism." As he remarked in the preface to *The Bias of Communication*, these studies "emphasize the importance of communication in determining 'things to which we attend' and suggest also that changes in communication will follow changes in 'the things to which we attend.'"[6]

The dialectical interdependence emphasized in this passage between changes in communications media, epistemological changes, and changes in the conditions that influence "the things to which we attend" constitutes a central element in Innis' analysis of the political economy of communication and militates against adoption of a crude, monocausal, deterministic perspective. Yet even in his study of the Canadian Pacific Railway, which is by no means dialectical in essence, Innis made a

number of observations that indicate an ecological awareness of the reciprocal interaction between communications and overall political–
economic development:

> Physical expansion of the [CPR] to a large extent determined, and was deter-
> mined by, the growth of traffic. . . . The addition of technical equipment
> described as physical property of the Canadian Pacific Railway Company was
> a cause and an effect of the strength and character of [western] civiliza-
> tion. . . . [In French Canada,] the *seigneurial* system, the effects of military
> struggle, the character of the St. Lawrence River Basin, the influences of
> language, religion and customs promoted the development of homogeneous
> settlement, and the growth of a distinct national feeling.[7]

In Innis' subsequent "staples" studies, a concern with the economic
implications of communications media and processes continued to occupy a major place in his thought. In one sense, this is not at all surprising: insofar as the pattern of Canadian political–economic development
has been heavily influenced by the character of staple exports that have
sustained and been sustained by that development, an analysis of Canadian history (like that of many "new countries") requires particular
attention to the sphere of circulation and hence to communications networks (transportational, informational, and financial) that have historically determined the character of the circulation process.

More concretely, the nineteenth century, during which Canada
emerged to continental nationhood, witnessed a fundamental shift in the
competitive position of maritime and continental transportation (evidenced most dramatically in the rise of the railroad, but also in development of roads, canals, and steam-powered vessels on inland waterways).
This shift was instrumental in the settlement and development of "countries of new settlement" and also in the eastward movement of the center
of gravity of European power, in particular toward Germany and Russia.
In addition, the particular staples industries studied by Innis (including
cod, fur, timber, wheat, gold, pulp, and paper) all posed distinct problems
of production and of "distribution" or "marketing," which enforced
a continuous concern with the range of problems of communication (in
the broadest sense of the term) that constituted preconditions for the
political–economic viability of different systems of staple production.

An extended preoccupation with the detailed historical analysis of
problems of staples production thus strengthened Innis' materialist understanding of the process of historical development. Moreover, just as
Marx's marginal German origins heightened his awareness of the significance of characteristic features of English capitalism in his day, and
as Veblen's marginal Wisconsin-Norwegian agrarian origins heightened
his awareness of the significance of emergent U. S. industrial and finance capitalism, so Innis' marginal Canadian and agrarian origins,
heightened by his experiences in World War I, sharpened his concern

with the dialectical relationship between imperial centers and colonial margins (insofar as Canadian development has been conditioned by successive subordinate relations to French, British, and U. S. empires); with interimperial competition; and with the internal center–margin dialectic that has characterized Canadian political–economic relations given the federal character of the Canadian political economy. In short, to the extent that Innis' later works in the economic history of communication involved a dialectical materialist scientific perspective, both the dialectical and the materialist roots of his communications analysis can be traced to his earlier staples analyses.

Perhaps even more significantly for the future theoretical development of the economics of communication, study of the staple exports that influenced Canadian political–economic development forced Innis to refine a core of distinctive and strategic analytical tools. These included a generalized concept of overhead costs; a recognition of historical consequences of differing time structures of capital; an appreciation of the importance of temporal and spatial problems of excess capacity as determinants of problems of "rigidity" or "bias"; an acknowledgment of the extent to which such "rigidities" and possibilities of joint production operated to undermine the effectiveness of the price system and related allocative mechanisms: an awareness of the ways in which monopolies of force and monopolies of knowledge have historically arisen in relation to the existence of such biases; and a sensitivity to the potential for political–economic centralization and decentralization incidental to the adoption and utilization of particular means of communication. All these tools had been developed in relation to problems raised by the so called "staples" studies by the time Innis embarked on his so called "communication" studies.

At a theoretical level, then, Innis' shift from the "staples" studies to the global analysis of the long-run economic history of communications constituted neither a discontinuous break with his previous historical concerns nor a fundamental theoretical or epistemological break with the analytical framework he had previously developed. Rather it was an attempt to provide an historical context for the understanding of contemporary trends that was as temporally and spatially extended as possible, and a sphere of analysis within which the tools of inquiry developed in his earlier studies could be pushed to their limits in the exploration of the role of communication (which Innis had identified by the 1940s as a strategic factor) in long-run political–economic development.

The peculiar role of two staples, gold, and pulp and paper, in Canadian and global capitalist development contributed in different but related ways to the extension of Innis' temporal and spatial horizons that culminated in the application of the early frameworks he had already developed to the economic history of communications in global civilization. Innis came to realize the strategic role gold played in the system of capitalist production,[8] precisely because it served as a principal medium for general exchange of commodities within and between economies based on commodity money, but he also realized the "cyclonic" and potentially disruptive consequences (for regions dominated by gold extraction) of the dependence of the international economy on the production of gold and other precious metals, as reflected in his ironic use of Keynes' term "liquidity preference" in describing the process.[9]

In related fashion, his study of the pulp and paper industry forced consideration of the nature of the demand for the product of the industry. The economics of pulp and paper is particularly complex. It requires a consideration of the joint production of pulp and paper and of hydro-electric power on the one hand, and a consideration of the determinants of the demand for pulp and paper (as newsprint, book paper stock, wrapping paper, and shipping containers), on the other. The first two sources of pulp and paper demand are directly related to the demand for information, to the prerequisites of the formation of "public opinion" within predominantly print-oriented capitalist societies.

It is hence arguable that the specific supply and demand characteristics of the Canadian gold and pulp and paper industries tended to lead Innis toward an intensified preoccupation with the strategic role of communication-related staple products in long-run political–economic development. His recognition that precapitalist and capitalist economic history of such staples and related communication media and processes had been seriously neglected in previous economic–historical studies pushed him to explore the economic history of the communications industry of western (and, to some extent, eastern) civilization along the lines of the industry studies he had conducted within a much narrower spatial–temporal compass in dealing with the principal Canadian staple products. What must be recognized, however, is that this extension of interest involved an extension of the range of application of analytical tools that Innis had already developed, rather than a fundamental break with the approach he had already hammered out,[10] even though he was quite conscious that in his final works he was pushing that analytical method to its limits. It must also be recognized that Innis' preoccupation in his later works with the preconditions for the spatial and temporal survival of historical empires, with the role of communications in sustaining them and with the possibilities for successful marginal resistance to imperial control, was not unrelated to the shift from British to United States imperial hegemony in Canada and globally during the twentieth century, of which Innis had become increasingly conscious during the 1930s and 1940s.

Innis' final studies of the economics of communication, in short, involved an approach to communication which, taken as a whole, was focused less on a notion that media in their technological aspects are ultimate determinants of political–economic development than on a social–ecological perspective in which communications media were seen as one principal determinant of long-run system development. Certain passages in Innis' later works, taken in themselves without reference to the whole of his writings on the economic history of communication, might appear to provide support for a reductionistic, technological-determinist characterization of his achievement. Yet in Innis' final writings, communications media were both broadly defined and intended to be understood in their systemic social–ecological relationship to other determinants of political–economic development. "Media" in Innis' sense comprehended not only technologies of communication in the narrow sense but also organizational media (such as priesthoods and the state) and the products of intellectual activity (from lyrics to locomotives to libraries to law). In short, Innis, in his communication studies, worked less as a "media determinist" than as a social ecologist with a focus on the ecological implications of transformations in the character of communications media.

The "economics of communication" in Innis' sense hence acknowledged the economic importance of geographical factors (as in his mediated extrapolation from the St. Lawrence to the Nile and the Tigris and Euphrates rivers); of military developments (such as the crossbreeding of speedy Libyan with strong Asiatic horses in the Middle East in the second millenium B.C.);[11] and of the interpenetration of developments in communication and in the general political economy.

Marx's analysis of the overall communications sphere of general economic activity, like that of Innis, displays an ecological perspective, although on a first appraisal (even for a careful student of Marx) the importance of this perspective in Marx's work may be less apparent than it is in the case of Innis. Marx's analysis in the first three volumes of *Capital*, for example, appears to focus principally on preconditions for reproduction and inevitable contradictions of capitalist production, and in one sense such a conclusion is not unwarranted. Even in this sense, however, it is difficult to ignore the centrality of Marx's concern with the "economics of communication" as previously defined:

> [There] are certain independent branches of industry in which the product of the productive process is not a new material product, is not a commodity. Among these only the communications industry, whether engaged in transportation proper, of goods and passengers, or in the mere transmission of communications, letters, telegrams, etc., is economically important.[12]

Even more to the point, *Capital* itself contains much communication analysis. Marx's analysis of the Commodity at the outset of Volume I of *Capital* is from one standpoint a brilliant logical historical analysis of the semiotics of money. Indeed, it is precisely Marx's recognition that money is a medium, a complex medium of social communication, which informs and gives depth and coherence to his entire analysis and warrants decribing him as one of the foremost monetary theorists in the history of economic thought. The second volume of *Capital*, moreover, treats the sphere of circulation of commodities in terms which emphasize in considerable detail the role of communications in capitalist development:

> . . . what the transportation industry sells is change of location. The useful effect is inseparably connected with the process of transportation, i.e., the productive process of the transportation industry. Men and goods travel together with the means of transportation, and this travelling, this locomotion, constitutes the process of production effected by these means. . . . But the exchange value of this useful effect is determined, *like that of any other commodity*, by the value of the elements of production (labour-power and means of production) consumed by it plus the surplus value created by the surplus labour of the labourers employed in transportation [italics added].[13]

It is this two-fold character of communication (as an independent branch of *production* and as a process in the sphere of circulation) that gives it a two-fold role within Marx's theoretical system. The shortening of the time of circulation implied by technical change in communications has ramifications (of unequal magnitude in different branches of production) throughout the system, since in itself it causes a fall in the final value of all transported commodities, under competitive conditions. Moreover, the increased speed of transportation tends to enable a reduction in the raw material inventories that constitute an element of constant capital,[14] thereby lowering the organic composition of capital and hence raising the rate of profit insofar as the rate of exploitation remains constant in the face of changes.

Of even greater significance in appreciating the role of communications in Marx's analysis and the affinities between Innis and Marx is the following extended passage from *Capital: A Critique of Political Economy*, Vol. II. Marx outlines how changes in communication alter the relationship between space and time; how the differential impact of communication developments on different centers results simultaneously in spatial centralization and centralization of capital; and how the extension of communication is both a product of and an impelling force underlying the continuing expansion of capital. Although improvement in communication reduces the absolute time of circulation of commodities it:

> . . . does not eliminate the relative difference in the time of circulation of different commodity capitals arising from their peregrination, nor that of different portions of the same commodity capital which migrate to different markets. . . . The relative difference remains, although often diminished. But the relative differences may be shifted about by the development of the

means of transportation in a way that does not correspond to the geographical distances. . . . In the same way the same circumstances may alter the relative distance of places of production from the larger markets, which explains the deterioration of old and the rise of new centres of production because of changes in communication and transportation facilities. . . . Moreover with the development of transport facilities not only is the velocity of movement in space accelerated and therefore the geographic distance shortened in terms of time. Not only is there a development of the mass of communications facilities. . . . The development tends in the direction of the already existing market, that is to say, towards the great centres of production and population, towards ports of export, etc. [pp. 253–254]

Marx was also continuously concerned with the relations between the economic bases of systems and the political ideological superstructures that emerge from them in mediated and potentially or actually contradictory form, and formulated some of the strategic problems in this sphere more clearly then anyone had before.[15] Yet his analysis of communications is less than comprehensive, not fully articulated, and not free of errors. In this context, Innis' theoretical advances in the economics of communication constitute one of the soundest bases for the resolution of critical gaps in Marx's theory

At a more concrete level, the penetration and profundity of Innis' historical insights stem in part from his systematic exploration of the economic history of communication in terms of an extension of the generalized theory of overhead costs he had refined in relation to his staples studies. The historical and theoretical importance of "fixed capital," particularly as it manifested itself in the rise of machine production (which Marx identified with the development of "capitalism" properly so called), was acknowledged by Marx, as was the significance of indivisibilities related to the existence of fixed capital in the sphere of communication. Marx also recognized, and analyzed to a considerable extent, the tendencies to absolute concentration and monopolization or centralization of capital incidental to the existence and nature of fixed capital and the process of capitalist competition.[16]

Innis, however, both grasped a number of implications of fixed capital more fully and certainly than Marx had, and recognized that many of these implications were also characteristic of the organization of precapitalist and noncapitalist economic formations. "Fixed capital," in Marx's sense, is capital that has been withdrawn from the sphere of circulation and "frozen," or fixed in a specific form, for an extended period of time, in the expectation it will provide the basis for future extraction of surplus value or profit and for continued accumulation, so that its value is only fully realized after a number of years. It is this intertemporal fixity in the form taken by capital (say, in the form of plant and machinery) that defines the time structures of production; and it is the rigidity of the physical form and the limits on the range of potential uses of such "fixed" capital that contributed to the intensification of the "realization problem," or of individual and general capitalist crises, with the extension of industrial capitalism.

Innis clearly recognized this aspect of fixed capital; indeed, his only partly tongue-in-cheek comment on the fate of the beaver following the extension of the fur trade is a classic statement of the principle:

> In the language of the economists, the heavy fixed capital of the beaver became a serious handicap with the improved technique of Indian hunting methods, incidental to the borrowing of iron from Europeans. Depreciation through obsolescence of the beaver's defense equipment was so rapid as to involve the immediate and complete destruction of the animal.[17]

Yet Innis extended the concept in a number of directions that have particular relevance for future development of the political economy of communications.

First, he recognized that, insofar as all historical political–economic organizations have an existence in space and time and involve a concern with their reproduction over time and the maintenance or expansion of their spatial extent, all human social organization partakes of the character of fixed capital.

Second, and more specifically, all communications systems and media necessarily manifest aspects of fixed capital and of overhead costs. The establishment and maintenance of any system or medium of communication (whether a spoken or written language, drum signals, Morse Code, a library, a theological system, a newspaper, a system of military or bureaucratic administration or control, an imperial road network, or a symposium on the works of Innis) necessarily involves certain original fixed, indivisible and irrevocable costs, as well as certain costs of maintenance, precisely because of the systemic character of communications media.

Third, given the systemic or indivisible character of all communications media and processes, the establishment of a system of communication involves problems of "externalities" and "joint production" in forms which pose intractable problems for neoclassical economic theory. Moreover, communication networks involve problems of capacity, which are manipulated in two distinct ways. Problems of *excess capacity* can emerge both spatially and temporally. Spatially, as Innis was aware, such problems arose in the Canadian fur trade, where the high value/bulk ratio of furs relative to trade goods inhibited settlement and encouraged the development of the timber trade, which (following the decline of the fur trade) promoted the settlement of Upper Canada. Temporally as well, seasonal and cyclical problems of excess capacity also encouraged innovation, as in the development of active maritime trading activity by New England fishermen in relation to the seasonality of the cod fisheries or in the development of the New York penny press by Benjamin Day in relation to the cholera epidemic of 1833. Problems of *pressures on capacity* can equally contribute to innovation (particularly "process innovations") or to system breakdown, if system rigidities and conservative tendencies are sufficiently powerful to prevent adaptation to quantitative or qualitative changes in the environment.

Innis articulated the preconditions for the survival of systems in space and time in terms of the dialectically related concepts of "control over space" and "control over time." "Control over space" relates both to the territorial extent of control by a system and to the degree of organization of the means of maintaining territorial control by the system. Similarly, "control over time" relates both to the systematic intensity of organization of time and to the adaptability, flexibility, or persistence of the system in response to changes in the configuration of its environment.

The dialectical relationship between control of space and control of time in Innis' analysis can readily be indicated by means of examples. On the one hand, Byzantine control of time was extended through concentration of its spatial extent; in this case there was a tradeoff between control of space and control of time. On the other hand, the consequences of New England's proximity to the cod fisheries implied a degree of control over space that was translated into increased control of time as exemplified in the success of the American Revolution, indicating the mutually reinforcing nature of control over space and over time in this instance. Similarly, the control over time of the Roman Church was reflected in increased control over space: "The Catholic church renounced the world and became the heir of the defunct Roman empire."[18]

Innis' concepts of control over space and control over time and the nature of their interdependence cannot be fully understood without reference to their relation to the spatial–temporal organization and demands of fixed capital. Excess capacity simultaneously involves a potential or actual drain on the strength of an organization and an incentive and the resources to promote innovation. Adoption by the Greeks of a twenty-two symbol consonantal Semitic alphabet, some letters of which had no phonemic counterparts in Greek, implied a situation of excess capacity that resulted in the Greek invention of vowels. A rise in the interest rate in relation to the existence of fixed capital is a signal of the necessity for the reorganization and concentration of control over time.

The indivisibility of fixed capital and of communications media involves massing of resources, emergence of organizational complexity, and potential or necessity for monopolization, hierarchy, and centralization as techniques of simplification. Monopolies of knowledge and monopolies of force in Innis' view are related to but not uniquely determined by the technical characteristics of the media that sustain and are sustained by them. Although it is true some media are technically more susceptible to monopolization (or present more substantial technical "barriers to entry") than others, organizational restrictions such as celibacy in the Roman Catholic Church are also of significance in the maintenance of such monopolies. Communications systems in their technical *and* organizational aspects, however, imply rigidities or biases (just as does any form of fixed capital). Preoccupation with defensive strategies in relation to such biases involves tendencies toward ritualization, conservatism and bureaucratization, inability to adjust to new forms of media or more general ecological competition, and increased potential for marginal development of new methods of competition, with responses involving repression, central innovation or collapse. The center–margin dialectic explored by Innis thus serves as a necessary refinement of and complement to Marx's analysis of class conflict.

The foregoing discussion constitutes the barest of sketches of some ways in which Innis' analysis of the economics of communication, founded on the concepts of ecological competition, the center–margin dialectic, and the general theory of fixed capital and overhead costs, can contribute to the articulation of Marx's theoretical framework and to the future development of Canadian political economy. Yet it may be suggested that the heuristic tools Innis developed (and which require further theoretical and historical development) constitute vital avenues of insight into the present global system. It may also be suggested that if the future analysis of Canadian political economists are not Innis capable, they will lose Marx; conversely, however, if their analyses are off the Marx, they will remain in Inniscence.

NOTES

[1]Parker, Ian. "Harold Innis, Karl Marx and Canadian Political Economy.": *Queen's Quarterly*, Winter 1977, pp. 545–563.

[2]Marx, Karl. *Grundrisse* (1857–1858), Harmondsworth, Penguin, 1973, p. 173.

[3]Innis, Harold A. *The Bias of Communiation* (1951). Toronto, University of Toronto Press, 1964, pp. 327–357.

[4]Parker, Ian. "Studies in the Economics of Communication." New Haven, Yale University, 1977, chapter 1.B.2. (unpublished doctoral dissertation).

[5]Parker, "Studies . . ." chapter 1.B.3.

[6]Innis, *Bias*, p. xvii.

[7]Innis, Harold A. *A History of the Canadian Pacific Railway.* Toronto, McClelland & Stewart, 1923, pp. 270, 287–288.

[8]Innis, Harold A. *Settlement and the Mining Frontier: Canadian Frontiers of Settlement* (1936). Toronto, Macmillan, 1956, pp. 327–357.

[9]Innis, Harold A. *Essays in Canadian Economic History.* Toronto, University of Toronto Press, 1956, pp. 327–357.

[10]Innis, *Bias,* pp. xvii–xviii.

[11]Innis, Harold A. *Empire and Communications* (1950), Toronto, University of Toronto Press, 1972, p. 75.

[12]Marx, Karl. *Capital: Volume II* (1885). Moscow, Progress Publishers, 1967, pp. 53–54.

[13]Marx, *Capital II,* pp. 54–57.

[14]Marx, *Capital II,* p. 146.

[15]Marx, *Capital II,* p. 137.

[16]See also Marx, *Grundrisse,* pp. 525–533, 692–695; *Capital I* pp. 621–628 and passages cited above in the text.

[17]Innis, Harold A. *The Fur Trade in Canada: An Introduction to Canadian Economic History* (1930). Toronto, University of Toronto Press, 1956, p. 5.

[18]Innis, *Bias,* p. 140.

10

IMPERIALISM AND THE STAPLE THEORY OF CANADIAN ECONOMIC DEVELOPMENT: THE HISTORICAL PERSPECTIVE

ROBIN F. NEILL
Carleton University

The problem that confronts us is the limitations of the staple theory of Canadian economic development. On the one hand economists can refer to the well-known power of the staple theory in explaining Canada's progress. On the other hand there are acknowledged nonstaple oriented factors in the country's growth, and there is considerable evidence that governments, federal and provincial, have adopted policies oriented to freeing the country from reliance on staples or otherwise interfering with normal development based on staples; this, too, is a nonstaple oriented factor in growth. Further, there is evidence that nonstaple factors have been regionally differentiated. Given the well-known importance of federal–provincial diplomacy in the formation of national policy, the ultimate desideratum is an account of the factors, economic and political, staple and nonstaple oriented, underlying the regionalized development of the economy.

A relatively simple answer to the question of centralization and decentralization is, at least, implicit in much of the literature. In the nineteenth century, staple exports of wheat and timber united the nation on an east–west trade axis connecting Canada to its metropolitan center in Britain. In the twentieth century, staple exports of wood products and minerals have fractionated the economy by creating a north–south trade axis connecting the provinces to metropolitan centers in the United States. The staple theory thus seems to provide an economic explanation for both the unity and the regionalization of the nation. The weakness of this answer is evident in the relative economic decline and political alienation of the Maritimes in the period of Confederation, the extent to which agriculture in Quebec expanded in isolation from staple exports, and the extent to which manufacturing in Ontario cannot be reduced to a forward or backward linkage from staple exports in the latter half of the nineteenth century and perhaps in the twentieth. There are, however, immense problems involved in measuring the more subtle contribution of these and other nonstaple oriented factors.

It has been argued that institutions developed in consequence of early reliance on staple exports have reinforced reliance on that type of development, leading the nation into a "staple trap" and entrenching its position as a dependent hinterland exposed to the disintegrating influence of increasing penetration by United States interests. Regionalization, in this view, is a consequence of reliance on staple exports. It can be argued, however, that the aboriginal condition of the nation was extreme regionalization and that, despite the presence of nonstaple oriented factors, its regionalized character prevented adoption of effective policies of nonstaple oriented, independent growth. This, combined with the rapid extension of its political boundaries, in competition with a much more advanced economy using the capital-intensive techniques of that economy at a critical moment in its own development, forced the nation into a compromise position involving substantial continued reliance on Imperial politics and political expansionism related to the Imperial connection, was the cause of continued reliance on staple exports. Reliance on staples has not caused regionalization. Regionalization has caused reliance on staples.

Canada's reliance on staple exports and theories rationalizing that reliance must first be understood in the context of the early nineteenth century liberalization of the British Empire. Britain was adjusting a mercantile empire to accommodate the rise of its manufacturing sector after 1750. The economic demands of the new economy were ill-suited to the political structure of the Empire in terms of its geographical extent and location, especially after 1776, and in terms of the structure of monopolies, tariffs, and navigation laws that had been built up in response to earlier economic and political pressures. The answer, in general, was the adoption of laissez-faire, or what has been called Manchester Liberalism. The advantages of free enterprise in a competitive environment, explained by the theory of exchange and the principle of comparative advantage (Smith cum Ricardo), lay in its power to efficiently allocate and locate resources and production, respectively, without a readjustment of the political geography of the Empire. Indeed, with free trade the political extent of the Empire would cease to have economic significance.

The thrust of the new policy was to substitute an economic for a political empire. The colonies were to continue as hinterland markets and sources of basic materials, as they had been under the mercantile system of the old Empire. Only the political institutions that had formerly supported that arrangement—or grown out of it—were to be dismantled. The colonies would be given self-government and would themselves carry the expense of their defence and civil administration. It seemed in Britain that the high ratio of land to labor and capital on the frontiers of the Empire, if not the world, would lead, under enlightened trade laws, to a natural and mutually beneficial specialization in land-intensive production in those areas: that is, reliance on "staple exports." Britain, the metropolitan motherland, having a high ratio of labor and capital to land, would continue to expand its "natural" specialization in manufacturing. A paradoxical liberal empire came into existence on the basis of an argument that economic and political laissez-faire would better serve Imperial ends.

Perhaps as a result of overweening ambition and unwarranted enthusiasm, typical of frontier regions, perhaps as a "natural" consequence of their relatively underdeveloped stage of growth, the British North American colonies recoiled not only from the immediate consequences of the liberalization of Imperial trade but also from the rationalizations and long-run implications involved. Political laissez-faire, appearing as "responsible government" for the colonies, was accompanied by the adoption of illiberal policies designed to accelerate balanced growth and reduce reliance on staple exports. The move was evident in the economic proposals of Joseph Howe, who led the "struggle" for responsible government in Nova Scotia, and in the ambitions expressed by Thomas McCulloch and John Young, whose letters were published in Howe's newspaper. It was evident in the general support for protectionism in Quebec where, perhaps, less sophisticated economic reasoning was buttressed by the enormous drive of a "conquered people" for complete independence. It was evident in Ontario where Imperial political liberalism expressed in fiscal independence produced the tariff of 1858. Finally, even in British Columbia it was evident in the time given to discussion of free trade and protection during the Confederation Debates of 1870 and in the adoption of protectionist resolutions.

Following Confederation heavy pressure was mounted for the adoption of a national tariff policy and a national currency policy. Although the arguments supporting these propositions were never coherently put together, except perhaps in the statements of Isaac Buchanan, they were consistent in their illiberal proposal of government interference on behalf of balanced and independent growth. The national, fiat currency scheme was intended to eliminate depressions resulting from reliance on external capital and to accelerate the development of the economy as a whole. The national tariff was intended to tax expenditures on imported consumer goods, reduce the risk in new investments in domestic manufacturing, realize economies of scale and provide revenue for the government's program of investment in transportation and other infrastructure. In short, the national economic policy was to be geared to nonstaple oriented balanced growth financed by domestically generated capital.[1]

On the assumption that an acceptable rate of increasingly nonstaple oriented independent growth was technically possible for the four original provinces of the Dominion, we may ask, what were the factors preventing that result? There is no reason to believe this assumption to be "heroic." Some questions may be raised about the matter of increasing independence, since there seems to be fair evidence that, as national Gross National Product per capita grows the world over, trade increases as a portion of GNP. Thus increasing "dependence" on foreign markets is associated with growth. This sort of "dependence" simply indicates the growth of a world rather than a national market. It in no way refers to the state of dependency or subordination of a capital-scarce, primary product, staple-exporting hinterland economy. There is a distinction between the staple theory and the export base theory. The latter does not take into account the power relationship and the consequent biased sharing of the risks and gains of trade that was explicit in earlier versions of the staple theory and still is explicit in Western Marxian versions. An export base theory that equally accounts for the growth of the Japanese economy in the mid-twentieth century and the Canadian economy in the early nineteenth century misses some important aspects of development.

If continued reliance on staple exports can be explained in this way, by political factors, room is left for consideration of the effects of nonstaple oriented economic factors in Canadian development. The appropriate counter factual question would be: at what rate and in what direction would Canada have grown if political factors preventing nonstaple oriented independent growth had not been present? The preliminary step in answering this question is the identification and sufficiently reasonable substantiation of the historical importance of the inhibiting factors.

A corollary to the assumption that independent, nonstaple development was possible is the assumption, supported by the historical events already referred to, that such development was contemplated and attempted. This implies, contrary to received opinion, that there was in 1867–78 little expectation of staple exportation from the Prairie region or British Columbia.[2] The annexing of the Hudson's Bay Territory and the entrance of British Columbia into Confederation were politically motivated, and so then was the building of the Canadian Pacific Railway. The political motivation derived in fair measure from imperialistic expansion on the part of Canada and from the birth of a new imperialism under Disraeli in Britain in 1870. The political goal was to hold vast areas of North America in the face of United States expansion after the Civil War. The means were the creation of a united British North America in a liberal Empire, bound together by a railroad that would be part of a band of steel rails and steam ships holding the Empire strong against the rise of continental Europe and the United States.[3] The consequent immense expansion of Canada so strained and allocated its resources that independent, nonstaple oriented growth became an impossibility. The weakness of private capital in the Canadas had been the occasion of government involvement in canals and railways. Indeed, part of the economic significance of 1867 can be found in the need to centralize the railway debts of the colonies. Confederation and the National Policy of 1878 may be interpreted as an attempt to use government to facilitate the saving-investment process. After the imperialistic expansion of the immediate post-Confederation era the possibility of independently generated balanced growth, even with government involvement, faded.

There were other factors. The preexisting regionalization of the economy, in part a matter of differences in geography but largely a matter of history, culture and politics, frustrated the attempt to organize for independent balanced growth at the national level. The establishment of a national currency system, that is to say a financial structure appropriate to the desired growth, was proposed in the period from 1866 to 1870, and some beginnings of the arrangement were put in place or suggested in the bill put before the House by John Rose in 1871. Rose's bill was defeated and the arrangements undone largely because Toronto and Canada West were ready to ignore the implications of the proposed new system in order to prevent Montreal from gaining financial hegemony over the country. Regional rivalries prevented effective action at the federal level.

The federal government began with a very weak basis of consent on Confederation. Its efforts to force political and economic expansion further weakened it. Nova Scotia was virtually legislated in and British Columbia cooperated, in fair measure, only with the urging of the Imperial government. For Ontario and Quebec Confederation was an act of separation. When the national currency policy foundered on the rock of regionalism the federal government was forced to fall back on the tariff as the only means of promoting growth, and on the formation of a heavily government-subsidized monopoly for politically motivated building of the CPR. These devices further alienated the Maritimes and created disaffection in the West itself. Both the Maritimes and Quebec complained that their resources were being used to finance expansion in other parts of the country. For the Maritimes, the contribution of the West to the economic growth of the country as a whole, a contribution that remained in doubt until the 1890s, would have to be measured against the losses incurred in their own relative decline following the transfer of jurisdiction, capital, population, and enterprise that accompanied Confederation, the National Tariff Policy, and the opening of the Prairies. While the West, the Maritimes, and Quebec complained, Ontario pursued its own ends of autonomy and territorial expansion, contesting the power of the federal government at every turn and eventually spearheading the acceptance of the Compact Theory of Confederation by a majority of the provinces at the Inter-Provincial Conference of 1887.

Although "resources," except in the North West Territories, had been put under provincial jurisdiction in the British North America Act, there was reasonable doubt that the provinces would have effective control since their position as agents of the Crown, rather than the federal government, was in grave doubt. The refusal of Ontario to accept subordination to Ottawa and the rebellion of the provinces expressed in their decentralizing proposals in 1887 were, at first, thwarted by Imperial rejection, but subsequent interpretation of the BNA Act by the Judicial Committee of the Privy Council recognized the natural decentralization of the nation. After 1887 the control of Provincial governments over resources was enforced. Considerable control over economic growth was thus regionalized and by 1910 most of the provinces were embarking on their own "national policies." If the north–south flow of trade based on "new staples" after 1900 has decentralized the economy it is in fair measure because aboriginal decentralization has created a facilitating political arrangement.

The result of these factors, demands for imperialistic political expansion and the hamstringing of national policy by regional interests, was rapid extensive expansion of the Canadian economy with considerable use of imported British capital. The borrowed capital had to be repaid and could only be repaid by earned British (or American) currency. Britian, having its own manufacturers, was interested only in buying primary products. After 1896 a number of technical advances in farming on the Prairies and in railroading and associated transport made wheat a viable staple. There ensued "a wheat boom" and a marked increase in imported British capital to build more railroads, many of which politically motivated and never became economically viable. The export of wheat was, nonetheless, sufficient to ensure the flow of capital in the first instance. What had begun in the 1850s and 1860s as a scheme for independent, balanced growth came to be a scheme for dependent growth in a staple producing economy.

The switch from a policy of independent balanced growth to dependent staple-oriented growth could not, on our presumptions, have been complete. The economic factors and the technical capabilities present in the 1850s and 1860s were not obliterated but continued, however diminished, alongside the new economy. Why those factors came to be downplayed or ignored in national policy and in explanations of national policy itself needs explanation. Again, the reasons seem to be political and related to both the aboriginal regionalization of the economy and the consequent strength of the Imperial connection.

The importance of Imperial power in bringing about Confederation and in keeping it in existence in 1867 and 1887 has already been mentioned. But the matter was more complex than that. Beginning with the Riel Rebellion and ending with the Manitoba School Question, serious differences had to be worked out between the French- and English-speaking populations. The West had to be kept English-speaking; the ultramountanes in the French-speaking wing of the Conservative Party had to be kept in line and western expansion had to be the priority. Thus a sort of alliance grew up between D'Alton McCarthy and his followers who opposed "French domination," Clifford Sifton who was responsible for settling the West, Van Horne of the CPR, and the Prairie provinces in general, all of whom benefited from pressing the Imperial connection.

With Imperialism in such high fashion (in important circles) in the 1890s, the National Policy of 1878 was reinterpreted as an attempt to establish east–west trade based on Imperial politics, capital and markets. The unity and cultural–political character of the country was thought to depend on it. In this light the great usefulness of the staple theory was that it provided an economic rationale for national unity and the Imperial connection.

Throughout the period from 1848 to 1878, Reciprocity and the annexation of the Hudson's Bay Territory notwithstanding, the direction of British North American policy was toward political and economic national independence. This accorded with Imperial political liberalism but not with Imperial economic liberalism. Following the assertion of Canada's fiscal independence with the 1858 tariff, A. T. Galt found himself apologizing to an Imperial audience that protectionism and illiberal government involvement in railway building in Canada would, in fact, lower transport costs and facilitate extension of Imperial trade. The illiberal policies of the colony were, he alleged, designed to support Imperial liberalism. A similar reinterpretation of the tariff of 1878 occurred in the staple thesis of H. A. Innis who, in his preoccupation with proving the "natural" unity of Canada,[4] was taken with the staples explanation of Canadian development, with Galt's argument and with "the necessity of development nationalization in Canada to support liberalism in Great Britain and the United States."[5]

It is a long way from the staple theory of H. A. Innis, which Watkins rightly asserts was a theory of exploitation and did allow for nationalist policies designed to offset the problems of reliance on staples,[6] to the neoclassical staple theory of Douglas North,[7] which reduces the illiberal policies of 1870–78 to a fiscal linkage from the wheat staple to railroads and manufacturing. The distance is at least the distance between Karl Marx and Alfred Marshall. That distance has been covered, however, and the explanation of the National Policy has been liberalized. The theory of Canadian economic development was reverted to a modified version of the Smith cum Ricardo theory that rationalized the liberalization of the British Empire more than one hundred years ago.

The problems associated with this theory are multidimensional. Nationalists, like Innis, who rely on the staple theory to demonstrate the economic basis of the unification of British North America in the nineteenth century, find their arguments favoring continental integration and decentralization in Canada in the twentieth. Conservatives, like Donald Creighton, who rely on the staple theory to rationalize the British connection in the nineteenth century, find that their argument favors the United States connection in the twentieth. Twentieth century nationalists, like Watkins, who accept the staple theory of Canadian development (or underdevelopment), have to fall back on Marxism to find an economic justification for their illiberal position. The weakness of all three positions lies in their common assumption that reliance on staple exports explains the emergence of the Canadian nation. For Innis and Creighton reliance on staple exports has been economically justified; for Watkins it has not: but all agree that the causation runs from economics to politics. In reality the causation runs the other way. Reliance on staple exports has been the result of political circumstances. Canada's staple-oriented economy is an economically second-best fall-out from political problems. Watkins is correct when he asserts that reliance on staples has not been economically justified, but the explanation of this is not to be found in the exploitative tendencies of international capitalism. Rather it is to be found in the aboriginal inter-regional rivalries that have precluded the pursuit of economically justified nonstaple oriented growth. The staple theory of Canadian economic and political development is a plausible explanation of the historical evidence, since we have in fact relied heavily on the export of staples; but why we have done so, whether it was the best alternative on economic grounds and what nonstaple factors were at work are matters which when given sufficient attention will lead to the conclusion that the staple theory, as we have received it, is a *merely* plausible explanation of what has taken place.

It is not enough, however, to proceed on presumptions and persuasive historical argument. The strength and character of nonstaple factors in economic growth have to be shown to have significance. This requires, in the first instance, the elaboration of a model of economic growth in which the nonstaple as well as the staple-oriented factors are specified in a measurable way. In the second instance, it requires their measurement.

NOTES

[1] The only adequate theoretical justification of this policy was given in John Rae's *New Principles of Political Economy*, Boston, Hilliard, Gray, and Co., 1934. Although there is no indisputable evidence that Rae's propositions were widely known in nineteenth-century Canada, similar and consonant propositions were, and it was from those statements of J. S. Mill that were drawn from Rae's work that Macdonald drew his argument when he first presented his National Policy to the House of Commons on March 7, 1876.

[2] K. Buckley asserts that the expectation of a wheat staple exported through central Canada was common in the early 1870s. K. A. Buckley, *Capital Formation in Canada, 1896–1930*, Toronto, McClelland and Stewart, 1974, p. 6. As proof he cites a Budget Speech of Tilley quoted in W. A. Mackintosh's *The Economic Background of Dominion–Provincial Relations*, Toronto, McClelland and Stewart, 1964. Reference to Mackintosh reveals a much more cautious statement and reference to the budget speeches of the early 1870s, of which Tilley's was supposed to be typical, does not confirm Buckley's assertion. There was *hope* that *some* commercial development would occur but there was considerable opinion that the Canadian Pacific Railway would never pay its way. The line was a political commitment that, according to G. E. Cartier, could not be met at too soon a date without overtaxing the resources of the country. Buckley himself at another point (p. 40) concurs that this was the case. P. Hartland has pointed out that as late as 1885 the *Economist* of London concurred. ("Factors in Economic Growth in Canada," *Journal of Economic History, 15*, 1955, 13–22, p. 18.) This is not to deny that agricultural interests, especially in Ontario, were anxious to annex the West in the hope of reviving expansion on the frontier that had run up against the Laurentian Plateau by the 1860s.

[3] This view is fairly substantiated in R. C. Brown, *Canada's National Policy*, Princeton, Princeton University Press, 1964; and J. M. Gibbon, *Steel of Empire*, Toronto, McClelland and Stewart, 1935.

[4] Innis, H. A. *Autobiography* (mimeo.), p. 110. Available in the Rare Books collection of the Sigmund Samuel Library at the University of Toronto.

[5] Innis, H. A. "Economic Nationalism," *Papers and Proceedings of the Canadian Political Science Association, 6*, 1934, 17–31, p. 30. See also Dales, J. H., "Canada's National Policies" in *The Protective Tariff in Canada's Development*, Toronto, University of Toronto Press, 1966, pp. 143–158, fn. 1, pp. 145–147; Galt, A. T., *Canada: 1849–1859*, London, Robert Hardwicke, 1860; and Innis, H. A., "A Defence of the Tariff" in Neill, R. F., *A New Theory of Value*, Toronto, University of Toronto Press, 1972, pp. 149–159.

[6] See Watkins, M., "The Staple Theory Revisited," *Journal of Canadian Studies, 12*, 1977, 83–96; and Innis, H. A., "The Penetrative Powers of the Price System" (1938) in *Essays in Canadian Economic History*, Toronto, McClelland and Stewart, 1956, pp. 252–272.

[7] North, D. C., "Location Theory and Regional Economic Development", *Journal of Political Economy, 63*, 1955, 243–258.

11

OVERHEAD COSTS, RIGIDITIES OF PRODUCTIVE CAPACITY AND THE PRICE SYSTEM

IRENE M. SPRY
University of Ottawa

> The importance of fixed capital equipment characteristic of modern industrialism, particularly in recently industrialized continental countries with emphasis on transportation, on hydroelectric power, and on the expansion of metropolitan centres, has emphasized the increasing significance of overhead costs. . . . The impact of overhead costs in increased production of raw materials and declining prices has coincided with the extension of fixed charges. . . . As a result of the importance of overhead costs, in its effects on inelastic supply and especially joint supply, the price level has become an uncertain and far from delicate indicator in adjusting supply and demand.[1]

So wrote Innis in 1934 in a characteristic comment. His studies of the fur trade in Canada,[2] the cod fisheries,[3] mining,[4] and pulp and paper industry,[5] agriculture,[6] railways[7] and other means of transportation,[8] and power generation[9] contain many illuminating references to "overhead costs," "rigidities," "unused capacity," and "fixed charges."

Problems of overhead cost and rigidity arise when it is impossible to adjust capacity to produce or the actual rate of output to match changes in the rate at which output can be disposed of. The reasons for such a lack of flexibility are many and diverse. An attempt will be made in this paper to analyze the more important of them, to disentangle the complex variety of circumstances, which underlie the rigidities that so greatly concerned Innis.[10]

"CAPITAL INVESTMENT ON A LARGE SCALE"[11]

The first type of inflexibility to be considered is a matter of the size of the smallest possible unit of investment, that is to say, of the minimum indivisible cost that must be met if production is to be undertaken at all, or, at least, undertaken on the basis of advanced technology that offers a possibility of low unit costs if a massive scale of production can be achieved.[12] Innis showed in *The Cod Fisheries* that an industry characterized by small units of investment, wooden sailing ships, had considerable flexibility, especially as each ship could adapt freely to alternative opportunities by sailing from one fishing ground to another and from one market to another as circumstances required. The contrast is sharp with a canoe route in the fur trade, a canal system, or a railroad.

The contrast is evident in the difference between the individual enterprise of a coureur de bois and the elaborate arrangements and massive, indivisible scale of investment needed in the highly developed enterprise of the Northwest Company. The trading system that linked the Athabasca country and the Pacific coast with Montreal and with sources of trade goods and credit overseas involved an annual rendezvous of brigades of canoes, posts, and forts, a supply of provisions and planned exploration all integrated into a coordinated whole.[13]

The smallest possible effective input of canal construction is a sequence of locks that is sufficient to overcome an obstacle or series of obstacles to through navigation from point A to point B. A lock that lifts a vessel ten feet adds nothing to the output of through transit services if the rapids to be by-passed or the height of land to be surmounted requires that vessels be lifted one hundred feet. Similarly, a railway designed to connect Montreal and Vancouver would add nothing to communication facilities between these two destinations if its length was limited to one thousand miles or any length shorter than the entire distance between the two cities.[14]

An analogous indivisibility in the massive input of resources that must be made to bring a hard-rock mine into production is in sharp contrast with the tiny unit of input of resources required for primitive placer gold mining, which made the industry a classic example of atomistic individualism.[15]

The requirements of the newsprint industry, again, imply "enormous capital equipment, in mills and power plants, heavy fixed charges, and serious problems of overhead costs."[16]

In all those cases (as in many more) the need for a massive, irreducible commitment of resources has created rigidities of a type that is characteristic of modern industrialism. The size of the indivisible unit of investment imposes severe limitations on the number of independent enterprises that are capable of mobilizing the requisite enormous capital and struggle for a share of a limited market. The result is oligopolistic competition among a few giant firms, which has very different results from the smooth, flexible adjustment of supply to demand that is envisaged in the economist's model of perfectly competitive markets. Insistent pressure by each firm to expand its share of the market, so full use may be made of its capacity to produce, creates a danger of price wars. This threat engenders "basing point systems, intensive advertising, and monopolistic arrangements."[17] Innis explored a classic instance of duopsony in his study of the violent competition between the Hudson's Bay Company and the Northwest Company for control of sources of fur supplies, which led to the merger of the two giant rivals in 1821.[18] Similar opposition (to use the old fur trade term) among the giants of modern industry has meant, as Innis wrote, that the "trust movement has solidified industrial development."[19]

RIGID FINANCIAL OBLIGATIONS
AND FIXED CHARGES

The necessity for huge capital investment by firms engaged in mass production and especially in canals, railways, and power plants resulted in "the introduction of long term credit through corporate and government finance,"[20] with fixed interest charges accompanying bond issues and government support of major projects. Heavy, rigid financial obligations were the counterpart of heavy, indivisible capital investment:

> ... the weight of overhead costs in relation to extensive capital equipment, and the heavy fixed charges involved in government ownership were evident in rigidities of railway rates and interest charges.[21]

State support added to the "rigidity of finances without benefit of bankruptcy,"[22] while the inflexibility of prices of manufactured goods, interest on debts, and railway rates in relation to prices of raw materials for exports exposed to world competition, meant an unequal spreading of the burden of indivisible costs in a period of depression.[23] The result was evident in the 1930s in "rigidities of freight rates and interest charges and shrinking income through drought and falling prices, and without a balanced economic structure."[24]

Though often called "overhead costs," financial obligations, however rigid they may be, are not costs at all in the economic sense. They certainly impose payments that have to be made, but the necessity to make those payments arises from a contract, a legal commitment. The payments would have to be made whether or not the debtor produces the goods and services he or she expected to be able to produce and sell when he or she entered into the contract with the creditor. The payments to be made do not disappear if nothing is produced; they do not increase if more is produced than had been anticipated.

COMMITTED RESOURCES AND FIXED CAPACITY

The confusion between obligations to make payments and cost may originate in the simultaneous decisions to commit massive resources to a particular kind of productive asset and the decision to secure the capital needed for this investment by borrowing it on the strength of certain promises to make specified payments in the future. Before the resources to be used in bringing the asset into existence are irrevocably committed, there is still a possibility of using them instead for some other project. Before they are sunk in building a canal, a railroad, a power plant, a satellite communication system or any other type of massive equipment for whatever the project may be, there are alternative opportunities open for the use of whatever capital sum is available for investment. There is, therefore, an opportunity cost in deciding to use that capital for a railroad instead of a canal system or mineral exploration or something else. If capital is borrowed to finance the construction of the railroad, the sum total of the capital plus the charges on it gives a measure of the value of the alternative possibilities that must be sacrificed to make the railway possible. At that stage the whole investment that will have to be undertaken is a true cost in the economic sense; there is still a choice to be made between the railway and alternative possibilities.

However, once the railway has been built, there is no longer any alternative possible. The resources put into constructing it have been irretrievably committed; instead of a sum of money that gives to those who dispose of it unfettered choice among all the possible ways of investing that sum of money—command over resources in general up to its total value—the investors now have a roadbed, tracks, locomotives, marshaling yards, roundhouses, and all the other apparatus that makes it possible for them to carry freight and passengers between the points that the railway connects. The owners of the railway have sunk the resources over which they had command in a complex of capital assets that together provide a highly specialized productive capacity that is likely to have a long life. During that lifetime what was, historically, paid to bring the railway into being is no longer a cost. There is no way in which the railway, once built, can be transformed into some other kind of productive capacity if it does not earn as much as was anticipated when the decision was made to construct it. Leaving the railway idle will not recoup the expenditure that was made on it. Only as its constituent parts wear out is there once more a choice: Should they be replaced or not? Again, once the choice has been made and resources committed, the expenditure made on those resources is no longer a cost. Paradoxically, a "sunk cost" is not a cost any more, once it has been sunk. To call such irretrievable commitments of capital "overhead costs" is equally misleading. Expenditures committed in the past to bringing into existence a durable, specialized productive capacity are no longer costs. Of course, if the capital assets in which resources have been embodied have more than one alternative use, then choices have still to be made between those possible uses, which means that there is a true cost—an opportunity cost—in terms of the sacrifice of one possible use in deciding on another. A hydro-electric generating plant can only be used to generate electricity, but the electricity it generates may be used for many different purposes.[25] The cost involved in using the electricity for one purpose to the exclusion of the others is the value of the alternative opportunities foregone, not the past expenditure on the hydro-electric installation.

Rigidities of productive capacity that are associated with the massive initial investment in specialized and long lasting productive capacity required by modern industrial development are commonly paralleled by rigidities of financial obligations in the form of bond issues and government guarantees of the principal and/or interest. The combination of inelastic productive capacity and financial inflexibility, associated with "unpredictability of development on a continental scale has seriously reduced the value of the price mechanism as an effective means of adjusting supply to demand."[26]

JOINT COSTS AND JOINT PRODUCTS

The limitations of the price mechanism are still more evident in relation to the cost of productive capacity that contributes to the output of more than one product. In such cases it is impossible to disentangle any part of the common cost as being incurred by reason of the production of any one of the several joint products. None of these could be produced without the services of the shared productive asset; all of them must be produced, in some quantity at least, if any one of them is to be produced at all. If it becomes necessary to produce more or less of any one of the joint products, then more or less of all the others must be produced as well. If rock that contains both silver and cobalt is dug out of a mine for the sake of the silver, then, whether or not the cobalt is wanted, it has been dug out of the ground too; it is unavoidably one of the outputs accruing from the operation. The cost of that operation cannot be divided between the silver and the cobalt; it is inextricably shared by both of them.

In some cases, it is true, it may be possible to make adjustments at the margin to produce a little more or a little less of one or the other joint product. The classical instance is that of changing the breed of sheep raised to one that yields a higher proportion of meat to wool, if more meat is wanted and less wool. The extra cost of the extra wool may then be identified, but the cost of the sheep is still a shared cost common to meat and wool. If the proportions in which several joint products are produced cannot be changed, then it is not possible even to calculate such an incremental cost at the margin. The process of digging a complex ore out of the ground costs the same whether or not all the minerals in it are to be used or some of them are to be discarded as wastes. This makes it impossible to calculate the individual cost of any one of the joint products; it is only possible to calculate the total cost of producing all of them together. Of course, if, at the next stage of processing the ore, there is an identifiable cost added for recovering cobalt as distinct from the silver, that cost is specifically attributable to the output of the cobalt.[27] It remains true, nonetheless, that the joint costs cannot be divided up among the various joint products; they are inextricably common to them all.

The problem has become increasingly complicated with the spread of modern technology with its intricate combinations of costs that are partly shared and yet can be used in varying proportions to help in the output of different products. What part of the cost of the roadbed and rails of the CPR was incurred to carry wheat and what part to carry mixed freight from east to west? It is impossible to say, just as it is impossible to allocate accurately the shared overheads of manufacturing, retailing, or other types of enterprise among the various joint products. The result, as Innis pointed out, is that overhead costs "have contributed to a lack of precision in accounting, and the allocation of costs between the purchaser of goods from department stores and the purchaser of the paper, or between the purchaser of paper and the purchaser of hydro-electric power from plants owned by paper companies, is extremely difficult to determine. In paying for electric light or for groceries one cannot be certain how much is paid for newspapers."[28]

UNUSED CAPACITY

Still another overhead cost problem is engendered by the inflexibility of capacity through time, while the output required fluctuates more or less violently. If, to meet a peak demand, capacity has to be expanded beyond what is needed in period of slack demand, there will be recurrent unused capacity, a problem characteristic of hydro-electric power generation, since the product cannot be stored and the demand for it changes from hour to hour, from day to day and from season to season. Gaps between peak capacity and an oscillating load in an electrical system, transport system, telecommunication system or any other case of regular irregularities in demand combined with inflexible capacity create strong incentives to flatten the peaks and fill the troughs of demand. Appropriate rate structures that penalize peak-hour consumption and encourage off-peak consumption and pooling diversified load patterns in different areas serve to mitigate the problem. Another possibility is to explore new uses for the product, such as the use of electricity on an interruptible, off-peak basis for steam raising in pulp and paper plants. Efforts may be made, also, to introduce some elasticity into the peak capacity, for example, by the storage of water for hydroelectric systems or pumped storage schemes. Despite much ingenious effort, the problem of unused off-peak capacity persists.

An analogous type of problem is that of unbalanced inward and outward freight in many transport systems. Such imbalances have beset Canadian economic development since the first arrival of Europeans and probably before that. Fishing vessels outward bound from Europe to the new fishing grounds were lightly loaded with fishing gear and salt; they had to carry ballast. Homeward bound, if they were lucky, they were heavily loaded with salt cod. Moreover, the number of men needed to catch the fish was greater than the crew required to sail the ship. Ship masters sought lading to use the unused capacity of the vessels on their way to the fisheries. Taking men out and leaving them to settle on the shores adjacent to the fisheries, though contrary to the policy of both government and West Country fishing interests, helped to solve both problems. Despite strenuous efforts to prevent it, settlement increased as a result, even in Newfoundland.[29]

The opposite problem characterized the fur trade. Ships outward bound from Britain to Hudson Bay carried heavy and bulky trade goods, supplies and provisions; the return cargo consisted of compact and valuable furs. Inland traffic from both the Bay and Lachine consisted, similarly, of bulky trade goods to be hauled upstream, while the downstream, return freight was lighter and easier to handle. Great emphasis was therefore put on the use of country produce and the local manufacture of bulky articles, such as kegs.[30]

The third great staple again reversed the imbalance of freight. Ships came out from Britain in ballast to take on a load of square timber at Quebec for the homeward voyage. To put the unused outward capacity to use, these "coffin ships" took on human cargoes of immigrants to the New World.[31]

Problems of unused canal and railway capacity were accentuated by the:

> basic importance of the production and export of wheat from the prairie regions. . . . Seasonal navigation implied rapid movements of grain and pronounced peak load of east-bound traffic. . . . The secular trend of expanding wheat production shown in long-run peak-load problems of transportation was accompanied by short-run problems of annual fluctuations of crop.[32]

Yet another type of unused capacity characteristic of the Canadian economy has been what Innis called "Overhead cost incidental to railway construction across the Precambrian formation."[33] So long as wheat was the dominant outward freight, the Shield contributed little traffic. When its mineral resources came to light, as a byproduct of the wheat economy,[34] and into production, they began to fill the freight gap, just as they contributed to filling the off-wheat-peak periods.

The combination of "lumpy" investment resulting from indivisibilities in units of productive capacity with "relatively inelastic limiting geographic factors such as power sites, ore bodies, or areas of land with a suitable climate"[35] has given rise to still another kind of unused capacity. To develop a power site, for example, usually means building the complete dam and headworks at once, even though it is not anticipated that the load will grow sufficiently for many years to require full use of their capacity. The upward jerk in generating capacity creates surplus power potential that can be absorbed only gradually as the load is built up. Indeed, it may happen that local needs for electricity based on requirements for the exploitation of other local resources, such as pulpwood or minerals, are never likely to absorb the whole capacity of a local power site. Unless there is a possibility of transmitting the excess energy to some other center of demand, efforts made to discover some possible use for the surplus may result in the development of new industries. Production of aluminum in the Saguenay region is an outstanding case in point. Such situations have provided a dynamic impulse to growth in the Canadian economy.

Capacity that is incompletely used, for whatever reason, exerts a powerful pressure to expand output. "In continental countries the importance of fixed capital, especially in transportation, and thus the importance of overhead costs, added to the importance of new sources of power [oil and hydro-electric], have involved a market increase in the production of raw materials and a decline in price,"[36] as Innis wrote in 1934. He had traced the operation of such pressures to expand operations and output from the days of the fur trade to the disastrous depression of the 1930s.

OVERHEADS, INSTABILITY, AND COMBINATION

He had observed, also, the countervailing pressure to limit output in order to check catastrophic price wars when the destabilizing effects of competition among giant oligopolists became apparent. Oligopolistic competition itself gives rise to a new sort of overhead cost, the cost of defensive and offensive measures against the opposition. In the struggle between the Northwest Company and the Hudson's Bay

Company, for example, each huge duopolist tried to outreach the other by establishing new posts to intercept supplies of furs from ever more remote sources, leap-frogging past each other into the far interior. Each sought to attach bands of Indians to itself by generous treatment, especially in the matter of supplies of spirits, and in other ways by which they tried to secure loyalty to the company. This rivalry imposed on both concerns uncontrollable and crippling costs. How great these were became apparent after the two companies had merged. Duplicate posts were closed, redundant personnel were terminated and an attempt was made to regenerate exhausted trapping areas by dint of drastic conservation measures. The costs of rivalry had not been at all responsive to changes in the demand for furs. While coalition between the duopolists did not eliminate all rigidities of costs and of capacity, it made possible at least some flexibility and the avoidance of some heavy costs,[37] but perhaps increased the difficulty of adjusting to future changes in the conditions of demand and supply.

The pattern is a familiar one in modern corporate complexes concerned, on the one hand, to build barriers against the entry of other firms into close competition with them, and, on the other, to absorb potential rivals in an attempt to effect sufficient centralization of control to secure at least some stability of output and of market outlets and of costs and prices to avoid the worst dangers of economic collapse.

The result is a dual price structure. Those types of production in which the pressure of indivisible costs and rigid capacity generate centralized control, government ownership or guarantees, and administered prices are in sharp contrast with that part of the economy which remains the sphere of personal, small scale enterprise, such as that of the family farmer growing wheat for export. Such a producer can have no control over total output and fluctuating prices, except to the extent that cooperatives, such as the Wheat Pool, or government intervention, as in the International Wheat Agreements, may reduce the extremes of instability. As Innis summed the situation up in 1934: "Prices of raw materials for export, exposed to world competition, crush the primary producer between declining returns and relatively stable costs in terms of prices of manufactured products, of interest on debts, and of railway rates."[38]

LOSS OF ADAPTABILITY
TO CHANGING ECONOMIC CONDITIONS

Attempts to meet the problem of increasing rigidities of costs and of capacity in a world subject to violent fluctuations in the conditions of demand and supply by recourse to rigid prices and rigid interest charges intensify those problems; they do not solve them. Producers locked into massive specialized and durable productive capacity that is the result of past heavy investment try desperately to protect their position in the face of unforeseen, unfavorable changes in economic conditions. Fearing disastrous losses, in terms of failure to realize the returns expected when existing capital structures, both financial and real, were set up, dominant firms resort to explicit or tacit collaboration and combination to defend their vested interests in the status quo. To write off or even scale down established productive capacity, or to accept lower earnings than had been anticipated is extremely difficult. The need for fundamental adjustments to changing circumstances means disappointment of expectations that is not readily accepted. Centralized decision-making power is likely to be used to stave off the need for change rather than to plan and implement changes quickly and flexibly, regardless of disappointment of financial expectations, in the manner that might be expected of the ruthless play of impersonal market forces. Heavy investment in specialized, long-lasting capital assets has brought about a profound transformation in the mechanisms of economic organization. In some sectors of the economy, monpolistic bargaining power and centralized decision-making authority, whether in the hands of corporate complexes or of governmental bodies, has given rise to what Innis called "the dangers of inadequate planning":[39]

> Planning in any one direction introduces certain rigidities the impact of which is felt throughout the whole economy, and in a violently fluctuating economy tends to produce inequalities and to create maladjustments which have serious consequences for the regions or classes most directly exposed to effects of world competition.[40]

Planning in relation to massive investment, whether by private or public monopolistic enterprises and authorities, seemed to him, therefore, to entail a danger of intensifying and prolonging maladjustments in conditions of change. In particular, Innis emphasized that: "Economic planning which characterized an era of expansion becomes inadequate and inefficient and serious for an era in which expansion ceases to play an important role."[41]

As yet we understand very little about the patterns of decision-making in corporate complexes. How far are they guided by profit maximization? How far by considerations of security? Or how far are they controlled by the impersonal imperatives of growth? Innis wrote of the "pronounced swing of economic theory to problems of monopoly rather than competition"[42] and stated that the handicaps of the price system "have been stressed to an increasing extent by economists who have been concerned with monopoly theory and with the decline of competition."[43] We may well regret that in the twenty-five years since Innis died, too little attention has been given to the dislocations and disequilibria characteristic of a world of oligopoly, imperfect competition, and monopoly in contrast to elegant and determinate models of perfect competition far removed from the contemporary exigencies of indivisibilities, discontinuities and rigidities of productive capacity, joint costs, and unused capacity, to say nothing of the inflexibilities of debt, interest charges, and prices in which they are reflected.

NOTES

[1]Innis, H. A. *Essays in Canadian Economic History.* Mary Q. Innis (Ed.). Toronto, University of Toronto Press, 1956, pp. 129–130.

[2]Innis, H. A. *The Fur Trade in Canada.* New Haven, Mass., and London, Yale University Press and Oxford University Press, 1930; revised ed., Toronto, University of Toronto Press, 1956.

[3]Innis, H. A. *The Cod Fisheries: The History of an International Economy.* New Haven, Mass., and London, Yale University Press and Oxford University Press, 1940.

[4]Innis, H. A. *Settlement and the Mining Frontier.* Toronto, Macmillan, 1936.

[5]Innis never published a book on the pulp and paper industry though he spent several years studying·its problems. His article, "Pulp-and-Paper Industry" in *The Encyclopedia of Canada,* W. Stewart Wallace (Ed.), (Toronto, University Associates of Canada, Ltd., 1935–49, pp. 176–185), is a useful summary of his findings. There are many references to the development of the industry and its problems in other works, for example in his Introduction to *The Canadian Economy and Its Problems,* H. A. Innis and A. F. W. Plumptre (Eds.), Toronto, Canadian Institute of International Affairs, 1934, pp. 19–21. (Reprinted also in *Essays in Canadian Economic History.*)

[6]See, for example, "The Historical Development of the Dairy Industry in Canada" and "The Wheat Economy" in Innis, *Essays,* pp. 211–219, 273–279.

[7]Innis, H. A. *A History of the Canadian Pacific Railway.* London, P. S. King & Son, Toronto, McClelland and Stewart Ltd., 1923; "Transportation as a Factor in Canadian Economic History" in *Essays,* pp. 62–77; and "Transportation in the Canadian Economy," in *Essays,* pp. 220–232.

[8]*Ibid.* and many references in *The Fur Trade.*

[9]Again, see scattered references, such as those in "the Canadian Economy and the Depression," in *Essays,* pp. 124–125.

[10]An earlier attempt to analyze the relationship of such rigidities to the structure of prices may be found in I. M. Biss (Spry), "Overhead Costs, Time Problems and Prices" in H. A. Innis (Ed.), *Essays in Political Economy in Honour of E. J. Urwick.* Toronto, University of Toronto Press, 1938, pp. 11–26.

[11]Innis, *Essays,* p. 117.

[12]The choice between flexibility of capacity and output and the hope of a low unit cost with indivisible equipment on a massive scale depends on how much a firm expects to be able to sell if the equipment is installed. The expectations on which the decision is based to use massive, indivisible equipment may, of course, turn out to be overoptimistic.

[13]See the discussion in *The Fur Trade* of the difficulties that beset the Northwest Company in establishing and maintaining its transcontinental system of trade.

[14]A "portage railway" only a few miles in length but connecting two waterways might, of course, provide a useful link in the system of communication between the two cities in what Innis called "the amphibian stage of transport history." *Essays,* p. 69.

[15]Innis, *Settlement and the Mining Frontier.*

[16]Innis, *Essays,* pp. 136–137.

[17]Innis, *Essays,* p. 270.

[18]Innis, *The Fur Trade* and *Essays*, p. 145.

[19]Innis, *Essays*, p. 132.

[20]Innis, *Essays*, p. 153.

[21]Innis, *Essays*, p. 154.

[22]Innis, *Essays*, p. 229.

[23]Innis, *Essays*, p. 127.

[24]Innis, *Essays*, p. 154.

[25]Biss, *Overhead Costs*, pp. 12–13, fn. 1.

[26]Innis, *Essays*, p. 138.

[27]The problem becomes even more complicated in the case of still more complex ores that may contain ten or more mineral constituents. The level of processing at which costs that are specific to a single product can be identified may be different for the different minerals. When to this is added the dual relationship of jointness and of marginally adjustable rates of output, the difficulty of calculating even marginal costs for each product becomes apparent.

[28]Innis, *Essays*, p. 267.

[29]Innis, *The Cod Fisheries* and *Essays*, pp. 141–142.

[30]Innis, *The Fur Trade* and *Essays*, pp. 142–147, 157–159.

[31]Innis, *Essays*, pp. 146–147.

[32]Innis, *Essays*, p. 151.

[33]Innis, *Essays*, p. 157.

[34]Innis, *Essays*, p. 88.

[35]Innis, *Essays*, p. 138.

[36]Innis, *Essays*, p. 133.

[37]Innis, *The Fur Trade.*

[38]Innis, *Essays*, p. 127.

[39]Innis, *Essays*, p. 82.

[40]Innis, *Essays*, p. 83.

[41]Innis, *Essays*, p. 81.

[42]Innis, *Essays*, p. 130.

[43]Innis, *Essays*, p. 270.

12

IMPLICATIONS OF OIL
AND GAS DEVELOPMENT
FOR ALASKA

ARLON R. TUSSING
University of Alaska

To scholars trained in the "new economic history," which emphasizes the testing of historical hypotheses with the aid of neoclassical economics, Harold Innis was one of those seminal historical philosophers like Marx, Turner, Schumpeter, and Rostow, who furnish grand hypotheses for later empirical scholars to support or disprove with algebra and factor analysis.

I am far removed from the study of economic history, and I have no firm opinion on the usefulness of Innis' concepts as tools for historical analysis. Innis' world view, moreover, evokes at least four protracted controversies about the meaning and worth of Canadian nationhood: French versus English, Native versus European, Eastern and Western Provinces versus the Middle, and Canadian versus the United States. As an ex-historian and a foreigner, it is probably best I not stir my spoon in that pot.

In any case, Innis' categories and concepts are at least as useful for thinking about and describing present Alaskan development as they were for the past development of Canada. Alaska spans about sixteen degrees of latitude, roughly the same as those of the Canadian "North." Ketchikan is less than two hundred miles north of Edmonton or Goose Bay. Juneau is abeam Fort Nelson, Churchill, and Ft. Chimo; and Anchorage is at about the same latitude as Whitehorse and Yellowknife. Fairbanks is about as far north as Dawson, Norman Wells, and Frobisher Bay; and Point Barrow at seventy-one degrees is north of everything in Canada save the Arctic Islands and the Bootha Peninsula. Yet, the history, demography, and economy of the two regions are vastly different.

Alaska, with more than 400,000 people, and with local ownership and political control over the most valuable single resource deposit in North America, is in Innis' sense both hinterland and metropolis. Alaska's urban core is more of the latter than the former: Resource exploitation in the North enriches the business class and the working people of Anchorage far more conspicuously and lastingly than their counterparts in Yellowknife, for example.

The great advantage Alaskans have in keeping wealth and power at home stems from the State's ownership of resources. Upon its admission as a state in 1958, Alaska received the right to choose more than one hundred million acres of federal lands. Much of that entitlement was used to select potential mineral lands, including the area where the Prudhoe Bay field was discovered in 1968. The State collects all the bonuses, royalties, and rentals from leasing of these lands, plus nine-tenths of the revenues from onshore federal lands; it also levies production (or severance) taxes—now at a rate of four to eight per cent—on oil and gas production from state, federal, and private lands alike. Self-government has also given the state a broad range of licensing and regulatory authority over resource development activity in general, whether or not it takes place on state-owned lands.

The question of the North's cultural future, which is being debated so furiously in Canada today, has pretty much been decided in Alaska. The State's Native movements have generally achieved their political demands: They have civil rights and civil liberties and home rule over large regions, all *within* the framework of European democracy. Village and regional Native corporations have also gained the ownership of more than forty million acres with substantial resource potentials together with a cash grant of nearly a billion dollars—here again *within* the framework of American capitalism.

The full story is not yet in on the investments of Native corporations, which include virtually every imaginable kind of asset: government and corporate securities; a new state bank and a controlling share in an existing national bank; hotels and other commercial and residential real estate; construction, trucking and air taxi firms; fishing vessels and fish processing plants. Some of these ventures have been quite profitable and others have been disasters. It would be surprising if the final reckoning were not a mixed one.

Those Natives who look to the land, their families, and their villages for sustenance and for meaning in their lives will not disappear. Indeed, they may still be and may continue to be a majority, cherished and (we may hope) protected because of family ties, sympathies, and nostalgia on the part of their more achievement oriented compatriots. There will also be hundreds of Native alcoholics, bullies, and other individuals who are failures by the measure of either culture, and their numbers may increase both absolutely and relatively.

Whether the indigenous culture would have remained more vital without any settlement, or with another kind of settlement, I cannot say. Nor am I sure whether the drunks, criminals, and dropouts would have been more or less numerous if there had been no cash grants, no regional and village Native corporations, no municipal self-government or local control over schools, no fee ownership of land, and no telephones or television.

One may regret the inevitable logic of the distinctive Alaska resolution of Native claims—the fact that social position in Native communities is to be measured by success in municipal and state government, power in the Native corporations, or bank deposits and real estate holdings in Anchorage. With the land claims settlement, however, the die has been cast. It is clear that the emergence in less than a decade of a real Native bourgeoisie, a real Native bureaucracy and real Native wealth is a direct outgrowth of this settlement. It is unlike anything I am familiar with in the Canadian North. Whether or not this story is the kind Canadians— Europeans or Native—want to look forward to, it is clearly a success story, at least on its own terms.

THE BOOM OF THE 1970S

Alaska's economy has just concluded a period of exceptional growth. In the six years between 1970 and 1976, average annual employment grew by 78,600, an increase of 84.4 per cent. During that same six-year period, gross business receipts quadrupled, from $2.8 billion in 1970 to $11.6 billion in 1976. Individual Alaskans were on the average prosperous: Mean income per capita in 1976 was $9,407 compared with the national average of $6,348. Taking into account the fact that Alaska's living costs were typically about forty per cent higher, real income per person seems to be substantially better than that for the United States as a whole.

The rapid growth of Alaska employment and business activity and the relatively high incomes of most Alaskans are due mostly to the state's rich per capita natural resource endowment. Of course, the most important direct stimulus to recent growth has been the construction of the Trans-Alaska oil pipeline. Although completion of the project caused a significant business slump in 1977, there is little doubt the economy will begin to boom again in 1978 or 1979 as oil royalties and taxes from the Prudhoe Bay field pour into the state treasury at a rate of more than $400 million a year. The boom will be further accelerated if the sponsors of the Alaska Highway gas pipeline are successful in arranging financing and the preparations for construction begin.

Development of Alaska's natural resources can be expected to sustain further growth of employment and income for years to come. Only two of the state's major sedimentary basins, Cook Inlet and the Arctic Slope, have seen significant exploration for oil and gas. Even in these two areas there are still many promising geological structures yet to be tested by the drill.

This is not to say that another Prudoe Bay field is a big probability. That field is the largest ever discovered in North America. Even on a worldwide scale such finds are random and rare occurrences. Nevertheless, it will be decades before Alaska's offshore and onshore petroleum prospects have been subjected to the same intensity of exploratory scrutiny as the lower forty-eight states or Canada's Western Basin. Exploration alone would sustain substantial economic activity, but is almost certain to generate a continuing and sporadic series of unspectacular reserve additions, which are likely to sustain the state's oil production at one, two, or more million of barrels per day well into the next century.

Alaska also has a significant percentage of U.S. coal reserves and its potential for copper, nickel, silver, and other non-ferrous metals is believed comparable to that of the Rocky Mountain heartland of the U.S. mining industry. Moreover, the Northeast Pacific Ocean and the Bering Sea adjacent to Alaska constitute the richest fishing grounds in the world measured by value of catch. Until the recent passage of federal legislation extending the United States' fishery jurisdiction to two hundred miles, Alaska-based fisheries were confined almost entirely to salmon, crab, and shrimp, leaving more than one million tons of bottomfish a year to be harvested by distant-water fleets of other countries. Even so, by 1977 these conventional fisheries had grown to the point that Unalaska (Dutch Harbor) was the number two fishing port in the United States (and apparently number four in the world) by value of landings. In the near future, development of a major Alaska-based bottomfishery is inevitable.

Analysis of a region's growth usually starts with a division of its industrial structure into an "economic base" and a "support sector." The basic industries in this view are not confined to commodities, but include any activity that brings outside money into the region; a basic industry, in other words, exports most of its product or serves mainly nonresidents. The economic base occupies the same role in the contemporary analysis of regional development that "staples" have in the writings of Innis and in Canadian economic historiography generally. In Alaska, these base industries are natural resources extraction and primary processing, the federal government, and tourism. Local payrolls, profits, and taxes from these industries are the ultimate source of revenue to the "non-basic" or "residentiary" industries that serve the local market, such as trade, services, and state and local government. These will grow as fast or faster than basic industry, but in the foreseeable future Alaska's location away from major trade routes and its high labor costs will prevent the development of a manufacturing industry serving outside markets.

The state's greatest power over future economic development is exercised through its policies regarding oil and gas leasing on state lands, its encouragement or opposition to federal OCS (Outer Continental Shelf) leasing, and environmental and taxation policies toward petroleum and other resource industries. But the impact of any given state action in these areas is uncertain and depends upon exploration luck, world market conditions, and other factors outside the state's control. Moreover, because of long lead times involved in major resource development projects, the total economic impact of any given project becomes evident only many years after the particular governmental action that stimulated the project.

For this reason, although resouce development issues are at the heart of Alaska's deliberations over growth policy, there is, nonetheless, no way that the state can precisely determine the rate or character of its economic growth through its policies toward resource development. Whatever the state government's actions may be with respect to natural resource developments, their impact on Alaska's economy is bound to come in fits and starts. There is no way to predict the timing or size of important new oil and gas discoveries or the impact of new federal policies, such as extension of fisheries' jurisdiction. And there is no way to spread the economic shock of building an oil or gas pipeline or a refinery or petrochemical plant over a decade or more. Each development of this sort will cause a massive and temporary injection of dollars into Alaska's still-thin economy, creating a surge of employment opportunities. Completion of each of these development projects will cause at least local layoffs and recessions. The state can do little to alter this situation short of the kinds of actions that would shut down the growth process entirely.

There is, of course, a substantial part of the Alaska citizenry who would do just this; they can be expected to have *some* influence on resource development policy and that influence will inhibit growth to some extent. In the past, however, the "boomer" elements have usually prevailed politically, and they will probably continue to do so in the foreseeable future.

As the state's economic base becomes more diversified, the influence of booms and periods of decline in basic industries will be proportionately less important, and Alaska's economic growth will become more stable, with its future less vulnerable to price declines or exhaustion of particular commodities. If the boom-and-bust cycle can be moderated in this way, there is reason to believe the long-term average rate of unemployment can be moderated too.

In economic base analysis, growth of business and employment in the basic industries is usually regarded as both necessary and sufficient to induce a proportionate growth in the residentiary or support sector. Analyses based upon this assumption are often valuable for projecting the full future impact on a regional economy of the establishment of new basic industry facilities. Despite the general validity of the economic base approach in explaining long term growth trends in Alaska, its usefulness is more limited in predicting the year-to-year state of the economy. Between 1967 and the end of 1973, for example, Alaska's economic base was largely stagnant or in decline, yet the overall economy showed a solid but continuing boom, mild as it may have been compared with the next three-year period.

Following the first North Slope oil exploration boom of 1968–1969, oil industry employment declined in every quarter, and in the fall of 1973 was less than half of what it had been in 1969 immediately after the Prudhoe Bay discovery. The timber and fisheries industries were also stagnant or in decline. Yet there was not a single quarter between 1967 and the third quarter of 1976 in which total employment failed to grow compared with the same quarter one year earlier. Over the whole "recession" period of 1969–1974, employment grew at an average annual rate of more than seven per cent. Neither the federal government (at that time the largest component of the economic base) nor the oil industry seemed to be in any direct way the engine of economic growth in Alaska; nor was there any other "basic" industry or group of industries that played such a role.

Several elements kept the state's economy growing despite the temporary decline in most of its major industries. One element was the spending of the bonus money—about $900 million—that the state received in its 1969 North Slope oil and gas lease sale. The second and most important cause of growth was the expansion and deepening of the economic support sector: improved retail trade facilities, expanding service industries, and an upgrading of housing.

The bulk of growth in both employment and in business receipts in Alaska in the pre-pipeline period was in trade and services. The bulk of construction was residential construction. Alaska was becoming a more comfortable place to live. It offered more of the amenities of modern life as costs declined relative to the other states. A bigger portion of each dollar received in Alaska tended to stay in the state. In technical terms, the decline of the economic base itself was more than offset by the increase in the size of the economic base multiplier.

There are indications that the state's economy is entering another such period, in which growth in the basic resource industries is at a lull but in which the support sector continues to grow. It is instructive that 1977—after completion of the pipeline—saw record levels of residential construction in both Anchorage and Fairbanks despite high vacancy rates. In summary, the growth of the support sector is, to a degree, self-sustaining and is guaranteed by growing state government revenues and expenditures.

FISCAL POLICY

The state government's potential influence on the growth of the support sector of Alaska's economy is more direct and predictable than its power over basic industry. Construction (other than the heavy construction trades that support the basic industries), retail and wholesale trade, personal and business services, transportation, communications, public utilities, and state and local government all tend to grow or contract quickly and directly in response to the demand for their services. That demand is in turn affected by the level of activity in basic industry; in Alaska it is also powerfully influenced by the way the state disposes of its surplus mineral revenues.

State spending reverberates through the entire Alaska economy, whether it be disbursed as salaries to civil servants, for highway construction, as unemployment benefits and welfare payments, as aid to local government or as business subsidies to encourage economic diversification and rural employment. If the State increases spending either on current account or on investments inside the state, sales, jobs, profits, and population increase. Conversely, if state spending declines, sales, jobs, profits, and population decline at least relatively.

In the immediately forthcoming years of large budget surpluses resulting from oil revenues, the state's discretionary spending power will be immense. This spending cannot be "fine-tuned" to offset the month-to-month or even year-to-year changes in basic industry spending in Alaska; any attempt at a "countercyclical" spending policy might well make the state's economy even more unstable if the lags in recognizing and acting upon cyclical changes were of the wrong length. In my judgment, a deliberately countercyclical fiscal policy is just as likely to zig when it should zag as to move in the right direction, but state fiscal policy can clearly have some stabilizing effect if only the growth of government expenditures within Alaska is smooth and predicatable.

In other words, state expenditures themselves need not duplicate the boom-and-bust cycles of the oil industry. This long-term stabilizing task is one of the main reasons the people of Alaska voted a constitutional amendment last year creating a Permanent Fund into which at least twenty-five per cent of the state's nonrecurring mineral revenues must be deposited. The legislature is now deliberating on a proposal to commit thirty per cent of oil and gas royalties and one hundred per cent of cash bonuses to the fund. Such a reservation acts to limit the stimulating effect of current state spending, and earnings from Permanent Fund investments can be used later to offset future state deficits. A carefully designed formula for contributions from the General Fund to the Permanent Fund (and in later years from the Permanent Fund to the General Fund) would limit fluctuations in state spending that would otherwise aggrevate the instability of Alaska's economy.

Thus far, there has been little demand for government-owned business ventures to play a major role in the development process. The federal government built and still owns the Alaska Railroad, but the only state enterprises have been the "Alaska Marine Highway"—an interstate and intercity ferry system—and a state housing authority. A state hydropower authority has been established, but it yet has no approved project and no funding; officials have from time-to-time considered buying a part of the Trans-Alaska oil pipeline or the proposed gas line, but neither proposal is likely to be executed.

The overwhelming preference of Alaskans is now to restrict the State's role in economic planning to land and resource administration, environmental—and some economic—regulation, and (perhaps) some limited development subsidies. On the whole, however, they are prepared to rely on market machinery and private enterprise to mobilize investment funds and decide what local industries have the greatest potential. Whether this preference can withstand several years of large budget surpluses is another issue.

UNEMPLOYMENT

Despite high average incomes and continuing economic opportunity, Alaska has chronically high unemployment rates. During the years from 1972 to 1975, the unemployment rate hovered around ten per cent; it dropped to about eight per cent in 1976; and rose to more than fourteen per cent in 1977.

Three major factors contribute to the unusually high levels of unemployment in Alaska. The first reason Alaska's unemployment rate is often the highest in the United States and the principal reason it was the highest among all states early this year is the unevenness of economic growth. This unevenness is a product of the state's exceptional economic dependence on a few extractive industries. The 1977 slump is easy to understand: Completion of the Trans-Alaska oil pipeline resulted in a net layoff of about 6,000 workers between the first quarter of 1976 and first quarter 1977. The pipeline boom and bust of the 1970s repeated on a larger scale the cyclical pattern created by fur harvesting, salmon fishing, gold mining, and military construction in earlier decades. One part of this cycle is the rapid immigration of new residents seeking boom-time wages. When industry (like pipeline construction) booms, new employment opportunities attract outside job-seekers. The "outside" workers who joined the ranks of Alaska's well-paid labor force during the pipeline boom swell the ranks of the "Alaskian" unemployed now that the project is over.

The second major feature contributing to high unemployment is seasonality. Construction, fishing and fish processing, logging, and tourism are industries in which employment varies radically over the year. There is simply no way that these sectors can keep the same number of people working around the year that they require in July and August. To the extent that construction workers, fishermen and other people in seasonal occupations stay in Alaska and in the labor force, drawing either unemployment benefits or welfare, official unemployment rates for Alaska will continue to be higher than those of other states with more moderate seasonal variations. In assessing this element in total unemployment, it is important to recognize that much of it is voluntary. Working overtime during the summer and taking it easy the rest of the year, with or without unemployment benefits, is an historic Alaskan lifestyle, and one which is regarded as a positive value by a large part of the state's population. Indeed, this pattern is probably increasing in importance, as newly developed urban amenities hold many workers in the state who earlier would have spent their winters in Seattle, California, or Hawaii.

The third particularly Alaskan unemployment problem evolves from the circumstances of Alaska's rural Native peoples: a combination of cultural attitudes and values at odds with the needs of conventional employment, isolation from the urban job centers, and inadequate education—all historically aggravated by prejudice and discrimination. Here again, official unemployment figures are little guide to the reality: On one hand, many Natives who are listed as "unemployed" are simply following a modernized version of a traditional pattern of sporadic or seasonal labor, while many others are not officially in the labor force only because they are not eligible for unemployment compensation or because they have become discouraged about the prospect of finding work.

In summary, the next few decades in Alaska will see the same trend as the last few years: population growth, economic development, and a profound transformation of the lifestyles of Alaska Natives, propelled by the distribution of lands and resources to the state and the Native corporations and by their respective petroleum revenues. These changes are occurring so rapidly and in such a unique institutional setting, however, that it is almost pointless to predict——much less try to control—events and conditions more than a few years into the future.

13

STAPLE PRODUCTION AND IDEOLOGY IN NORTHERN CANADA

PETER J. USHER
Clayton, Ontario

Harold Innis demonstrated that the nature of staple production leaves its mark on the entire economy and society of the hinterland. I would like to examine the specific case in which the production of one staple is replaced by another and the impact of that replacement process on the hinterland. As well, I will explore the way in which the metropolis generates ideological justification for both the process and its consequences.

STAPLE PRODUCTION AND NATIVE PEOPLE

The production of fur as a staple in northern Canada brought Native people there into a dependent relationship with European, and later North American, capitalism and created a distinctive economy and society that persists in modified form to the present day. It transformed Native people into producers of goods for exchange yet, to some degree at least, allowed them to retain a subsistence mode of production. We need not dwell here on the regional variations in this pattern, nor on the fact that wherever subsistence and exchange production conflicted the trading companies encouraged the latter, even at the expense of Native peoples' well-being. Nor need we dwell on the use of coercive authority by metropolitan institutions to extend their control over Native peoples' lives and land.

In the most favorable circumstances, Native people were, and in

177

some instances still are, able to increase their standard of living and general well-being by producing commodities such as fur, fish, wild rice, handicrafts, and so on for trade in addition to obtaining the bulk of their food, shelter, warmth, and clothing through subsistence production. The production of both trade and subsistence goods could be combined largely by using the same skills, the same resources, the same mode of production and the same internal socioeconomic arrangements. Today, what Native people commonly refer to as their traditional way of life is the society and economy of the fur trade era, not of some unremembered aboriginal past.

This fur trade system of production broke down all across the North around the middle of the twentieth century, primarily due to externally initiated forces. Although the timing and circumstances varied considerably from place to place, the general pattern of disruption included the following five features: First, there was the assault by metropolitan interests on such resources as timber, minerals, water, oil, and gas, the production of which frequently conflicted with traditional resource harvesting and generally resulted in a greater integration of the frontier to the metropolis by virtue of new transport and communication links. Second, there was increased white settlement, resulting in growing competition for the traditional fur, fish, and wildlife resources. Third, there were rising costs coupled with falling fur prices. Fourth, universal schooling was introduced, resulting either in the breakup of the family as a productive economic unit or in its displacement to population growth centers in which it could no longer effectively function. Finally, there was the rapid introduction of industrial capitalism's universal welfare system to a society neither industrial nor capitalist. Not all of these events were directly or causally related. They were, however, the chief features of a major phase in the extension of metropolitan control to northern Canada, during which radically new forms of staple production were introduced, requiring new economic and political arrangements.

Not surprisingly, these things had a profound (and generally adverse) effect on preexisting economic activity in the North. Many studies of the northern economy in the 1950s and 60s documented remarkably low cash incomes from trapping and commercial fishing. Since these activities were the main source of employment and cash, these low returns, especially in the face of rising prices for imported commodities (including the means of production) were cause for alarm. These studies, like almost all that have followed, either asserted that the production of country food was small or declining or made no attempt to include this subsistence production in their quantitative evaluation of the Native economy. Policy makers and academics alike quickly concluded that the old economy was dead and, moreover, could never again hold any possibility of sustaining Native populations. With the advance of civilization, the future of Native northerners was seen to lie in education and wage employment. Native people had allegedly crossed the Rubicon to "modernization," and there would be no turning back.

But what was the real nature of the crisis in the Native economy? If we examine the economics of exchange and subsistence production separately, we see the crisis in subsistence production occurred chiefly under circumstances of rapid urbanization and depopulation of surrounding areas, that is, where Native people were effectively deprived of access to their traditional hunting areas. In many of these cases, social and technological readjustment has allowed Native people to regain access to these areas, with the result that in many northern areas probably more food is being harvested now than was the case twenty-five years ago.

On the other hand, the adverse trend in costs and prices for exchange production has at best moderated rather than reversed, so that only in exceptionally favorable circumstances can the majority of Native people earn the bulk of their cash requirements by producing fur or fish for exchange. The value of subsistence produce to the producer is great, as I will demonstrate below; the value of exchange production generally rather less. The income realized from the sale of fur and fish today is by and large inadequate to finance the traditional mode of production; that is why many Native people find it necessary to obtain wage employment. Jobs enable them to hunt; they are not substitutes for hunting. In the context of the traditional economy, based on diversity of opportunity, jobs are not careers to be pursued single-mindedly; they are just one more option, to be taken up and left off as circumstances dictate. To the degree that they are consistent with participation in traditional activity (i.e. in the proper location, at the proper time, and relying on familiar skills) and contribute to overall economic security without detracting from one's ability to exploit other opportunities, they are welcome options. Unfortunately, conventional economics, due to its inability to understand and analyze a subsistence, nonmarket economy, has made a substantial contribution to the misunderstanding of the northern Native economy.

Our materialistic view of culture has also contributed its share to this misunderstanding. We see only with our eyes, and today the traditional life is no longer visibly in evidence. Dog teams are rare, skin clothing nonexistent, and the old fur trade posts have turned into modern general stores. The isolated hunting camps have been mostly abandoned. Instead one sees Native people living in prefabricated houses with refrigerators and television sets, working for wages from nine to five (or drawing unemployment insurance) and driving trucks, taxis, and snowmobiles. It is easy for the casual observer to assume that the old ways are dead, and with them Native involvement with the land. Indeed, public policy has for at least twenty-five years been based on precisely this assumption.

Yet despite almost complete urbanization, massive government drives to move Native people into the wage economy and growing amounts of cash flowing into northern communities in the form of wages and transfer payments, country food is still common fare at meal times in much of the North, and men with steady jobs are often to be found out on the land on weekends and holidays. Recent confrontations with government and industry over land use priorities have revealed a depth of feeling and concern perhaps previously unarticulated by Native people and unsuspected by whites. In fact, the Native economy is not dead, only hidden from the eyes of most whites, largely because the evidence of it is what people do in the bush away from the settlements, and what they eat in their own homes, and few white people have occasion to observe either of these things.

A few facts about this hidden economy, gleaned from recent research, are in order. First, land use and occupancy studies conducted by several northern Native organizations have documented that the overall use of lands and waters by Native northerners is still very extensive, geographically, although many specific changes have occurred.[1] Second, the rate of participation in subsistence hunting and fishing, if not in trapping, is still high, even by those with full-time jobs. Because trapping embodies a way of life, and is not merely an occupation, many people still call themselves trappers even if they do not actually trap.[2] Third, the volume of production remains high. Conventional means of measuring production through the use of official statistics has been found invariably to produce underestimates. The best documented estimates, for a number of individual community studies all across the North as well as from more comprehensive estimates for Nouveau-Quebec, the Mackenzie Valley, and Western Arctic, suggest that subsistence production provides Native northerners with substantially more protein per capita than our own industrial system does for us.[3] As well, if the value of this protein is imputed at its replacement cost (that is, if Native people had to buy more or less equivalent imported protein), subsistence production contributes several thousands of dollars of real income per year to a northern family.[4] When economists ignore or belittle this contribution, they arrive at the conclusion that Native people are impoverished and therefore in urgent need of the jobs that only "development" can bring. Finally, this quantitative evaluation, important as it may be, tells us nothing of the social and cultural significance to Native people of their traditional mode of production, which is after all not simply an economy but a way of life. These considerations have been well documented in recent years and I need say no more about them here.[5]

THE IDEOLOGICAL BASIS OF NON-NATIVE "KNOWLEDGE" AND POLICY

Our misunderstanding of the traditional economy, however, derives not simply from incorrect but relatively obscure academic methodologies. The continuing commitment of Native northerners to their land is increasingly discomforting news to the metropolis, already embarked on a massive assault on the material and energy resources of the North. This commitment is inconsistent with our most deeply rooted notions about hunting peoples. They are, after all, supposed to be at the other end of man's evolutionary scale, living a primitive, barbaric, and unpleasant life that we of European ancestry abandoned thousands of years ago. Since the long march to civilization has allegedly brought us wealth, security, and ease, it follows that peoples so unfortunate as to remain hunters in the twentieth century must lead lives of poverty, insecurity, and hardship, as indeed the very word subsistence implies. We imagine the northern hunter to be balanced precariously at the top of the food chain, entirely at the mercy of biological cycles, migration changes, and climatic catastrophes. In his primitive state, he must resort to infanticide and forced marches to avoid starvation, yet given the least advantage over his prey, like a rifle or a fishnet, he will destroy his balance with nature, by overexploiting the very resources on which his life depends. The hunger exists in a classic Malthusian trap, from which only a civilized political economy can save him. Hunting, fishing, and trapping are thought to produce such meager returns for such strenuous and unremitting effort as to be akin to the task of Sisyphus. Constantly stalked by hunger, the hunter, during his nasty, short, and brutish life, is condemned to spend his every waking moment scrabbling for his next mouthful; he has no civilization because he has no leisure time to develop it. Moreover, the hunter experiences such personal discomfort, risk, and unpleasantness that he must be only too ready to seize the first opportunity to escape his predicament of grinding poverty and hardship.

If at first this seems a caricature, try a little introspection. Virtually all the people I have met who have gone among Native northerners, or who have been responsible for the administration and development of them or their lands, have held some variant of these views, and with much sincerity and conviction. Can it be surprising that industrial man's impulse toward the hunter is to save him from his own economy and invite him to participate in another, and moreover to be offended if he does not accept? How else to explain the astonishing fact that the peoples of Europe and America, daily bombarded by accounts of cruelty and atrocities among their fellow human beings, can afford to focus so much of their wrath on a handful of men in the outports of Newfoundland, who every spring go among the ice floes to earn a living in the manner of their forefathers? It is this underlying mythology that has contributed to our "scientific" misconceptions about the Native economy in the North, to say nothing of the ideological justification for removing hunting peoples from the path of industrial development.

It would be convenient to suppose that the industrial system has arrived in the North just when it was most sorely needed—to fill the vacuum left by the unfortunate collapse of the fur trade economy. What I am suggesting is that the subsistence basis of that economy never really collapsed and that many Native northerners adhere to that mode of production today by preference. In fact, the industrial system has been imposed on the hinterland and, if we examine its mode of production, we see at once that it is entirely inconsistent with that of the Native economy and is in sore need of ideological justification for its effects.

The very isolation and "primitiveness" of the North requires the metropolis to deploy its most capital intensive, technologically sophisticated, and tightly organized techniques of production there. The North is thus a land of incredible contrasts, between tradition and modernity, small and large, simple and complex, diversity and specialization, Native and white. The simultaneous existence of both modes of production (i.e. subsistence-domestic and industrial-capitalist) in the hinterland means that there are two sets of political and economic institutions there, each with separate ideological foundations. Participation in each is largely a matter of ethnicity: Whites in the North engage in the industrial mode, most Native people engage in a mixture of the two.

The industrial mode, and its attendant political institutions and systems, has gained hegemony at all levels—federal, territorial or provincial, and municipal, often in that order chronologically, as might be expected under circumstances of colonial penetration. The subsistence mode, and particularly its traditional political institutions and practices, must exist either as sanctioned by the dominant polity, or covertly.

This situation is sometimes incorrectly characterized as a "dual economy," in which the two systems are seen as separate enclaves, unlinked to and unaffected by each other's activities. The logical outcome of that analysis is that the traditional economy is seen as being plagued by inherent (rather than externally generated) problems which are, in effect, barriers to Native people receiving the full benefits of "development." Accordingly, the sooner that economy is fully integrated with (i.e. replaced by) the industrial system, the better. Until that happens, there should, on humanitarian grounds, continue to be a "free choice" as to what economy Native people will engage in. Incorrect as it is, this "dual economy" analysis is nonetheless consistent with such social scientific theories or ideologies as pluralism, acculturation, positive economics, and econometrics, and is hence not surprisingly the basis of public policy in the North today.

In fact, both modes of production are manifestations of capitalist expansion on the frontier, and their apparent separateness in the 1950s and 60s was transitory if not illusory. That situation has given way to one in which there is now direct competition between the modern and traditional sectors for all productive factors: land, labor, and capital. The extensive nature of modern resource exploration and development, and its potential for widespread chronic and catastrophic pollution and environmental degradation, is already posing an unprecedented threat to traditional Native use of the land. Even where the right to harvest fish and game belongs exclusively to Native people, "development" in its many forms every year is preempting an increasing proportion of the harvest. As more non-Natives take up residence in the North, they demand direct access to these resources as well. At the same time, government and industry are seeking to enlist Native people into the industrial labor force, as the predominant mode of production in the Native or traditional economy becomes less compatible with the dictates of metropolitan activity in the hinterland.

One of the original justifications for training Native people to become wage laborers was to create a resident skilled labor force so that massive migrations of southern workers would be unnecessary. In the outcome, as modern resource extraction in the North has proved on the one hand to create relatively few jobs and on the other to require such specialized skills and motivations for those it does, the emphasis of Native job training programs is increasingly oriented to making Native people more mobile, so that they will be able to move easily from one part of the North to another, or even out of the North entirely.

THE CONSEQUENCES OF CONFLICT BETWEEN THE TWO SYSTEMS OF STAPLE PRODUCTION

The "needs" of the modern industrial system in the North— of this late stage of Canadian internal expansion—dictate that hunters, and the animal populations on which they rely, must be progressively restricted and circumscribed in the interest of development activity. In short, this is a modern version of the enclosures. Native people are to be effectively separated from their traditional land base, uprooted from their communities, rendered a political minority in their own territory and incorporated into the lowest levels of the national class structure. The great majority of Native people will become members of a dispossessed town proletariat in the larger centers, left behind in the wake of a development process which, however orderly and humane it may seem in the plans and policies of Ottawa and Calgary, will be chaotic and ruthless in Inuvik, Baker Lake, and Frobisher Bay.

The development of the modern sector is thus directly dependent on the degradation of the traditional sector. All the social costs that have typified such processes in other parts of the world may be expected to follow: racism, crime, violence, alcohol and drug abuse, economic privation, self-destruction, cultural loss, and the breakdown of family and community life.

The growth of Native organizations and their focus on the issue of land claims has been one of the most important hinterland responses to metropolitan dominance in recent years. Yet the prospects today are, in my view, not good. Every land claims settlement to date (Alaska, James Bay, and the tentative Western Arctic settlement) has in effect given Native people title to certain lands *in exchange for,* rather than *for the protection of,* their traditional resources, notwithstanding whatever sentiments are expressed in the preambles of these documents. Those Native groups such as the Dene Nation or Inuit Tapirisat, which are seeking much more far-reaching settlements including political control, have made no progress at the bargaining table. Increasingly, the federal government's strategy is to separate the issues of land ownership and political power.

The process of colonization on the frontier has already created class divisions and factions within Native society. The formation of regional elites within the hinterland, with a direct interest in collaborating with metropolitan forces, has already begun. These are relatively recent events, by and large post-dating the formation or rejuvenation of most Native organizations in the late 1960s and early 70s, but strongly encouraged by the strategies and activities of both government and industry, particularly through the educational system. There have been many instances in the North recently where initial opposition to industrial development has been effectively defused or defeated by the calculated exploitation of latent divisions and conflicts by corporate developers and government agencies.

The federal government's current model for land claims settlements, which is essentially a mixture of cash, minor land and resource transfers, and increased local government responsibilities, all requiring disproportionate bureaucratic administration relative to the benefits gained, is a recipe for the creation of a petit bourgeois and bureaucratic class among Native people. Accordingly, the continued pursuit of a purely ethnic solution must be called into question. True, the extension of metropolitan control and the replacement of one type of staple production by another has had adverse consequences primarily for Native people rather than whites. Yet the current dynamics of class formation within Native society, the likelihood of that frustrating the goals of a settlement as most Native people conceive them and the implications of that to Native–white relations in the future can no longer be ignored. I am not suggesting that Native people should be expected to build model alternative institutions and structures while surrounded by a sea of industrial capitalism. I do believe, however, that Native claims settlements have taken on a somewhat magical aura as a solution to a number of problems they cannot realistically be expected to solve. Serious reassessment of the actual situation and the necessary solutions is very much in order.

That is a problem primarily for Native people. In the meantime, whites should awake to the true nature of the ideological justifications that are invariably required by the advance of the frontier, and the putting of new lands to new uses by new peoples (or as some might call it, theft). These justifications have been well developed in the course of five hundred years of expansion into southern North America, Africa, and Australia. Today we hear them repeated in the Middle East, interior South America, and the far North; they are probably also expressed in Siberia and Western China, doubtless with only minor variations. Most people like to believe they are doing good, hence theories about the nature and well-being of peoples who live by hunting and trapping in our own North become rationalizations for individual behavior, government policies, and corporate priorities there.

We in the metropolis must start re-examining these attitudes, because so long as they prevail we will be blind to the real consequences of what we do in the name of progress on the frontier. I think it is possible to create a real dual economy in the hinterland, in which the Native economy can, by its viability and integrity, be truly coequal with the industrial economy. In such a situation, the needs of the metropolis could be served without the degradation of the society and economy of the hinterland. A real reordering of the relations between metropolis and hinterland must ultimately depend on metropolitan action, however. If we fail to achieve that goal, Canadian society will pay the price. I know of no people in history who have gratefully acquiesced to the theft of their land and the destruction of their culture and society. I think we would be quite mistaken to suppose it will be any different in Canada.

NOTES

[1] Milton Freeman Research Ltd. *Report, Inuit Land Use and Occupancy Project.* (3 vols.) Ottawa, Dept. Indian Affairs and Northern Development, 1976; Brice-Bennett, Carol (Ed.). *Our Footprints are Everywhere.* Nain, Labrador, Labrador Inuit Association, 1977; Sieciechowicz, K. "The People and the Land are One; an Introduction to the Way of Life North of 50." *Bulletin, Canadian Association in Support of the Native Peoples,* 18:2, 1977, pp. 16–20; Nahanni, P. "The Mapping Project." *Dene Nation,* M. Watkins, (Ed.). Toronto, University of Toronto Press, 1977, pp. 21–27.

[2] Berger, T. R. *Northern Frontier Northern Homeland, The Report of the Mackenzie Valley Pipeline Inquiry: Volume Two—Terms and Conditions.* Ottawa, Supply and Services, 1977, Chapter Two, "Renewable Resources," pp. 7–43; Usher, P. J. "Renewable Resource Development in Northern Canada." *Northern Transitions,* J. B. Wilson and R. F. Keither (Eds.). Canadian Arctic Resources Committee, Ottawa, 1978, pp. 154–162; Rushforth, S. "Country Food." *Dene Nation,* M. Watkins, (Ed.). Toronto, University of Toronto Press, 1977, pp. 32–46.

[3] Berger, *Report;* Usher, "Renewable Resource Development"; Weistein, M. S. *What the Land Provides.* Montreal, Grand Council of the Crees (of Quebec), 1976; Ballantyne, P. *et al. The Land Alone (Aski–Puko).* Federation for Saskatchewan Indians, n.p., 1976; James Bay and Northern Quebec Native Harvesting Research Committee. *Research to Establish Present Levels of Harvesting by Native Peoples of Northern Quebec.* Part I, A Report on the Harvests by the James Bay Cree (2 vols.), Part II, A Report on the Harvests by the Inuit of Northern Quebec, Montreal, 1976; Rushforth, "Country Food."

[4] Usher, P. J. "Evaluating Country Food in the Northern Native Economy." In *Arctic,* 29:2, 1976, pp. 105–120; Ballantyne, *The Land Alone;* Interdisciplinary Systems Ltd. *Effects of Exploration and Development in the Baker Lake Area.* Winnipeg, Department of Indian Affairs and Northern Development, 1978.

[5] Brody, H. "Land Occupancy: Inuit Perceptions." In Milton Freeman Research Ltd., *Report, Inuit Land Use and Occupancy Project,* Vol. 1. Ottawa, Department of Indian Affairs and Northern Development, 1976, pp. 185–242; Brody, H. "Permanence and Change Among the Inuit and Settlers of Labrador." In Brice-Bennett, *Footprints,* pp. 311–347; Usher, P. J. "The Significance of the Land to Native Northerners." *Proceedings of the 1973 National Convention.* Calgary, Canadian Society of Exploration Geophysicists, 1974, pp. 170–177; Sieciechowicz, "The People and the Land"; Nahanni, "Mapping Project."

III

COMMUNICATION, CULTURE, AND THE INTERDISCIPLINARY PERSPECTIVE

> I have attempted to suggest that Western civilization has been profoundly influenced by communication and that marked changes in communications have had important implications. . . . As modern developments in communication have made for greater realism, they have made for greater possibilities of delusion.
>
> —Innis

Previously in this volume, reference has been made to an early Innis, preoccupied with political economy, and a later Innis, concerned with the role of communication technology in world history. The view that these two interests represent points on a continuum rather than the opposite sides of an intellectual divide has already been expressed by several writers. This perspective also characterizes the following section and is accompanied by an examination of its bearing on Innis' later communication studies.

The concern with making serious inroads into an area as uncharted as the history of communication involved Innis from 1945 until his death in 1952. The major source for many of his later writings was a thousand-plus page manuscript entitled *The History of Communications*, slated to be published in several volumes in the near future. From this base emerged *Empire and Communications* (1950), *The Bias of Communication* (1951), and *Changing Concepts of Time* (1952). These contributions are suggestive rather than definitive. They attempt to explore a new field of research, not to frame and hand down to subsequent generations a specific theoretical perspective. Thus, there is much to discuss, critique, and build on with respect to the later work, as the articles in this section will ably demonstrate.

In opening for investigation the relationships between communication and society and history, Innis found the perspective of any one discipline would not suffice. What he labeled academic monopolies of knowledge had rigidified the viewpoint of both the social sciences and the humanities. His criticisms were directed not so much at the structure and focus of the traditional disciplines but at their unwillingness to exchange insights or collaborate on relevant problems. As a result, he called for an interdisciplinary perspective well before the idea became popular during the late 1960s and early 1970s.

Unlike his earlier work on the Canadian Pacific Railroad, the fur trade, and the cod fisheries, which could be readily accommodated into the traditional disciplinary structures of history and political economy, the later communication studies do not fall within orthodox academic venues. These studies draw from a vast number of disciplines and Innis' familiarity with some of these disciplines was only slight. Despite the revealing perspective that emerged out of the communication studies, they had little impact at the time Innis wrote and in the decade following his death. During the 1960s, interest in this aspect of Innis' work began to increase. Although a number of factors were responsible, and the papers that follow deal with them, two should be mentioned at the outset. First, the writings of Marshall McLuhan, despite their shortcomings, have stimulated interest both in Innis and communication–society–history relationships; second, the increasing stress being placed on interdisciplinary research and teaching, particularly in the social sciences.

The papers that follow emphasize the richness and diversity of concerns to be found in Innis' communication studies. Although the writers come from many disciplinary backgrounds, their focus is inherently interdisciplinary. Today a discipline of communication can house such ventures; this was not the case when Innis was writing and this lack of disciplinary identification is perhaps one reason why a number of former colleagues were, and in some cases still are, uncomfortable with the later work. Despite the fact that we now have a discipline of communication, it has yet to fully assimilate the Innis legacy. One goal of the editors of this volume is that its publication will help to extend the dimensions of a discipline for which the work of Innis provides a founding contribution.

In leading off the section, Liora Salter outlines important connections between Innis' contribution to political economy and the later work on communication. In so doing, she provides a useful explication of some basic Innis concepts. Her analysis manages to mesh the two diverse, but not uncomplimentary methodologies of Innis into a revealing analysis of several problems that beset Canadian broadcasting. The accent of her study is on relationships and contradictions that exist between mass media and public broadcasting. This approach ties together the macrohistorical insights that are a part of the Innis legacy with his concern for policy and the impact of things technological on actual human communities.

The relationship between communications and communities is also a theme in the paper by Gail Valaskakis. She uses an Innis-inspired perspective to analyze an area that forms a conspicuous gap in his work: implications of the extension of empire on the native peoples of Canada. In examining the Innuit of Baffin Island, she deals with the successive waves of domination in terms of the role communication techniques and technologies played in the drama. Of particular note is her application of the Innis model of the shift from time-binding to space-binding traditions to a well-studied, small-scale historical context. Her paper ends with a brief assessment of the impact of electronic communication on the region, an assessment that merits further development.

The paper by Don Theall concentrates almost exclusively on the later Innis. Like Salter, Theall is concerned with explicating some basic Innis concepts, an exercise of no small importance. Theall's point of departure is a comparison between the perspective of Innis and Innis' more well-known student, McLuhan. This critique entails an analysis of the Innis style, particularly with respect to the types of discourse he employed. Insight is also provided into the several humanistically inspired ways Innis used the concept of culture as a critical tool in both historical analysis and social criticism. Innis, the historical analyst and social critic, also forms the subject of David Crowley's paper. Crowley's analysis draws from and defines connections between the ideas of Innis and more recent critical social theory. He is also concerned with the epistemological status of Innis' communication studies, particularly the relationship between the method and its intended, versus its actual implications.

Finally, Paul Heyer closes the section by looking at earlier writers, not necessarily influential to Innis or to one another, who dealt with communication–society–history relationships; he shows their contributions to be a discontinuous tradition in modern social thought. His paper also examines several unsuspected biases in Innis, biases that at times steered the implications of an analysis away from Innis' original intent. Heyer concludes his analysis by highlighting an important theme implicit in most of the papers in the volume: That despite the provisional and ambiguous nature of Innis' work, it constitutes a rich and innovative source from which the contemporary social sciences and humanities can profitably draw sustenance.

14

"PUBLIC" AND MASS MEDIA IN CANADA: DIALECTICS IN INNIS' COMMUNICATION ANALYSIS

LIORA SALTER
Simon Fraser University

Unlike his earlier studies on political economy, Innis' work on communication is not specific to Canada. Nor does it focus sharply on the nature and development of mass media systems as we know them today. Only by extrapolation can we view his communication analysis, as some authors have done, as a guide to understanding satellite development. Satellites were science fiction and television was in its infancy when Innis died. More important, perhaps, Innis' communication analysis is an impressionistic painting on a wide canvas worked through with examples and insights that span cultures and epochs. Even McLuhan, who claims both the Canadian and international legacy, wrote relatively little specific to Canadian media. Thus it is not surprising that many scholars who draw heavily on Innis' political economy find the communication analysis either peripheral to the main body of his work at best, or speculative and disjointed at worst.

Yet to cut off Innis' work on communication from the rest of his writing does both Innis and Canadian political economy a disservice. Innis, perhaps alone among Canadian scholars, dealt extensively with the relationship between public and private capital: Canadian broadcasting divided as it is between public and private sectors reflects the tension of this relationship. Innis explored the impact of distributive technology on what could or would be transmitted; current Canadian literature underemphasizes the factors mediating content and control in media systems. Innis believed that creative, expressive use of small format media could offset the alienating impact of mass media. Interestingly enough Canada is at the forefront of community media experimentation. If Innis' Canadian political economy can be brought together with his more general communication analysis we would all benefit.

Unfortunately, few scholars have developed Innis' studies on the relationship between public and private capital. The effect of that relationship on Canadian broadcasting must await further background research. More has been done on the impact of distributive technology and on community media. These studies form a basis for an analysis of Canadian media that focuses on what Innis termed the dialectic of "time" and "space" communication and what I will call the dialectic of "public" and mass media. Following Innis, I will argue that developments in distributive technology and the context of community media experimentation in Canada have ensured that authority would come to rest in the process of media production. As a result, those who have expertise in and control over access to the technology of production increasingly control the legitimacy of explanation as well, although they may never exercise that control through directive or censorship. "Public" media, creative use of media technology not subject to advertiser sponsorship constraints, provide no exception.

THE POLITICAL ECONOMY OF MASS MEDIA

Innis' contribution is generally regarded in two parts, the early work on staples and the later communication analysis. In both cases, the work is treated as if it formed a coherent theory—or at least two somewhat unrelated theories. Innis himself was more eclectic. His work bears the stamp of his fascination with a series of consistent problems examined in a multitude of settings and epochs. His liberal bias, his preoccupation with feuding liberals and Marxists at the University of Toronto and his search for a "judicious balance" took precedence over theory. He distrusted theory.[1] He felt it often led to the creation of new dogma, new "rigidities" and new monopolies of knowledge.[2] His work is more usefully approached as a series of essays and as a collection of analytical insights.

Nonetheless, this approach should not mask our perception of the coherence of his work. He abstracted processes and patterns in a variety of situations and epochs. Throughout his work, he was fascinated with the role of transportation and tended to view communication as the transportation of ideas. He explored links between production (of staples), transportation and developing technology.

He was preoccupied with dialectics, which he defined as the opposing tendencies in any social or historical situation which serve to create conflict and tension. His preoccupation extended to his methodology. If others stressed a Marxian interpretation, he would stress: "pushing of the Marxian conclusion is its ultimate limit, and in pushing it to its limit, showing its limitations."[3] He viewed conflict as productive change, and destructive of boredom. He stated: "In the clash between types of monopolies, an unpredictable freedom has been achieved, supported and destroyed."[4] and continued: "The limitations of any culture, in point of duration, are in part a result of the inability to muster the resources of a people to the point where stagnation can be avoided and where boredom can be evaded."[5] Unlike the economists whose work he had criticized at length, he began from the perspective of the colonized. When he explored the underlying dynamics of economic and communication history, he did so by situating his analysis in detailed social histories of those peoples affected by major shifts in power and systems of control. His is without doubt an analysis from the hinterland.

Innis focused on the concept of empire. Even when he wrote his major works (1930–50), empire was a strange concept. In general parlance it referred to imperial systems like Germany or Rome. His reference was much wider. Empire, as he used the term, was simply the institutionalization of a system of power. Empire could refer to specific states,[6] to primitive cultures[7] or to historical "empires" like Byzantium.[8] He used it to describe the church in the middle ages[9] and the colonizing impact of specific market in a world economy at a particular stage of capitalist development.[10] The integration of the Canadian economy, into the colonizing efforts of first Europe and later America for example, had more to do with the conflicting pressures and demands of a shifting distribution of power in the capitalist world system than with the national agenda of any one country.

The shift in Canadian history from a European dependency to an American one reflected changes in capitalism, with concommitant new technologies and new distribution routes.[11] Although Innis' work might be used to support a "nationalist perspective" on Canadian development, it did not assume that empires into which Canada has been integrated were always consonant with nation–state organization.[12]

Empires of one kind or another had almost always existed. The term encompassed both geographic conquest and tradition bound hierarchical organization. If empire could be equated with "metropole" (as many current writers suggest) it was only because metropole could be viewed as a system of power and control. If empire could be used to describe capitalism, it was because capitalism was without doubt a system of power with conflicting bases and demands at different stages of its development.[13] Monopoly and empire could be seen as two perspectives on the same phenomenon. If empire was the institutionalization of power, monopoly represented the nature and means of control exerted. "Rigidities," a term used throughout Innis' work, were viewed first as constraints imposed by the demands of empire (as a series of often conflicting pressures imposed by the demands of successive empires) and second as inherent tendencies in any institutionalization of power to resist change and adaptation. Empire had to be viewed in two lights, as a succession of historical epochs and as a constant interplay of conflicting centers of power within any period.[14] All empires sought to extend their control, over space as in the case of Rome, or through time as in the case of the church, by restricting access to particular staples or distribution routes or through the development of new technologies.

Innis began with a pragmatic sense of human activity. "Culture," he claimed, "is concerned with the capacity of an individual to appraise problems. . . ."[15] Activity itself is an essential characteristic of human beings; activity is problem solving; adaptation and resistance to control are essential human characteristics. Technology is viewed as an extension of activity: It is instrumental. Like the activity of which it is a part, technology is grounded in specific social and economic conditions; it is tied to relations of production, kinds of markets, and vested political and economic interests.[16] Technological systems function as an integral part of production, are developed to meet the needs of specific forms of production, and contribute to the maintenance of control. At the same time, they can be used as weapons of resistance. New technologies, such as radio, extend the reach of the American empire across national boundaries. They also decentralize information and are developed at the periphery of empire.[17]

To Innis then, the distinction between simple and complex technology was beside the point. Specific technologies relate to patterns of distribution.[18] A complex technology like newspaper production had quite different social consequences than a similarly complex technology like radio. The differences were linked to their different distribution characteristics.[19] Innis' analysis of the canoe, railway, and radio are therefore very similar.

Because mass communication systems display characteristics that parallel, extend, and complement his earlier analysis of railway development, it would make sense to trace the pattern of railway development as an introduction to Innis' contribution to understanding the nature of the Canadian media system.

First, of course, railway development tied the west to Toronto, and Toronto more tightly to the conflicting needs of American and European markets. A series of chain-link relationships was set up, the chain-links in this case being a series of successively greater dependencies. The west, and Toronto in turn, functioned as suppliers of staple products, while the central metropoles utilized the railway to extend their control over both staple production and the staple producing areas. Distribution systems, in staple producing areas like Canada, were inherently linked to the creation of dependency. Each dependency could be seen as part of a constantly changing pattern of relationships.

In his staple theory, the nature of the distribution system is critical: "We can suggest that changes in technique and improvements in the waterways and types of boats were responsible for rather wide fluctuations in economic development through the dependence on staple raw materials."[20] Distribution systems facilitated access to specific staples, gave competitive advantage to new powers and therefore essentially shaped the nature of staple export at any one period. New technologies, and new distribution routes following from their use, opened up new areas for exploitation and changed the pattern of dependency relations from one metropole to another.[21]

At the same time, distribution systems facilitated control over new resource producing areas. They were themselves instruments of expansion and colonization. The railway opened up the west, but it also linked the west more closely to the control centers in Eastern Canada, especially with the concurrent development of the telegraph. It became easier to centralize control when information could be transmitted over long distances and throughout local areas. Distribution technologies were, Innis argued, instrumental in the creation of new monopolies. As a result, local regions invariably lost much of their autonomy.

Mass rapid information transmission (a form of what Innis called "space-binding" communication) also facilitated control of distant regions under centralized authority, and generated dependency of the margins upon the center. In Canada, it facilitated a similar chain of dependency relationships between the west and Toronto, Toronto in turn on the United States. Computer data transmission or television standards would be matched to the needs of the metropolitan area; the shape and problems in communication systems were generated in the demands of the metropolitan system. Paradoxically, however, mass communication systems also decentralized information. News became available from any part of the globe and was made available without discrimination to new and diverse publics. The rapid growth of information transmission systems was paralleled by the growth in information being transmitted (and with the concommitent growth, in time, of anticolonialist or nationalist movements).

Mass communication systems, then, tended first to reduce the significance of locality and the autonomy of regions even as they increased the scope and coverage of information made available. The impact of the technological form was felt in the kind of information transmitted, because information had to be adaptable for easy transmission. The significance of regional class, or national experience, or the complexity of on-the-spot data, or even the richness of complex interrelationships of many levels of data would be reduced to that which could be expressed in broad general categories, categories common to all localities and with no specific ties to workplace or neighborhood:

> The radio appealed to vast area, overcame the division between classes in its escape from literacy, and centralization and bureaucracy. A single individual could appeal at one time to vast numbers of people speaking the same language and indirectly, though with less effect, through interpreters speaking other languages.[22]

Innis argued that expressive language would not travel well through mass communication systems, but masses of data did.[23] Although both satellites and television were developed after his death, they are good examples of what he called "space-binding" communications. Had he known their capabilities, he might have forecast their link to the expansion of American capitalism, noted their power in the extension of colonialism, noted the increasing flatness and consistency of the information transmitted, and commented upon their inability to encompass the richness and wealth of local experience. As he put it: "Superficiality became essential to meet the various demands of larger numbers of people and was developed as an art by those compelled to meet the demands."[24]

If space-binding communications facilitated efficiency of control over vast expansion of territories, "time-binding" communications, as Innis called them, extended empires through tradition-bound hierarchical social orders. Time-bound systems were based in societies with a rich oral tradition, or with sophisticated writing technologies that limited access to "knowledge" to the privileged few. Time-bound communication systems were based in societies with a strong sense of continuity and community; they transmitted tradition and, with tradition, the idea of an unchanging social order. Although time-bound systems tended to stifle individualism as a dynamic of change, they allowed for an individualism inherent in the rich expressiveness of language and the range of human emotion: "An oral tradition implies freshness and elasticity but students of anthropology have pointed to the binding character of custom in primitive cultures."[25]

Time and space functioned in a dialectical relationship within one era, or in successive epochs. Both time- and space-binding communication systems tended to become monopolistic and engendered their own rigidities. Rigidity, in the case of communications, was inherent first in the nature of the technology used, second in the use to which technology was put, and third in the derivation of information that would be transmitted. Communications technologies not only distributed information but also legitimated certain kinds of knowledge through the process of distribution. Three levels of rigidity could be distinguished:

First, time-bound societies tended to stultify enterprise, mobility, and change, and they lacked political unity.[26] Space-bound societies lacked community, a sense of place and continuity. As a consequence both time- and space-bound societies were alienating. Second, both medieval scholar and computer expert functioned within a system of control in which they held technical expertise. How their expertise was used has little to do with their personal views and more to do with the nature of control exerted. Third, those with expertise in any technology and access to organizations or institutions that could control the use of their technology developed increasing monopolization over what would be considered "information" and over what explanations would be available through media for the interpretation of experience: ". . . science lives its own life not only in the mechanism which is provided to distribute knowledge but also in the sort of knowledge which will be distributed."[27]

In the case of the church, the role of the monk and his relation to the church and to a system of legitimated explanations is well understood. In the case of mass communications, the relationships are more complex. Access to and expertise in the use of technology introduces a separation between producer and receiver.[28] Through this separation (which is increased with growing limitations on access to technology) the viewer loses the right to the interpretation of his or her own experience. With monopolies of knowledge, explanation and interpretation of experience are separated and knowledge shifts to something generated in and defined by the way it is produced.

News can be considered news in part because it is collected and disseminated through news-gathering and disseminating organizations, in part because it is prepared by those with access to and expertise in the use of news-gathering communication systems. The wire service, increasingly controlled by the metropolis, defines what is available as an explanation of events throughout an increasing proportion of the world. News is what has been transmitted through its technological system. Those who prepare news require a narrower range of skills as technological systems introduce a greater division of labor. The technical development of the wire service, its nature as a distribution system, its centralization of control and its sophistication cannot be separated from the content of information that wire services disseminate.

Other authors have located the underpinnings of bias in the practices of work within media organizations.[29] In the Innisian argument, they extend to the technology of distribution. As shared experience, class, region, locality, and collective interpretation are made irrelevant with mass rapid information transmission, authority comes to rest (as it did under the monopoly of knowledge held by the medieval church) in the process of its own production. Those who control the process and support its development hold authority although they may never actively intervene to control media content.

PUBLIC AND MASS MEDIA: DIALECTICS IN COMMUNICATION SYSTEMS

In concentrating on Innis' description of technology as a tool of empires, one might easily overlook his extensive commentary on technology as tool of resistance to these same empires. Technologies, he claimed, could be adaptive to, or productive of, change. Their use of resistance and adaptation were as critical as their uses for consolidation and expansion. New technologies often developed at the margins because they could be both instrumental in and responsive to the relative freedom from constraint there. Margins existed in empires created over space (in distant territories) and over time (in pockets of intellectual and cultural dissent). For Innis, this hinterland response and the dialectic relationships between metropolitan and hinterland pressures were central to the staples thesis.

At this point, I want to pose a rough equation between what Innis might have called a "hinterland dynamic" in media systems and "public" media, and to suggest that the "hinterland dynamic" appears operational in critical journalism and in the development of noncommercial media. The "hinterland" in media systems is both territorial and cultural. The response from the margin is a response from rural territories and cultures and from those in intellectual cultural and political rebellion to the extension of empire. There is strong empirical support for the equation: Community media in Canada have been largely rural or native phenomena. Counter cultural, political, and artist groups use urban community media facilities more than any other sectors of the public. Counter culture, political, and artist groups provide constituencies for those who attempt to function critically in the media system; in a few cases these groups hold individual writers accountable for their work.

Interestingly, the current literature on community media in Canada parallels Innis' description of the adaptive characteristics of time-bound systems, although it was written some fifteen or more years after his death. It also parallels some of Alvin Gouldner's recent commentary on the role of the public in the creation of mass media systems.[30] If "public" media is to be useful as an analytical tool, the commentaries of Innis and Gouldner will be helpful in fleshing out the description.

Innis, for example, stressed the simplicity of time-bound systems and their use as a means of escape from control.[31] Currently, community media are seen to function as a critique of the media system, and as a means of overcoming some of the alienating and atomizing characteristics of urbanization. Innis noted that activity, not passivity, was sustained in audience relations in time-bound systems, and current literature suggests that a defining characteristic of community media is audience participation. Time-bound communications were seen by Innis to be specific to particular localities or constituencies; community media appeal to local or specific constituent audiences. Time-bound systems, Innis noted, stress "the spirit," freedom, creativity, and change yet are, paradoxically, conservative.[32] Community media are viewed now as catalysts for social change and artistic experimentation, but a number of commentators stress the inherent conservatism of many citizen participation efforts.[33]

Gouldner suggests that the development of mass media was instrumental in the concommitant development of a "public."[34] This "public" is engaged in and defined through its participation in the political process, but is, Gouldner suggests, ironically an outgrowth of the privitization of family and work life. When news "defocalizes" events and imposes an artificial separation between experience and its explanation, the "public" as a political force has been contained and the internal dialogue between constituent groups and individuals who make up "the public" has been destroyed.

If, as Gouldner suggests, media systems particularize events and isolate individuals within a collective "public" whole, community media efforts would be those that generate dialogue between constituent groups and individuals who make up the public. Community media efforts could be seen as those that regenerate the contact between explanation and activity as portrayed through technically mediated communication systems. The "mirroring capacity of small format video," as expressed in many commentaries on community media, can be seen as a counter force to the alienating impact of media systems. The "public" dialogue that Gouldner claims was brought into being with the mass media would re-emerge transformed through a dialogue of publics responding to the very nonpublic nature of the system that created it.

Public media, as a hinterland dynamic in media systems, can be seen as media not responsive to ratings consideration. They are, by definition, reactive to the needs and aspirations, experience and explanation systems of the constituent groups who produce and use them. They may stimulate public dialogue or engage producers and audience in creative expression. By definition again, public media assume the audience is situated and responsive in many dimensions to programing. Some news and public affairs programing on CBC radio is public; a small proportion of CBC television or commercial media production is public as well. Also there are journalists who can be said to act within the public domain, although they write for commercial media. Those who work in community radio and cable systems and edit or publish small journals work in public media. Clearly, the source of funding is not itself a determinant, although funding has its effect. Neither is the size of the community being served, since constituent groups may include class or interest groups. A sizable proportion of the Canadian media system, then, is public.

The suggestion that public media exist, nevertheless, does not imply a mindless pluralist description of a media system that contains both public and mass elements. In an Innisian sense, public media constitute the dialectic within the media system. The relationship between public and mass media is oppositional, dynamic, and mutually reactive and both are part of a media system that depends on advertiser sponsorship and elite consolidation. In the first place, community media experiments are encapsulated within social and economic development programs sponsored by governmental agencies whose goals stem from a model of growth dependent upon further staples export. Second, contextual pressures on community media ensure that the community will be viewed as a special interest group and the public as a minority or collection of minority group interests. These two points require clarification.

Innis' "plea for time" reads like a humanist overlay on a critical analysis of the dynamics of control. Literature on community media, mainly descriptive and prescriptive, has the same character.[35] The analyses of experiments in Canada have been conducted (if at all) as if it were important to isolate the experiments from the impact on the communities they service. Usually descriptions of experiments focus on the work of the experimenters and the group process of the project. As a consequence, the descriptions seem hollow; their optimism only echoes back to satisfy the proponents of the experiments. A critique of community media based simply on a reading of the literature would be easy but facile: A community radio station, organized and operated by northern Ojibway people, may broadcast only the same country and western music as its American counterpart.[36] Regional or local programing may provide only local discussion of decisions being made in Toronto or New York.

Public media in Canada have had strong financial and regulatory support. Many critical journalists find work and community media experiments have been well funded. Cable operators complain but they contribute about ten per cent of their gross annual revenues to local programing that gives them no sales advantage. The National Film Board and several governmental agencies have conducted large experiments using film as a medium of community development or change. Occasionally, the resultant programing is highly critical, or even explicitly Marxist, but the evidence of censorship is more astonishing by its absence than by isolated examples of its existence.

Only a few community radio stations are flourishing, however, and films produced through the National Film Board or community cable systems seldom generate national or local controversy. Although CBC radio programs have generated widespread public debate, community programing, which by definition is closer to local needs and aspirations, has not. The limitations of community media are surprising given what ought to be the strength of their appeal, an hypothesized need for a "balance of time and space" (Innis), new publics (Gouldner), or an end to alienated labor (Marx cum Fromm).

Part of the reason lies in context in which community experiments are developed. Urban experiments tend to be funded on a short-term basis through job creation programs, while rural experiments tend to be funded as a component part of rural economic development projects. Experiments follow on the heels of resource development and government financed infrastructure support for resource export. The same agencies that fund resource development fund community media: Manpower, DREE, ARDA, The Department of Indian and Northern Development, and the governments of Alberta and Newfoundland have all been more active in funding experiments than the citizen-participation-oriented Secretary of State. The list of funded projects reads like a keyed index to major resource development: Major media experiments have been funded in Newfoundland and Labrador, northeastern New Brunswick, rural Quebec, Fort McMurray, Alberta (the Tar Sands development), the Mackenzie Delta, and recently, the Yukon. The level of funding seems impressive until the total costs of the accompanying project are taken into account.

Experiments emphasize community self-sufficiency and control but are funded by programs whose goals center on the development of an industrial work force and labor mobility. In the clash of perspective between those who work within and those who support projects, conflicts are created which are beyond the ability of experimenters to resolve. The experimenters may reject high technology models of development and argue for self-sufficiency as they did in Newfoundland. They may concentrate on community animation and political development as they have in Alberta. They may even quote from Innis, as they did in the

Mackenzie Delta. The underlying conflict has its impact, however. Goals of the experiment shift, implicitly or explicitly, to group process or political development among experimenters. Shifting goals is a means of coping with the disjuncture between experiment and context in a situation where experimenters are relatively powerless. Gradually group process becomes an end in itself. The descriptive, prescriptive literature describing community media in terms of participant group skills is a result of, not an introduction to, the experiments.

Regulatory support for community media supports this shift in experiment goals. The broadcast regulatory agency imposes a "tax" on the revenues of the private system to support community media. The "tax" on cable, for example, is the ten per cent of gross revenues that cable systems are asked to donate to community programing in return for monopoly protection of their franchise. The "tax" on radio broadcasting is a weekly FM program devoted to community access. Community programing is viewed by the agency as expressly local and as catering to the needs of particular or special interest groups.[37] The agency demands it be produced by amateurs and be noncompetitive with commercial or entertainment programing. In this light, community programing becomes, at best, an adjunct to the basic service, at worst, a duty of the licencee performed to protect a commercial franchise.

In early broadcast regulation in Canada, the demands of the public service were assumed to take precedence over the needs of the private sector. The CBC acted as the national broadcasting service and as the regulator of private broadcasting. The continued existence of private broadcasting after the creation of the CBC was justified on the basis that private broadcasters could provide an explicitly localized service filling gaps in programing left by an inadequately funded CBC. Now the relationship between the public and private sectors has been reversed and the shrinking public service has been encapsulated within a broadcasting environment characterized by and responsive to the demands of private development and consumer choice (ratings). Even the noncommercial CBC radio is programed with references to ratings and the CBC now viewed as filling the gaps in service left by private broadcasting. Instead of regulation by and in the national interest, the national service is regulated along with private broadcasting in an ill-defined public interest in which consumer choice again is a major variable. Cable transmission has integrated all forms of broadcast signal into a single system; the consumer chooses among apparent equivalents. Community cable programing has become an expressly localized service. It is expected to fill the gaps left by both private and national service by providing for special interest and minority group tastes. What is now considered public, in the eyes of regulatory agency and audience alike, includes noncommercial aspects of CBC programing and community cable programing. More importantly, public broadcasting has come to mean broadcasting that caters to special interests.

Constraints within the private sector support a definition of the situation where public broadcasting caters only to special interests. In part to minimize investment risk and in part because of the underlying goals of an advertiser-sponsored system, private broadcasters seek a predictable audience and equate predictability with mass media appeal. The relatively homogeneous minority of the population making up the commercial radio audience or the relative homogeneity of interest met through entertainment-based television programing ensures enough predictability to outweigh any risk the broadcaster might have in attempting to locate a constellation of multiple publics or multilevel needs. The untapped majority is viewed in terms of the diversity of its publics and interests and thus as a minority or collection of minorities. Class and regional interests are subsumed in this perception of diversity. Access programing, which views public interest as minority group interests, is equated with community programing.

Innis emphasized that it was in the separation between production and reception that monopolies of knowledge are created. He was talking of mass communication systems but he might have been talking equally of public or community media. In community media, the audience becomes a participant in production, but production is separated from audience relation. Media production and group process become ends in themselves. *How* something is produced overrides consideration of audience relations. In experiments that emphasize technological form or internal group participation, the monopoly of knowledge remains with the media system, which continues to control the availability of explanation available for the interpretation of experience. Those who provide support for the experiments are often integrated into political and economic elites but they maintain their monopoly without exercising direct control over media content.

When public programing is viewed as an adjunct to the basic media service and community programing caters only to special interests, the experience of the public becomes "exceptional." When community programing is conceived as access programing and the public is viewed in terms of its diversity, the collective experience of shared situation becomes irrelevant. The public becomes "people with special interests." When community programers and supportive regulation suggest that programing responsive to the needs and aspirations of its audience can only be of interest to the select few, the public has become a minority group.

Innis claimed monopolies of knowledge robbed the public of

legitimacy in the interpretation of its own experience. Here the very media that enable the audience to produce programs, to respond actively or to engage in public dialogue serve to cut the public off from a collective sense of its own reality. Public media become part of the media system under these conditions. These conditions, and the relationships they engender, mediate content and control. System constraints are extended far beyond the boundaries of commercial media, and advertiser sponsorship and elite consolidation extend their impact into the very content of noncommercial media.

NOTES

[1] Innis, H. A. *Bias of Communication*. Toronto, University of Toronto, 1951, p. 90.

[2] Innis, H. A. *Essays in Canadian Economic History*. Toronto, University of Toronto, 1956, p. 292.

[3] Innis *Bias*, p. 13.

[4] Innis, *Bias*, p. 133.

[5] Innis, *Essays*, p. 198

[6] Innis, *Bias*, p. 4.

[7] Innis, H. A. *Empire and Communications* (1950). Toronto, University of Toronto, 1970, p. 115.

[8] Innis, *Bias*, p. 53.

[9] Innis, *Essays*, p. 206.

[10] Innis, *Essays*, p. 220.

[11] See Innis, *Essays*, pp. 141, 168.

[12] There is a similar argument involved in O'Connor's attempt to specify imperialism's relation to capitalism. See O'Connor, James. *"The Meaning of Economic Imperialism."* In Robert I. Rhodes, *Imperialism and Underdevelopment*. New York, *Monthly Review Press*, 1970, p. 108.

[13] See Innis' discussion of radio and newspapers in *Bias of Communication*, p. 60.

[14] Innis, *Bias*, p. 85.

[15] See Innis, *Essays*, p. 83; and *Bias*, p. 138.

[16] Innis, *Bias*, p. 4. Canada is best known for innovation in communication and transportation technology.

[17] Innis, *Bias*, p. 78.

[18] Innis, *Bias*, p. 82.

[19] Innis, *Essays*, p. 74, 220.

[20] Innis, *Essays*, pp. 367–368.

[21] Innis, *Bias*, p. 82.

[22] Innis, *Essays*, p. 383.

[23] Innis, *Bias*, p. 82.

[24] Innis, *Bias*, p. 4.

[25] Innis, *Bias*, p. 10.

[26] Innis, *Bias*, p. 192.

[27] Innis, *Bias*, p. 140.

[28] Innis, *Bias*, p. 85.

[29] Smith, Dorothy, Bosswood, Kevin, Jackson, Nancy, & Webster, Sylvia, "B. C. Community New Project Report," British Columbia Department of Labour, Mimeo, 1975.

[30]Gouldner, Alvin W. *The Dialectic of Ideology and Technology*. New York, Seabury, 1976.

[31]Innis, *Bias,* pp. 34–40, 124, 130, 191–192.

[32]Innis, *Essays,* p. 192.

[33]See Emond, P. "Environmental Protection Laws." In *Osgood Law Journal,* Vol. 13, No. 3, 1976, p. 782.

[34]Gouldner, *Dialectic of Ideology and Technology,* p. 113.

[35]A good example would be Henaut, Doroth Todd, "Films for Social Change: The Hammer and the Mirror" and Martin, Gail, "Raven: Intermediate Communications and Rural Isolation" both in Theall, D., and Robinson, G., *Studies in Canadian Communications.* Montreal, Programme in Communications, McGill University, 1975. See also *Resources for an Active Community* published by the CRTC (1974); Yin, R. K., *Citizen Participation in Planning,* New York, Rand, 1973: Mandelbaum, Seymour. *Community and Communications,* New York, W. W. Norton, 1972; *The Seminar on Access to Information,* Ottawa, Supply and Services, 1971; Singer, Benjamin. *Feedback and Society,* Lexington, Mass., Lexington Books, 1973.

[36]Kenomadiwin, one of the first licensed community radio stations, operated from a truck in six communities in Northwestern Ontario and broadcast country and western music.

[37]Canadian Radio-television and Telecommunications Commission. *Annual Report 1975–76.* Ottawa, Supply and Services, 1976, p. 3.

15

THE OTHER SIDE OF EMPIRE: CONTACT AND COMMUNICATION IN SOUTHERN BAFFIN ISLAND

GAIL GUTHRIE VALASKAKIS
Concordia University

The later writings of Harold Innis represent a conceptual approach to history. Examining culture, Innis presents ". . . a systematic explanation of the relationship between communications media and the societies surrounding them."[1] Drawing a critical connection between modes of communication and social change, Innis legitimizes communication as a research approach and reinforces its potential as a research tool.

Innis is primarily interested in explaining dominant cultural trends. He analyzes social change from the perspective of Western development as a generalized cultural shift from time-binding modes of communications to space-binding media. Innis' initial interest in communications stemmed from awareness of its role in Indian/European contact.[2] Innis discusses "the disturbances which have characterized a shift from a culture dominated by one form of communication to another culture dominated by another form of communication," as Western movement from oral tradition to print communication and acknowledges but never analyzes "the dangers of the intrusion of one culture on other cultures," which occurs as a result of this shift.[3]

From the Native perspective, this is the critical nexus of social history in the North. The change that is important to understand and act upon arises in the interface of Inuit and Euro-Canadian cultures.

Innis' conceptual approach is clearly relevant to the expansion and control of Euro-Canadian culture in the Arctic. As part of historical process, Inuit communities received the media and knowledge monopoly of an empire expanding spatially. The North formed part of the margin as control solidified in centers and the Inuit became marginal to the authority of Euro-Canadian presence. The time-binding bias of oral tradition was broken and Inuit culture shifted toward a spatial orientation. As Innis would expect, however, the process of cultural change was not one of neat, unidirectional shift.

This paper looks at that process on a micro-level, relating Innis' concepts to "the other side of empire." To understand the impact of literacy on the cultural shift of Inuit in southern Baffin Island, I relate the new medium to changes in social organization—those relationships in a community—organized in terms of concrete, goal oriented social direction. Because contact occurred in Baffin three hundred years before literacy was introduced, patterns of interaction between Inuit and Europeans, and among Inuit had already begun to change Inuit social organization. Of course, interaction patterns and modes of communication were mutually reinforcing; both emerged from the perspective of literate European culture. In southern Baffin Island, however, literacy took a particular form: syllabic script. As the new medium shifted Inuit associations, its syllabic form redirected and diffused Inuit cultural orientation. This paper focuses on two aspects of the communication process: interaction and the mode of communication. I have not considered other important aspects of contact and communication, such as the potential and actual meeting of messages.

COMMUNICATION AND CHANGE AGENTS

With an historical framework, contact can be conceived in terms of sets of people who move into the North: change agents present to act upon the mandate and motives of outside institutions. Accounts of change generally follow the sequence of explorers, whalers, missionaries, traders, and government personnel, beginning with the Royal Canadian Mounted Police (originally the North-West Mounted Police) and enlarging to include various specialized personnel of contemporary settlements. Although agencies overlap and order differs, the conception is useful to understand agency roles in the contact process.

The relative importance of change agents shifts, of course, according to the focus of specific research or region. In historical analysis, institutionalized trading usually emerges as the most important influence on Inuit social change.[4] Traders brought the technology to sustain both trapping and trading on a large-scale and consistent basis: steel traps, guns and ammunition, boats and other trade goods. Although the whalers before them had introduced the essential technology and forged a certain dependency upon trade goods, the traders provided the basis for a generalized trapping adaption and exchange economy. The process of trapping solidified new hunting techniques and residence patterns; the process of trading established new forms of community leadership and interaction.

However, from the perspective of communication, the critical role of agency impact transfers to the missionaries. The interactional basis for new residence and leadership patterns is set in the missionary period. In addition, the missionaries introduced Inuit to literacy and print and, in southern Baffin Island, they did so almost simultaneously.

Although there was considerable European activity East and South of Baffin Island before the mid-sixteenth century, the first meaningful contact between Inuit and Europeans begins with Martin Frobisher in 1576. On three major voyages, he initiated a pattern of incidental contact that included barter, combat, and kidnapping. After Frobisher's voyages, the search for a Northwest Passage gained new momentum. For the first thirty years of the seventeenth century, it concentrated on Hudson Straits and by 1670 ships traveled through the Strait on a regular basis transporting furs and goods for the trading empire to the South. Sailing conditions along the southern shore of Hudson Strait encouraged a sea route, which followed the northern coast from Resolution Island to Big Island or, the Cape Dorset area. There, ships crossed a narrow section broken by islands and continued South or West.

When English exploration resumed in the nineteenth century, interest in a Northwest Passage began to focus on the northern Baffin region. With traffic already established in the Strait, contact continued to increase. In the mid-1800s, two Europeans moved from the controlled environment of ships exploration to the land. John Rae, in a series of expeditions between 1846 and 1854, was the first European to use Inuit technology and learn Inuit skills and in 1860 Charles Hall moved beyond the adoption of Inuit techniques to living among Inuit. Boas followed this tradition in 1883, but the general pattern of contact remained incidental.

As the exploration period involved Inuit in additional contact, trading became the interactional set for Inuit/European encounter. Violence decreased and cooperation increased as European technology began to motivate Inuit exchange. Relative to Inuit, Europeans controlled the frequency of interaction and its pattern and outcome. Trading from the secure closed system of the wooden ship, explorers determined trade items, market price, and interactional set for exchange. Technology gave them authority and incidental trading set the stage for Inuit to redefine social position in terms of access to European technology.

Whaling normalized the trading process between Inuit and Europeans and initiated conditions of dependency that foreshadowed institutionalized trading. Extending authority through technology, the whalers shifted European control from directed interaction to directed change. The potential of the whale fishery off the east coast of Baffin Island was recognized as early as the seventeenth century and in the early nineteenth century whalers moved into the area. Activity focused on Davis Strait and Cumberland Sound and, in 1852, a British whaling station was built at Kekerten. By the turn of the century, there were whaling stations in the Sound and southern Baffin Island was part of the fishery.

Except for the few explorers who had used Inuit as pilots or lived on the land, Europeans had not attended to native skills. With the whalers, Inuit in southern Baffin became a potential labor force to extract resources. "Because whalers almost never wintered along this coast, and only one whaling station operated briefly, contact was restricted almost entirely to summer. It was at first sporadic and unpredictable, but after 1898, when the whaler *Active* began to exploit the natives as summer hunters and whaling crews, contact occurred annually."[5]

The basic migratory model of Inuit lifestyle was not originally affected by whaling in southern Baffin but, with a summer whaling station at Lake Harbour, mobility patterns accommodated European presence. Entire families traveled throughout the summer on whaling ships and wooden boats were traded for Inuit skills. New experience and techology meant Inuit traveled further and more frequently. As interaction among Inuit expanded and diversified, where and how people traveled was almost entirely controlled by Europeans.

Whaling captains chose certain Inuit to perform the necessary functions of piloting the ship, securing Inuit services and, to a lesser extent, interpreting for Europeans. The whalers initiated the concept of "contact agent"—Inuit delegated by Euro-Canadians to act as community go-betweens, direct native activity to suit the needs of agency—maintained in this role through Euro-Canadian authority and technology. Contact agents became the "whaling bosses" who, in response to captains, directed Inuit participation in the hunt. European authority was supported by navigation skills, English language, technology, and trade goods.

Traditional Inuit leadership met an initial challenge through this system, but critical social change probably did not occur in southern Baffin Island. Pit-soo-lak, a shamen or angakok in the Lake Harbour area, told the first missionary to arrive there that ". . . on board the whaler he was the captain's 'voice.' The captain told him what he wanted and he, Pit-soo-lak, then arranged for the Eskimo to carry out the captain's commands."[6] During the whaling period, the man who was doctor, lawyer, politician, and priest to the Inuit community could easily transfer to the new role of contact agent, as he did in Lake Harbour.

Whaling declined quickly just after the turn of the century. Synthetics were discovered to replace baleen in the manufacture of clothes and heavy activity had begun to deplete the fishery. As whaling became less profitable, the agency diversified into trading and mining and the summer station at Lake Harbour included both a mica mine and a store. Shortly after 1909, when missionaries arrived in southern Baffin, whaling all but ceased.

Within a seasonal context, the whalers set the hierarchical structure of a change agency upon the Inuit community. Through contact agency and the exchange of harvested products and services for technology, new levels of control emerged. Social position in the Inuit community began to shift toward people who had not only access to technology but also access to authority.

In the summer, whaleboats and campsites brought close contact and created conditions which were new in scale if not in fact. With the whalers, disease and alcohol spread. Captains who felt moral responsibility for the contagious diseases—"the invisible invaders," as Crow calls them,[7]—invited missionaries, the subsequent change agents, to combat this social fallout.

From the period of earliest contact in Baffin, Europeans were committed to Christianizing and educating Native people. The first missionary who preached to Baffin Inuit accompanied Frobisher on his third voyage and, in 1852, the Kekerten whaling station requested a Moravian missionary. A missionary wintered in Cumberland Sound in 1857, but the Moravians withdrew. In 1894, a second whaler invited an Anglican mission on Blacklead Island. The same year, Rev. E. J. Peck established a critical change agency in Baffin. Peck continued to work out of Cumberland Sound and, in 1909, he brought A. L. Fleming and J. W. Bilby to Lake Harbour to build a second mission in southern Baffin Island.

Although the *Active* had supported the summer whaling station since 1898, Fleming notes that he and Bilby were the first Europeans to winter at Lake Harbour. They stayed twenty-seven months on this first trip and, along with two others, maintained European presence at the mission until 1915. Missionary impact was so substantial that Inuit "missionaries"—called lay readers or catechists—continued the agency. When Fleming returned in 1920, there were ". . . never fewer than thirty-two adults at any service and generally there were forty to sixty."[8]

LITERACY

As Stevens suggests, Protestant missionaries tended to include more Western values in their definition of Christianity than Catholic.[9] Literacy, already a vital part of European life for four centuries, was central to these values. Literacy provided for a singular aspect of Protestantism: personal consultation of the Bible.

> The Word could be conveyed by preaching, but in that situation, the listener relied partly on the authority of the speaker. Should not the convert be able to determine matters of salvation for himself in reference to the Supreme Source as revealed in the Holy Scriptures? Was not literacy required. . . ?[10]

From the perspective of European culture, literacy was not just a method to spread Christianity and Westernization. The mode of communication had a particular function in the process of directed change: the transfer of Christian authority from ministers to individual converts.

James Evans, a Methodist missionary, is usually credited with initiating native literacy. Working in Norway House in 1846, he devised a way for Cree converts to read the Bible. Using a character to represent the sound of each syllable, he created a syllabic system to write the Cree language. Peck adapted syllabic script to the Inuit language. Working in northern Quebec, Peck learned Inuttitut and began writing a grammar and translating religious texts before he moved to Baffin Island.

Through the overlapping autobiographical accounts of Archibald Fleming and Peter Pitseolak, we have a rare if limited opportunity to look at social change in southern Baffin Island. The former was a critical change agent; the latter became a contact agent, but not a "Christian boss." Pitseolak's autobiography is the first unassisted personal account from a Baffin Inuk. Written in syllabics, it was translated and published in 1975, after his death.

When Fleming arrived in Lake Harbour, he found many Inuit already knew syllabics, although only a few had been to the Blacklead Island Mission. None were baptized and the great majority was "pagan."Literacy diffused to southern Baffin Island from areas both North and South of the coast.[11] Peter Pitseolak, born in the area just after the turn of the century, writes: "I was born when Christianity had already come to Baffin Island. . . . Even before I was able to talk I had learned all the alphabet songs by listening to people sing them."[12] The medium was the message, the missionaries met the challenge by asserting authority through print.

In 1909, the cases containing a new and enlarged Service Book for the missionaries were lost in transit. The book included a translation of the Book of Common Prayer and one hundred and fifty hymns in Inuttitut. Without it, Fleming ". . . resorted to the simple method of having the people, young and old alike, memorize the prayers and hymns as well as many portions of the Scriptures and he spent much time copying the hymns from Bilby's book and making reproductions on 'Jellograph' . . . to provide every family with at least one copy of each hymn."[13] When the books arrived the following year, print was well established as an authoritative source.

As Innis would suspect, the immediate impact of the new communication mode followed the pattern of earlier interaction and authority transferred to European missionaries. Stefansson writes that Inuit looked "upon the missionary as the mouthpiece of God."[14] Aware of this generalized authority, Fleming comments: "They came to me with their joys and sorrows, their aches and pains, their successes and failures, their problems and, yes, their private quarrels, and seemed content to follow my advice."[15]

Literacy continued to spread and, within the decade, syllabics were widely used by Inuit in Baffin Island, northern Quebec and into Labrador and the Keewatin. Graburn writes: until the coming of the schools in the mid-twentieth century, "at least 99% of adult Takamiut [in the Sugluk area of northern Quebec] were literate in Eskimo."[16] In 1924, Jenness noted that oral tradition had declined to the point that "the professional storytellers are gone, and with them any notion of prestige for their art."[17]

In Innis' terminology, syllabic literacy initiated a shift from the time-biased culture of oral tradition to the space-biased culture of written tradition. As print established an authoritative source, oral tradition met the initial challenge of literacy in southern Baffin Island. Relationships defined through shared knowledge, group participation, and interdependence began to shift in response to spatially oriented media; but the missionaries introduced different writing systems across the North and Inuit adaptation was limited.

In the Western Arctic, literacy was taught "using the letters of the English alphabet."[18] As early as 1863, Father Emile Petitot had compiled a grammar of the Mackenzie dialect, but his brief stay in the area did not initiate literacy. In the early 1870s, Rev. W. C. Bompas, working among the Eskimo of the Lower Mackenzie, began to translate prayers, hymns, and the Bible into Eskimo using Roman characters. After 1896, when Rev. I. O. Stringer established a mission at Herschel Island, literacy spread throughout the Mackenzie region.

Moravians, too, adapted Roman characters to Inuttitut. They taught literacy to Inuit through their Labrador missions and, opening a mission in Port Burwell on Hudson Strait in 1904, they brought their system further East. Having developed through earlier mission work in Greenland, the Moravian system used the Danish alphabet.

Unintentionally but effectively, then, three different Inuttitut writing systems were established in the Canadian Arctic. The wider Inuit community was even further affected. In all, six different orthographies developed as adaptions to dialect and European language demanded: Roman characters adapted to the Greenlandic dialect, the Kuskokwim dialect in Alaska, the Labrador dialect, and that in the Mackenzie district; the Russian alphabet adapted to the Aleuts; and syllabic script adapted to the dialects of Baffin Island and parts of northern Quebec and the Keewatin. Even picture writing emerged. In Northern Alaska, two Inuit missionaries developed a pictographic writing system because "the older people who could not read nor write, needed a way to remember the new verses [of the Bible]."[19] The method spread and by early in the twentieth century two general styles had developed.

Within this diversity, the syllabic region became defined and bounded in the Eastern Arctic.

As Inuit interest and initiative spread literacy, missionary pragmatism led to literacy regionalism. Writing systems reinforced substantial dialect differences to further divide Inuit areas. Baffin Island became a "lonely island of Peck syllabics hemmed in between two larger and more populous regions"[20] and Baffin Inuit could not use literacy to communicate with other Inuit. And as they learned syllabics, they mastered a system that discouraged the transfer of Inuit literacy skills to the English language. In fact, this was an unintended outcome of missionary agency.

As Berkhofer notes, "To the missionaries . . . Protestantism was an inextricable component of the whole idea of civilization."[21] Christianity and Westernization were interrelated issues in missionary effort to direct change and "the argument over the method of propagating the Gospel was reduced to a simple precedence of procedure in the dissemination of two desirable effects."[22] Syllabic literacy and eminent Christianity had begun the process, but English-language literacy was needed to extend it. European cultural perspective called for education, and education aimed at acculturation depended heavily upon learning the English language.

Inuit literacy did not transfer to English-language learning. Only contact agents learned even rudimentary English, and there is no indication that any Inuit could read the language. Jenness reports that in Labrador as early as 1884 "all Eskimos along the Atlantic coast . . . could read and write their own language, and some . . . could speak a little English."[23] Somewhat later, the situation was similar in southern Baffin Island. Pitseolak writes: "Annie Keemilu had been in the white man's land; that was why everyone thought she understood the language. She was just like us; she could not understand."[24] Fleming, noting that early in the twentieth century "I myself had a library of over 200 volumes at Lake Harbour" never mentions Inuit who are literate in English.[25]

Missionaries in the Baffin region found themselves in a double-bind. While Christianity was advancing, general acculturation was not. Inuit were dependent upon missionaries for reading material. As it became clear that syllabic script was an ineffective method to accomplish broader change, the missionaries considered it a short-term investment and disregarded translating secular material into Inuttitut.

Concurring with the missionaries, new change agents did not popularize syllabic script. In 1931, the Hudson's Bay Company published probably the first secular book in Inuttitut: *The Eskimo Book of Knowledge,* and the Canadian government published *The Book of Wisdom for the Eskimo* and *Q–Book* in the post World War II period. Including these three straightforward attempts to accomplish the acculturation that did not occur through literacy, fewer than a dozen books were printed in Inuttitut prior to 1972.[26] Significant agency use of syllabics to communicate with Inuit began in the last decade.

Because communication between Inuit and Euro-Canadians could not proceed in English and did not proceed in Inuttitut, the general Inuit community was effectively removed from control as change agency brought bureaucratic hierarchy to the North. Inuit were neither allowed nor able to adapt their institutions to Euro-Canadian agency. Generalized authority remained the domain of change agents and they continued to select Inuit contact agents to direct it.

As syllabic script became dysfunctional for broad communication and acculturation, however, it was reinforced as a necessary Christian instrument.

> It was unfortunate that the first missionary to settle in the Eastern Arctic, the Rev. E. J. Peck, printed his hymns and prayers in the syllabic script . . . and taught the system of writing to the Eskimos of northern Labrador and southern Baffin Island. It left the rival missions subsequently established by the Roman Catholic church no alternative but to use the same system, and thereby entrench it among all Eskimo communities from King William Island to Hudson Strait and James Bay.[27]

Before missionaries reclaimed authority through control of print, social position in the Inuit community began to transfer to those who had access to literacy.

INTERACTION

Inuit interest and incentive diffused literacy and it spread ahead of the missionary presence. The status it conferred upon those who became literate lead to reoccurring periods of religious fanatacism which Pitseolak calls "religious times." The first "religious time" in southern Baffin took place in 1901, eight years before the mission was established at Lake Harbour, but after "the people had seen Okhamuk (Rev. Peck) and a few—only a few for at this time they were just starting to learn syllabic—had learned to read the Bible."[28]

Read individually, religious material was obviously not subject to the social control of personal contact and group interpretation. As Pitseolak noted in the initial stage of literacy, those who had access to the mode of communication became self-designated leaders:

> Simigak was the chief in the Etidliajuk area . . . and he was in charge. But when they gathered in the big new church, Simigak's cousin, Keegak, was outdoing everybody with the ceremony. In that church the leadership passed to Keegak—'the messenger,' that was the meaning of his name. He became the leader because he strongly believed that Simigak has seen Jesus. He thought of a Keegak as a person who was looking after all the people like a God. Keegak was the God in the first religious time. . . . Martha and Keegak had never been powerful but all of a sudden power was waiting for them. . . . Keegak was just like a white man—bossing everybody—he was a big boss now and has a white man's jacket made out of sealskin.[29]

As literacy threatened angakok leadership, the missionaries entered southern Baffin and displaced shamen through contact agency. To the whalers, Christianity was obviously not a criterion to select men who, either themselves or through the camps they influenced, could provide required services. Since such men were often angakok, the spiritual dimension of their authority made them totally unacceptable as missionary contact agents. In Fleming's perception, "An anagakok has nearly always attained his position by the force of character and his ability to control the people . . . in the 'teacher' who sets forth a different way of life he recognizes a rival if not a foe."[30]

Fleming's description of an early encounter with Pit-soo-lak illustrates the early role of the angakok leader and his exclusion from the missionary change agency:

> A man named Pit-soo-lak, a powerful angakok or conjurer, had been for some years the boss man for Captain Murray for the Whaler *Active*. Pit-soo-lak was, of course, a pagan and was without doubt the most influential hunter in the region. He now came to us and proposed that he and his family should have their dwelling near the mission house and that he would see to it that the people brought us all the fresh meat that we required. Then there would be no need for us to leave the station to visit the villages, he said.
> To his surprise we politely but quite definitely declined the offer. But Pit-soo-lak was not easily defeated. He had set his heart on this scheme so he went on to explain that on board the whaler he was the captain's voice. The captain told him what he wanted and he, Pit-soo-lak then arranged for the Eskimo to carry out the captain's commands. He explained that he would act in the same way for us, which would be best for everybody.[31]

Pit-soo-lak, like many shamen, used techniques to communicate with supernatural spirits aimed at "manipulating the social life of his people" and, as a shaman, his relationship to the group was maintained "in terms of his attempts to control a) environmental threats endangering the group; b) individual or group crises; c) interpersonal relations; and d) his own prestige among his people."[32] It was his communication with supernatural powers and his constituency that upheld his authority and maintained group cohesion.

As print stabilized missionary authority, the angakok became increasingly powerless, isolated, and suspect. Pitseolak writes: "Before I was born there were so many shamans—Okhamuk (Rev. Peck) had told them to repent—but they were still sneaking around behind his back."[33]

Shamanism was a generalized traditional value: "The entire Eskimo community is educated and geared to Shamandom. However, not every adult may be regarded as a full and actual Shaman. To be a Shaman, it is necessary that a person be able to perform in public."[34]

As the angakoks shifted from a dominant to marginal social position, communication with them and the spirits they mediated became illicit. Distrust and suspicion were reflected in wider community relationships. Carpenter notes that, among the Aivilik, "a general loss of faith in the magician's tools led to their discard. By 1950 magic was almost completely a thing of the past, a memory. Yet witch-fear was everywhere," causing "a great insecurity in interpersonal relations."[35]

Within this set, missionaries designated lay readers or catechists as Christian contact agents. With the new criterion, young men might be chosen without regard for hunting skills, healing powers, or family relationships. And, as Inuit became functionally literate within a religious context, the role of contact agent expanded. Working through literacy, the missionaries—more than the whalers before them or the traders after them—transferred their authority to these "Christian bosses." Lake Harbour illustrates the effectiveness of this transfer. Although Lake Harbour was without a European missionary between 1915 and 1920, Christianity flourished.

As the first permanent change agents in southern Baffin, missionary presence encouraged settlement development. The Hudson's Bay Company established a post in 1911. Phillips summarizes the leadership shift which, through whaling bosses, Christian bosses and, in the trading period, camp bosses, introduced a new pluralism in Inuit society:

> Another change was the institution of camp boss. Eskimo society had chosen its own leaders generally on the basis of skill in the hunt, though other considerations such as age, entered into the selection. The leader's power was tempered by much collective decision-making. The white man, however, wanted to deal with a single person, not necessarily the man who would be chosen by Eskimo standards. The new camp boss had to be amenable to the white man's needs, and quick to pick up some English. The reflected white light would ensure his position among the Eskimos. He was instrumental in eroding or eliminating the process of local decision-making, except on those matters well outside the white man's interest.[36]

The role of contact agent led to new activities and functions that demanded new skills: interaction skills. As these were acquired, used and diffused through families, access to authority created distinguishable sets of Inuit.

The missionary period introduced a rudimentary distinction between those Brody refers to as Inummariit—"the real Eskimos"—who "lived in camps, close to the land" and who were self-reliant and interrelated, and the Inuit who lived in or near white settlements.[37] Those Brody calls Inummariit, Vallee refers to as the Nunamiut or "the people of the land" and, in his Baker Lake study, Vallee found they could easily be distinguished from the Kabloonamiut—the "people of the whites"— who had adopted more Euro-Canadian language and custom through their association with change agents.[38] As additional change agencies joined the missionaries in southern Baffin, conflicting authority figures became absorbed in a pluralism which recognized those who were contact agents and those who were not.

This paper cannot detail the spiraling process of agency. Subsequent Euro-Canadians were interested in commerce, sovereignty, and services, so mandates and immediate goals were adapted. Sharing cultural orientation based on literacy and the generalized motive to sustain and control Inuit interaction became a model for change agency in southern Baffin. Introduction of syllabics as the form of literacy placed the Inuit in a position of undefined and unstable cultural disorientation.

IN RETROSPECT

From the perspective of communication, contact in southern Baffin Island reflects increasing Euro-Canadian control through authoritative interaction and media which shifted Inuit social organization. In the missionary period, conflicting cultural orientation emerged within the Inuit community. Print reinforced by contact agency effectively broke Inuit continuity in time, which was critical to traditional cultural orientation. Literacy brought knowledge monopoly and Christianity replaced shamanism and became, as Brody pointed out, the "traditional" widely regarded "as an important aspect of things that are essentially Eskimo."[39]

Religion, characteristic of a time-binding culture, was associated with a space-binding medium. However, syllabic literacy did not extend in space much beyond the Baffin region or religious texts. As it localized cultural orientation, the process of secularization associated with literacy was redirected; syllabics, too, became "traditional."

The mode of communication did not allow adaptive social development to space-oriented culture. Because literacy did not transfer to the English language, access to authority continued to define social status. The mode of communication conferred additional status on "traditional" people, and two distinguishable sets emerged within the Inuit community.

Losing the cultural orientation based on relationships solidified in time, and the Inuit lost their identification with the past. History became what was written; the post-contact became "traditional." And since little secularization occurred, little was written: no historical documents, no community policies, no precedents in law, no educational materials. Euro-Canadian control generalized as it solidified. European literacy goes back generations; the first unassisted autobiography of an Inuk from southern Baffin was published in 1975. Given access to the medium, Euro-Canadian definitions of Inuit identity, history, and traditional lifestyle differ from those held by Inuit. Inuit were placed in a certain cultural limbo. As Euro-Canadian authority made it different for them to understand or accept their cultural change, Euro-Canadian control made it impossible for them to adapt to it.

REFLECTIONS ON THE PRESENT

This short chapter cannot consider the complex process by which electronic modes of communication entered southern Baffin Island. It is important to note, however, that a brief overview indicates a similar pattern and, as a result, there is continuing Inuit cultural disorientation.

As empire expanded in space, broadcast radio reached the North on a relatively consistent basis by the 1930s. Agency activities increased in the post-war period and, in 1958, the CBC formed its Northern Service section.

Since 1960, Northern development in Baffin has increased in pace and quantity. Inuit communities have been drawn into settlements through expanded change agency. In 1967, television programing reached the first seventeen communities in the Western Arctic through delayed transmission of video tapes in four-hour packages. The service extended to one Eastern Arctic community in 1972: Frobisher Bay. The following year, the Anik satellite program introduced broadcast television to the North. Southern Baffin, Frobisher Bay, Pangiritung, and Cape Dorset currently receive broadcast television and direct telephone service; Lake Harbour does not.

As electronic media expanded to serve change agency, Euro-Canadians maintained control. The first Inuttitut radio broadcast occurred in 1960. By May 1972, just over sixteen per cent of CBC Northern Service short wave programs were broadcast in the Inuit language.[40] AM broadcasts from Frobisher Bay have extended Inuit access, but television service carries only one hour of Inuttitut programing weekly. Given this context, electronic media have not removed the barriers to Inuit spatial adaptation. Without significant access to and control of media, Inuit communities have additional pressure from Euro-Canadian education.

NOTES

[1]Duffy, Dennis. *Marshall McLuhan*. Toronto, McClelland and Stewart, 1969, p. 15.

[2]Carey, James W. "Canadian Communications Theory: Extensions and Interpretations of Harold Innis." In G. Robinson and D. Theall (Eds.). *Studies in Communication*. Montreal, McGill University, 1975, p. 49.

[3]Innis, H. A. *The Bias of Communication*. Toronto, University of Toronto Press, 1951, p. 141.

[4]See also Brody, Hugh. *The People's Land: Eskimos and Whites in the Eastern Arctic*. Harmondsworth, England, Penguin, 1975.

[5]Ross, W. Gillies. "Whaling and Eskimos: Hudson Bay 1860–1915." *Ethnology*, No. 10. Ottawa, National Museums of Canada, 1975, p. 60.

[6]Fleming, Archibald L. *Archibald the Arctic*. New York, Appleton–Century–Crofts, 1956, p. 75.

[7]Crowe, Keith. *A History of the Original Peoples of Northern Canada*. Montreal, Arctic Institute of North America and McGill–Queen's University Press, 1974, p. 124.

[8]Fleming, *Archibald*, p. 263.

[9]Stevens, Michael E. "Catholic and Protestant Missionaries Among Wisconsin Indians: The Territorial Period." *Wisconsin Magazine of History* 58:2. Madison, The Historical Society of Wisconsin, Winter 1974–75, p. 145.

[10]Berkhofer, Robert F. *Salvation and Savage: An Analysis of Protestant Mission and American Indian Response 1787–1862*. Lexington, University of Kentucky Press, 1965, p. 4.

[11]Fleming, *Archibald*, pp. 53–54.

[12]Pitseolak, Peter. *People From Our Side*. (Dorothy Eben.) Edmonton, Hurtig, 1975, p. 40.

[13]Fleming, *Archibald*, p. 70.

[14]Stefansson, Vilhajmur. *The Three Voyages of Martin Frobisher* (1913) (two volumes). London, Argonaut, 1913, p. 410.

[15]Fleming, *Archibald*, p. 176.

[16]Graburn, Nelson H. H. *Eskimos Without Igloos*. Boston, Little Brown, 1969, p. 204.

[17]Jenness, Diamond. *Eskimo Administration; III Labrador*. Montreal, Arctic Institute of North America Technical Paper No. 16, 1965, p. 179.

[18]Jenness, Diamond. *Eskimo Administration; II Canada*. Montreal, Arctic Institute of North America Technical Paper No. 14, 1964, p. 16.

[19]Ray, Dorothy J. "The Bible in Picture Writing." *The Beaver*, Winnipeg, Hudson's Bay Company, 1975, pp. 20–24.

[20]Jenness, *Eskimo Administration*, No. 14, p. 121.

[21]Berkhofer, *Salvation*, p. 7.

[22]Berkhofer, *Salvation*, p. 6.

[23]Jenness, *Eskimo Administration*, No. 16, p. 39.

[24]Pitseolak, *People*, p. 86

[25]Fleming, *Archibald*, p. 358.

[26]Mayes, Robert G. "Mass Communication and Canada's Eskimos." *Polar Record*, Vol. 16, No. 104, 1973, p. 683.

[27]Jenness, *Eskimo Administration*, No. 14, p. 121.

[28]Pitseolak, *People*, p. 43.

[29]Pitseolak, *People*, pp. 40–43.

[30]Fleming, *Archibald*, p. 75.

[31]Fleming, *Archibald*, pp. 74–75.

[32]Balicki, Asen. *The Netsilik Eskimo*. Garden City, N. Y., The Natural History Press, 1970, p. 229.

[33]Pitseolak, *People*, pp. 27–29.

[34]Frederiksen, Svend. "Some Preliminaries on the Soul Complex in Eskimo Shamanistic Belief." In Victor F. Valentine and Frank G. Valle (Eds.). *Eskimo of the Canadian Arctic*. Toronto, McClelland and Stewart, 1968, p. 51.

[35]Carpenter, Edmund. "Witch Fear Among the Aivilik Eskimos." In Victor F. Valentine and Frank G. Valle (Eds.). *Eskimo of the Canadian Arctic.* Toronto, McClelland and Stewart, 1968, pp. 56–67.

[36]Phillips, R. A. J. *Canada's North.* Toronto, Macmillan, 1967, pp. 79–80.

[37]Brody, Hugh. *The People's Land: Eskimos and Whites in the Eastern Arctic.* Harmondsworth, England, Penguin, 1975, p. 125.

[38]Valle, Frank G. *Kabloona and Eskimo in the Central Keewatin.* Ottawa, St. Paul University, 1967, p. 140.

[39]Brody, *The People's Land,* p. 139.

[40]Mayes, "Mass Communication," p. 93.

16

EXPLORATION IN COMMUNICATIONS SINCE INNIS

DONALD F. THEALL
McGill University

The title of this paper almost seems to invite a discussion of the relation of Harold Innis to Marshall McLuhan, since McLuhan is the most visible figure in the study of communications who has consistently praised Innis' brilliance. The possible conclusion of such a discussion might be that Innis is the "spiritual" father of the Center of Culture and Technology at the University of Toronto. The McLuhan–Innis relationship has been extensively commented on by many scholars in Canada as well as elsewhere and I have even written, somewhat more negatively than most, on the direct influence of Innis on McLuhan in *The Medium is the Rear View Mirror*.[1] In fact, as I have argued further in an article on Canadian communication theory, it is most likely that Innis and McLuhan shared similar interests because they shared a similar milieu. One of the prime characteristics of that milieu was a kind of marginality to the mainstream of North American influence today—the United States.[2]

Although the relation between McLuhan and Innis might conceal some important potentialities in the legacy of Innis, this is less of a fear today than it was ten years ago. Rather, the situation now is such that some of Innis' major challenges for future communication studies may be overlooked in the process of separating his later work from the ways in which McLuhan discussed it. Although it is important to keep in mind that McLuhan and Innis diverge sharply when Innis' critical quality and his social consciousness are stressed, many of the important challenges in Innis' work have some relation to those areas of McLuhan's work that are still of interest to communication theory.[3] Both share a common bias about how to write a history of communications; both manifest an interest in the classical tradition and its significance to the human sciences; both relate communication to a concept of culture as a value-oriented term; both view modes of communication as formative processes in the growth of knowledge and the structures of feeling in a culture; both would insist on a major esthetic factor being involved in the development of communication theory; both had a profound distrust of what mechanization was doing to the contemporary world; and both finally wrote history or theory with a sense of irony and the comic perspective.

It ought to be remembered that Innis can be profoundly ironic about the writing he is doing in the later works. The epigraph for *The Bias of Communication* is taken from Hegel's *Philosophy of Right*. The full text of that citation, however, has not been compared with Innis' possible attitude toward his work:

> One word about giving instruction as to what the world ought to be. Philosophy in any case always comes on the scene too late to give it. As the thought of the world, it appears only when actuality is already there cut and dried, after its process of formation has been completed. The teaching of the concept, which is also history's inescapable lesson, is that it is only when actuality is mature that the ideal first appears over against the real and that the ideal apprehends this same real world in its substance and builds it up for itself into the shape of an intellectual realm. When philosophy paints its grey in grey, then has a shape of life grown old. By philosophy's grey in grey it cannot be rejuvinated but only understood. The owl of Minerva spreads its wings only with the falling of dusk.[4]

Innis' ironic reflection on his own activity, which he indicates by the selection of such a title, is connected with an important principle that he developed in the history of communication—the application of what Kenneth Burke called "perspective by incongruity."

McLuhan comments on the "humor" which characterizes the "flavor of Inniscence." Such humor is "of the essence of his aphoristic association of incongruities." Thus, Innis' writing of history is associated with a major characteristic of modernism—the use of devices such as juxtaposition of forms as a technique of discovery that naturally results in "dramatic surprise."[5] That Innis himself recognized some of these issues is reflected in the annotations he prepared for a later edition of *Empire and Civilization*. In those notes he associates the comic spirit with Athenian democracy and he relates the oral tradition to multilayered presentations: "Oral tradition permits painters on vases to attempt to show several scenes at once, but written tradition compels a concern with time and painters use scenes with fixed space and time."[6] Consequently, Innis was interested in pursuing what McLuhan would later call the "mosaic" approach because he sought a form of discourse that could be validated in a conversational encounter between individuals, which would at the same time balance the demands of space and time. His interest in Wyndham Lewis' argument that the spatiality of modernism resulted in the predominance of a time-denying mind exemplified by Bergson's concern with the present moment led him to the point of lamenting the mechanization of learning. Addressing the Conference of Commonwealth Universities at Oxford, Innis observed:

> Mechanization has emphasized complexity and confusion; it has been responsible for monopolies in the field of knowledge; and it becomes extremely important to any civilization if it is not to succumb to the influence of this monopoly of knowledge to make some critical survey and report. The conditions of freedom of thought are in danger of being destroyed by science, technology and the mechanization of knowledge and with them Western civilization.[7]

These new monopolies of knowledge were focused in economic institutions such as the textbook publishers who Innis so rightly feared. Their subsequent mushrooming into the multinational, multimedia publishing and communication conglomerates only further intensifies Innis' position that: "Literature and other fields of scholarship have become feudalized in a modern manorial system. Monopolies of knowledge have been built by publishing firms to some extent in cooperation with universities and exploited in textbooks."[8] Perhaps somewhat naively Innis admired the university as an institution, and therefore could still lament that "The relative adaptability of various subjects to mechanical transmission has threatened to destroy the unity of the university."[9] In the process Innis also recognized the profound gaps that were made visible as a result of this process—gaps which his own "mosaic" approach of exploring history made more evident.

His opposition to the mechanization of learning and the monopolies of knowledge were supported by his bias towards the oral tradition "especially as reflected in Greek civilization."[10] The oral tradition constituted for Innis a dialectical corrective to a preoccupation with writing and the mechanization of knowledge—a corrective that meant to reassert an interest in form, a condition of mutual respect for time and space, oral and written, unity and disunity. The "mosaic" method was meant to deal with the contemporary problem of the segmentation of the sensory experience of man. This is a position for which Innis found support in Wyndham Lewis' *Time and Western Man*:

> The separation and separate treatment of the senses of sight and touch have produced both subjective disunity and external disunity. We must somehow escape on one hand from our obsession with the moment and on the other from our obsession with history.[11]

McLuhan, at least according to his own statements, certainly did not do this, for his work lauded the new age of tactility in which he thought the book would die. He left no place for the merging of the written tradition and visual perspective with the new potentialities of multimedia communication. Innis, on the other hand, insisted on a concept of balance in which his "mosaic" style played a significant role, just as his decision to write the history of communications as a critique of economic history—in fact, of the practice of history as he understood it—played an even more major role.

Innis' style is different from McLuhan's because it is associated with a fundamentally different methodology. Innis is genuinely trying to find a strategy for allowing a multiplicity of levels of discourse to interact with one another while simultaneously presenting an argument which is not "linear" but is rationally defensible. In other words, he tries to retain the flexibility suggestivity that he associated with the oral mode in a printed book. The purpose behind his strategy in writing is to attempt to keep copresent in the reader's mind the interrelation he sees between the various discontinuous and disjointed bits of historical information. Consequently, political, economic, cultural, and intellectual aspects are blended within the consideration of the history of communication.

Innis was inconsistent and contradictory when it came to facing the problem of contemporary disunity, for like many of his generation he was committed to an ideal of a unified sensibility. Yet that very fact led him to recognize and grapple with the facts of disunity and segmentation in the interests of which he developed his particular mode of presentation. For him it provided a way of dealing with a problem that obsessed him, a problem that reflected this disunity. The mechanization of knowledge was rapidly producing an overload of information which Innis, presumably following Graham Wallas, argued was effectively stultifying human thought:

> He [Wallas] pointed to the danger that knowledge was growing too vast for successful use in social judgment since life is short and sympathies and the intellect are limited. . . . He assumed that creative thought was dependent on the oral tradition and that conditions favourable to it were gradually disappearing with the increasing mechanization of knowledge. . . . The quantitative pressure of modern knowledge has been responsible for the decay of oral dialectic and conversation.[12]

Innis' attempt to reconstruct the conditions of oral dialectic and conversation led him to become interested in a method for writing the history of communication as a means of relating contemporary knowledge to people's capability to make social judgments. This raises the problem of disunity to a critical point. If there is a genuine disunity present within the contemporary world, is it possible to make genuine social judgments from some totally unified perspective? Innis' mosaic style provides him with a way of controlling the qualitative complexity of modern knowledge as a basis for social judgment in the absence of a totally unified perspective which he sought. Unfortunately he died before being able to question successfully the basic contradiction between the disunity that he recognized in the world around him and his own relatively un-questioned conviction that there had to be a return to a unified culture such as that of the Greek city states. In the process, he introduced into communication studies the problem of discontinuity and disjunction in the process of writing a history of how men communicated and how that interacted with their sociopolitical and economic situations. If we are convinced that Innis does not fully escape from a determinism because of his obsession with media as such, then there remains the challenge to write a history of communications which is itself a critique of history as it has been written and a history freed from the false unities and totalities that are usually imposed on historical writing. Or as Innis puts it, there is a need to escape the "obsession" with history, just as there is a need to escape our "obsession with the moment." Although Innis' own obsession with mechanization, like that of Mumford, Giedion, and McLuhan, may be an "obsession" of the moment, there remains the further challenge of exploring how mechanization in communications can continue to be offset by allowing people the potentialities of those transverse forms of communication on which not only social judgment but also human sanity are based.

His own style developed in a series of unquestioned commitments to balance and harmony. The varying periods of his prose forms derived from the British tradition of the essay as a weighing of the contents of the mind in action. This strategic method allows the author to explore the conflicts and reconciliations between the demands of space and time, of writing and print, of monopolistic control and the freeplay of thought. One of McLuhan's better insights was to take Innis' style seri-ously. McLuhan realized that Innis believed what he said when he ar-gued that it was necessary to work against the mechanical tendencies implicit in the form of the book. Innis' style is awkward and complex unless approached as an attempt to achieve the effects of oral discourse in writing. Leaving aside the problem of balance and harmony for the moment, this style of Innis' raises the problem of how to communicate about communication since the process of communication cuts across a wide variety of fields or disciplines. The examination of discourse in France by such writers as Michel Foucault and Gilles Deleuze[13] has just begun to raise many of the problems of discourse that were implicit in Innis' shift from economic history to the history of communication and in his development of a style designed to record discontinuities. The questions implicit in Innis' work concerning historical discourse raise significant questions for future communication studies in North America, providing that discussion is related to the socioeconomic con-test and the biological, social, and psychological aspects of the nature of human communication. Innis' analysis never suggested that all the prob-lems he raised would somehow be solved if the mechanization of knowledge were eliminated, for he realized only change in the actual conditions of producing and communicating knowledge could bring about a restoration of dialogue and debate adapted to a new set of conditions of everyday life. Finally, he located the problems of producing and communicating knowledge in relation to the problem of power and control, which was reflected in his analysis of what he called monopolies of knowledge.

The development of culture is essential as an antidote to this power and control, according to Innis. Culture as a theme introduces both of his major studies of the late 1940s—*Empire and Communication* and *The Bias of Communications*. Culture, as Innis conceived it, was a positive force, which involved what he took to be the sense of balance and harmony and an understanding of how to use the past. Like social judgment, it was a value concept and not merely a descriptive concept. Although he was familiar with such writers as Weber, Veblen, Kroeber, G. H. Mead, Mosca, Pareto, Sorokin, Spengler, and Toynbee, his particular development of the concept of culture is most indebted to his understanding of the classical tradition and to the writings of John Dewey, George Herbert Mead, and Ernest Cassirer.[14]

Fundamentally, though, Innis' concept of culture is closely tied to the concepts of community and communication. The first of these, as we have seen, he roots in the regional democracy of the Greek City States and ties to the oral dialectic and the conversational mode of interaction. Dewey also shared a view of culture that depended on this type of regional democracy that was related to the communal and that insisted on the simultaneous interaction of a large variety of factors within the social structure. Innis is writing around the same time that Raymond Williams wrote *Culture and Society*. Like Williams, he attempts to reconcile some of the literary and aesthetics aspects of the concept of culture with the importance that culture has in the formation of communities through the processes of communication. But Innis develops his concept of culture directly from classical scholars rather than through the British debates concerning culture, which developed between 1750–1950. One writer most influential to certain key aspects of Innis' treatment of culture was his former Toronto colleague, the classicist, Eric Havelock. He is not the only classicist who influenced Innis, but he is the one specifically mentioned in the Preface to one of Innis' later books. Havelock's discussion of *Prometheus Bound* in *The Crucifixion of Intellectual Man*, according to Innis' reading, is concerned with exactly the same arguments about power and its corrupting influence as Innis himself is:

> Intellectual man of the nineteenth century was the first to estimate absolute nullity in time. The present—real, insistent, complex and treated as an independent system, the foreshortening of practical prevision in the field of human action, has penetrated the most vulnerable areas of public policy. War

> has become the result, and a cause, of the limitations placed on the forethinker. Power and its assistant, force, the natural enemies of intelligence, have become more serious as the mental processes activated in pursuit and consolidating of power are essentially short range.[15]

Innis saw classical concepts of *urbanitas* and *humanitas* as the principle that would shape a culture, that would prevent the ascendancy of power and force by counteracting them with a sense of community and the sensitivity formed from undistorted communication. This, then, is the next challenge that Innis has left for students of communication: the exploration of a more adequate concept of culture than he himself was able to develop. Probably the most integrated statement he made concerning these matters was in "A Critical Review," a paper he presented to the Conference of Commonwealth Universities. He described his method as being related to Marx, a Marxian interpretation of Marx which stopped short of pushing "the Marxian conclusion to its ultimate limit."[16] In this he paralleled Raymond Williams, whose analyses of base and superstructure led him to the position that cultural studies are an essential aspect of Marxian analysis.

Therefore, it is important to examine those points that Innis actually raises with respect to culture. His initial essay in his final collection of essays, *Changing Concepts of Time*, is entitled "The Strategy of Culture," which is an analysis of the Massey report and its recognition of the cultural problems in U.S.–Canadian relations. The title essay of *The Bias of Communications* begins with a reference to Kroeber's *Configuration of Culture* and the first essay in that collection is entitled "Minerva's Owl," which, as well a referring to Hegel's *Philosophy of Right*, as we have seen, refers more obliquely to the Hegelian philosophy of history with its respect for Greek culture. Culture, therefore, is not an anthropological concept for Innis, but a description of a certain critical sense and a certain set of values that he located in ancient Greece. There culture was closely tied to the oral tradition and its liberating activity:

> It is suggested that all written works, including this one, have dangerous implications to the vitality of an oral tradition and to the health of a civilization, particularly if they thwart the interest of a people in culture and following Aristotle, the cathartic effects of culture. 'It is written but I say unto you' is a powerful directive to Western civilization.[17]

Innis here sees culture as an active principle associated with the purging of the social body, even if elsewhere he treats it in a more sociological manner. The strategy of culture, though, is obviously linked to a consciousness of cultural forms and the ability to employ that consciousness in the making of social judgements:

> Culture . . . is designed to train the individual to decide how much information he needs and how little he needs, to give him a sense of balance and proportion, and to protect him from the fanatic who tells him that Canada

> will be lost to the Russians unless he knows more geography or more history or more economics or more science. Culture is concerned with the capacity of individuals to appraise problems in terms of space and time enabling him to take the proper steps at the right time. It is at this point that the tragedy of modern culture has arisen as inventions in commercialism have destroyed a sense of time.[18]

What Innis calls culture subordinates ideologies and political institutions to constant criticism.[19] There is a limited kind of optimism implicit in the possibilities of such a critical stance. Innis never was able to complete his theory of culture and communication but he appears to have been grasping for a concept of culture as a constitutive social process, creating specific yet different "ways of life." He provided still greater depth for such a concept through an emphasis on material social processes. Communication provided a way of linking the material social processes and the creation of specific and different ways of life in that it itself was rooted in language, the human communication system par excellence. Consequently, Innis' concern with communication is dialectically grounded in the material relations of communication and the symbolic forms of communication, beginning with stone and hieroglyphics.

Innis' culture linked to humanism and involved an ethics subordinated to intellectual qualities, for he interpreted Werner Jaeger as indicating that: "Humanism subordinated technical efficiency to culture and distinguished between technical knowledge and power and true culture."[20] Therefore, Innis' concern with the question of the developing mechanization of knowledge and with the culture industries is tied to the challenging of technical knowledge and technical efficiency in the interests of culture. Innis never abandoned a concern with the material social processes, but he did come to see the equal importance of cultural form, and even as his readings show, of the socioesthetic dimensions involved in the understanding of the problem of human communication. Prometheus has been mentioned before, but it is highly significant that Innis selected an interpretation of a dramatic text as a powerful development of his general argument—an argument embracing the military implications, the propagandistic designs, and the subtle legal and constitutional challenges implicit in the United States as an empire. In the dialectic of insight and power Innis developed, culture is finally the process of the forethinker in the activity of criticizing the technical power, which it is possible for him to develop.

Innis implicitly evolved a dramatic method for examining the relation of the material social processes to the cultural activity, realizing the inherent dramatic basis of the oral dialectical processes. This enables him to see the historical connectedness of cultural form and esthetic form—to realize the centrality of literary, dramatic, and rhetorical knowledge in the understanding of the symbolic processes that are

mediated by the processes of communication. In this sense, as misleading as his development of Innis may have been, it is significant and
important that McLuhan was the medium of his introduction into communication studies and into humanistic and cultural studies, for McLuhan at least appreciated the central role that a critical understanding of
the cultural process had for Innis.

This discussion has tried to raise certain aspects of Innis' work that
still require exploration by students of communication. His method of
writing a history of communication, his theory of style, his search for a
critical concept related to "true culture" and his appreciation of the
dramatic and socioesthetic aspects of communication raise specific questions requiring further discussion. In closing, I want to return briefly to
a previous point I made about Innis' style. Like a Renaissance Senecan
essayist, he probes, and like a Baconian he tries to render forth the
critical processes of his mind in the act of thinking. He uses literary form
to embrace complexity in such a way as to value insight and to avoid
transforming knowledge into power over others. That openness reflected in his style deserves to be stressed, for the worst perversion of
Innis might well be to attempt premature closure of his own openness.
At least there McLuhan appreciated him and transmitted that appreciation to others. An example of that openness is Innis' own ability to
sustain the problem of not having indicated how an oral tradition could
be sustained in the contemporary world. It is McLuhan who misleads
when he makes Innis the basis for saying the electronic age will lead us
back to an orally based tribalism. Innis clearly indicates instead that it is a
dialectical problem for cultural studies, which have to criticize the place
in international society today of the super-writing of the electronic
world, for even the transmission of film or television to a passive audience is closer to an extention of the written tradition rather than the oral.
McLuhan, intuitively the greatest respecter of Innis' genius, ironically
became the instrument for turning Innis upside down.

NOTES

[1]Theall, D. F. *The Medium is the Rear View Mirror: Understanding McLuhan.*
Montreal, McGill–Queen's, 1971.

[2]Theall, D. F. "Communication Theory and the Marginal Culture: The
Socio-aesthetic Dimension of Communication Theory." In *Studies in Canadian Communica-
tions.* G. J. Robinson and D. F. Theall (Eds.). Montreal, Programme in Communications,
McGill, 1975, pp. 6–25.

[3]I have outlined these in an address to the International Communications
Association, Berlin, May 1977, which is to be published next year.

[4]Hegel, *Philosphy of Right* (translated by T. W. Knox). Oxford, Oxford University Press, 1942, p. 13.

[5]McLuhan, H. M. "Introduction" to Innis, H. A. *The Bias of Communications*. Toronto, University of Toronto Press, 1951, p. xiv.

[6]Innis, H. A. *Empire and Communications* (1950). Toronto, University of Toronto Press, 1972, p. 69.

[7]Innis, *The Bias of Communications*, p. 190.

[8]Innis, *Empire and Communications*, p. 163.

[9]Innis, *The Bias of Communications*, p. 84.

[10]See especially chapter on Greece in Innis, *Empire and Communications*.

[11]Innis, *The Bias of Communications*, p. 90.

[12]Innis, *The Bias of Communications*, p. 191.

[13]Deleuze, Gilles, *Anti-Oedipus* (Viking, 1977); Foucault, Michel, *The Archeology of Knowledge* (Tavistock, 1972).

[14]Innis, *Empire and Communications*, pp. xiii, 3 and passim.

[15]Innis, H. A. *Changing Concepts of Time*. Toronto, University of Toronto Press, 1952, pp. v–vi.

[16]Innis, *The Bias of Communications*, p. 190.

[17]Innis, *Empire and Communications*, p. xiii.

[18]Innis, *The Bias of Communications*, p. 85.

[19]Innis, *The Bias of Communications*, p. 195.

[20]Innis, *Empire and Communications*, p. 83.

17

HAROLD INNIS
AND THE MODERN PERSPECTIVE
OF COMMUNICATIONS

DAVID CROWLEY
McGill University

The death of a scholar, especially one whose work carried a quality of mystery about it, invariably leaves a scholarly cottage industry in his aftermath. Harold Adams Innis, perhaps because he tackled both the subject matter of political economy and that of communications sequentially in his lifetime, left the major puzzle of their interrelationship as well. For the most part it was the thesis of political economy that profited from this circumstance. Innis' infatuation with communications, it has been said, could be accounted for in one of two ways. By those who knew him well, communications was seen as an eccentric, if profound and incomplete, indulgence of his later years. Others, largely political economists, allowed that there was indeed a connection between his concern for political economy and communications and that connection was political economy.

Recently, however, new interest has surfaced over the significance of Innis' turn toward communications, especially its wider implications. In fact, given his consistent search for nothing less than a corrective to the state of social scholarship in North America, the thesis on communications may well be worth considering, less for its marginal status than for its contribution to understanding some central quandaries of modern social thought. I would like to raise three themes in contemporary communications thinking by way of example.

THE COMMUNICATION THEORY OF HISTORY

The basic ideas Innis worked with are accessible enough. The usual point of departure for disciple and critic alike is his thesis that history could be perceived as a series of epochs radically differentiated from each other by biases. These biases, in turn, are characteristic of internal antagonisms that are both system-maintained and system-maintaining. It is the interplay of such biases that constrain and transform the nature of organization and action. At differing levels of analysis, Innis has described these relationships in terms of knowledge monopolies, historical empires, and competing forms of social and cultural order. Within particular epochs, certain biases prevail and these dominant biases function to direct and provide limits on social relations and on what therefore count as legitimate forms of thought, expression and practice within their conceptual domains. It was Innis' claim that overall biases characteristic of each epoch could be identified materially in terms of the dominant forms, or media, of communication employed. What was to be demonstrated by such preferential media of communication was not so much the causal nexus of change as the way in which holistically distinct realities arose out of former ones. The task he set for the historian was the mapping out of these epochs in terms of the conditions and consequences attending the shift from one form of communication to another.[1]

It was in two such epochs, those of classical Greece and Byzantium, that Innis claimed to have found evidence for the necessary equilibria of communication biases in the maintenance of a flexible and durable social order. Classical Greece he found close to the ideal. In his characterization of that society, the opposing tendencies of oral and written traditions in thought and action constituted a relationship of complementarity, where the hierarchy of organized life in the polis nonetheless continued to depend upon intersubjective modes of interaction and direct discursive forms of reason. Byzantium, by contrast, achieved a less ideal but equivalent balance through a manageable tension between decentralist features of the church and centralizing forces of the state bureaucracy. Caesaropapism maintained in Byzantium a benign symmetry, a relationship in which the media preferences of the church for parchment and the state for papyrus underwrote these opposing tendencies, but not their escalation.[2]

In subsequent epochs bridging the empires of both Rome and Charlemagne, the opposing tendencies of church and state deepened into profound antagonisms. Important new uses of paper identified functionally an emerging institutional hegemony where interpersonal affinities became increasingly open to expression in terms of administration and law. This period, which gunpowder ushered in and which was, in turn, ushered out by the printing press, contained for Innis the most potent transformation in Western culture. It demarcates that period of struggle between a dominant religious order characterized by temporal stresses on ritual and memory and an emergent secular order with its desire to base society on the control of history rather than on its remembrance. Science rather than metaphysics arises as a master idea that directs the conceptualizing of thought, representation, and action. It is this epoch, foreshadowed in the secularizing forces of Gutenberg, Adam Smith, and John Locke, which ultimately deepens into the administrative hegemony of the modern industrial scientific order.

The "control of space," Innis' euphemism for the rise of technological expertise and popular interest in the conquest of external nature, identifies a characteristic of modern social order in which the cultural forms of communicating become linked ever more closely to the functional values of transportation—quantity, mobility, efficiency. In this converging traffic of goods and ideas the countervailing force of human social relations based in continuity and place loses its centrality. What results is a profound institutional reorganization and repression, where concerns for identity and place on many levels of social life become subordinate to preoccupations and judgments grounded in the technologies of information control and the synchronic grammars of the administered life.

In all this there is much that links Innis' melancholy assessments of the age to other modern epochal historians who view the present as strictly unfolding from the precedents of the past. Yet, by virtue of the distance his communicational history keeps from the way such views of history give rise to interpretations either of "decline" or "success story," Innis remains at once both more structural and more equivocal. And if psychologically informed reflections on his conservatism and his classicism continue to provide informative accountings for the biographical issues in this posture, Innis' conception of order and change, informed and abetted by transformations within the modes of comunication, contains epistemological implications which, though present in much of his thinking, go significantly beyond the theoretical range of such criticism. Of exemplary importance here is his claim that these biases of communication are not just precedents from the past through which we can appreciate the necessary evolution of social and cultural order, but are in fact a critical means for identifying the objective structures of authority itself.

Media of communication, through which the conceptual systems of a given historical epoch are directed and constrained, disclose as well the blueprint for its domination. What are to be dominated at every stage are matters of the margins—peoples, regions, forms of experience and representation, differences maintained by remoteness, isolation, or incomprehensibility. This is a matter not of "ruling classes" or "master societies," but of those elites enfranchized to name knowledge and, as experts, empowered to set the "limits of performance" on the lives of others.[3]

This is a cultural monopoly of knowledge. Innis' amalgam of political economy and epistemology indicates the empassioned focus of his historical work. Through this notion the conceptual framework of his communication theory of history indicates its deeper critical intent: that since dominant media of communication bear so closely upon the material conditions inhering in all human interactions, their analysis can reveal something of the empirical enclosures within which the expression and even the rationality of a given epoch is fashioned and constrained.

THE COMMUNICATION THEORY OF SOCIETY

Marshall McLuhan did the first notable reworking of the communication theory of Harold Innis. McLuhan's accomplishment, which culminated in his own *Understanding Media* in 1964, went beyond Innis to examine the role of current media technologies, especially those designated by the electronic metaphor. The pursuit of public notoriety has long since overshadowed much of McLuhan's own unique scholarly contribution, and that notoriety has occasionally reached out to Innis as well. Yet, this promotion of the "folk science" of an emerging discipline paradoxically provides much of the initial public legitimacy on which subsequent growth of the discipline depends. Exemplary of this popularization in communication studies was McLuhan's idea that electronic technology bring about complex sensory reorganization, a notion many found fruitful in understanding the youthful protagonists in the generational crisis of the early 1960s. The drift of his concern, then and since, has been a continuing exploration of these concatenated domains of technology and subjective perception. McLuhan openly questioned whether the effects of electronic media could maintain, let alone deepen, psychic identities with our past and responded by emphasizing the future importance of accommodation and re-education. When McLuhan could propose with finality that identity was not compatible with electronic technology, Innis' earlier proposals that authority and monopoly were the important concomitants in the rise of new communication media seemed to many just a bit abstract.[4]

In attempting to harmonize at a perceptual level the very relationships Innis had found so antagonistic at a structural level, McLuhan provided little resistence for the liberal and practical marketing of these ideas. The departure from Innis is revealed by almost any passage from McLuhan's writing of the period. In psychologizing the effects of technologically assisted communication, the structural antagonisms of historical bias seemed to make way for psychic revision. Unlike Innis, McLuhan's position appeared unequivocal. Older generations were re-proved for forsaking the benefits of a media transformed and media transforming future. As James Carey has argued, it was increasingly toward the reformative powers of media that McLuhan was drawn at the time, media "that not only orient us to the world but tell us what kind of world exists; that not only excite and delight our senses but, by altering the ratio of sensory equipment that we use actually change our charac-ter."[5]

This is one manner in which the communication theory of history, with its epistemological implications, came to be popularized as a theory of technology effects and perception and where, as a consequence, the problem of authority and its deeper constraints on social order gave way to the less complicated surface of events and the more painless reforma-tions of the moment. Perhaps less noticed in the dramatic turn McLuhan gave to the role of communications and its study was the very problema-tic manner in which subjectivity had been added to communication theory.

In McLuhan's revision the disjunctive feature appears to be the underlying conception of culture and society. It is not the content of his political attitudes but the concepts within which McLuhan carries out the reformulation of Innis that matter. What is radical in Innis comes not from his political attitudes but from his concepts. This disjuncture, be-tween what Russell Jacoby calls the truth content of concepts and the social and political views of those who employ them, identifies both the means and the necessity of defending Innis' concepts from the climate of opinion they have both occasioned and served.[6]

Innis' concern for media-maintained and media-maintaining con-tradictions in society might have received wider recognition earlier were it not for McLuhan's naming of the avenues of potential harmony. Still, McLuhan pushed, as few others did, the limits of critical scholarship in the early 1960s. In fact, whether by historically induced alliance or common argument, McLuhan's work became part of the mounting criti-cism, inspired by a sort of humanist revival at the time, that it was the very links between culture, society, and individual that scholars were neglecting, most notably in the discourse of mainstream social science. Though this humanist critique had as its target a variety of methodologi-cal and philosophical behaviorisms of the day, in retrospect it is worth remembering that the more radical positions emerging in this period

reflected a different view. What these new critics of society found revealing in the objectifying tendency of the social or human sciences was
curiously enough its very disregard of social and human values. Even at
the extremities, where rat psychologies reconstructed role psychology
into the hypothetical society of stimulus and response, these new critics
repeated the earlier contention of Frankfurt School sociology and the
unfreedom of such approaches was wordless testimony to the prevailing
unfreedom of the times. What they pointed out in the use of these
objectively detached and unreflective methods was their implicit critique
of the individual. It was not a question of whether the individual was
mere illusion, as Skinner proclaimed it, but simply that the popularity
for all manner of behaviorist solutions at the time was itself a compelling
kind of historical evidence that the individual some wished to humanize
and many others to eliminate located a profound conflict, perhaps ultimately an irresolvable contradiction, at the prevailing center of our social thought and practice.[7]

This conflict is as central to Innis' concern with the past as its
accommodation is central to McLuhan's concern for the future. Innis
had resisted the temptation to harmonize the contradictions his theoretical concepts revealed as much as he resisted the urge to psychologize
away the antagonisms of the present. Like Nietzsche, whom he quoted
with approval, he had a sense of the critical predicament: "Knowledge of
the past is at all times needed only to serve the present and the future,
not to enfeeble the present or to tear the roots out of the vigorous
powers of life for the future."[8] If Innis has remained outside the mainstream of communication study, this can best be understood in terms of
the general predicament of historical rationality within the changing
intellectual currencies of the day. The emergence of communication
study in the 1960s, characterized as it too had been by the struggle
between humanizing and objectifying discourses, was part of this deeper
betrayal. What was to be repeatedly questioned and resisted by the dis-
senting voices of the 1960s was the very tendency in mainstream thought
that the critical historical core of Innis' work had identified and condemned a decade earlier: namely, the guiding presupposition of the
dominant communications paradigm that, content aside, the study of
communication media was inseparable from its praise.[9]

Innis consistently tried to see the authority of media emerging
from its systematic and largely unconscious operation in the history of
society. That here were objective features to be uncovered in media was
what the concept of communication bias proposed to reveal. Innis never
believed in an easy dissolution of such biases, especially as he perceived
more clearly their operation in our own time; nor did he advance any

special vision of the future. In this he remained faithful to his concepts. He drew no cyclical theory of history from it all and he did not bridge the antagonisms between what his theory saw and the content of his own political conviction. It was a purposeful defense of humanism that seems to have occasioned the reformulation of Innis—and this largely in the interest of addressing contemporary social anxiety. By adding subjectivity to his formulations, humanisms of the moment, such as that offered by McLuhan, revealed not their particular weakness so much as humanism's own unacknowledged positivism as the uneasy promoter of those new values that facilitated the disappearance of older human, moral, and political ones.

The troubled nature of contemporary humanism reveals itself in such circumstances. It is not that defense of the human subject is in any way an unworthy pursuit but that, in its own unreflective forms, humanist thought can degenerate into a defense of the purely subjective. This loss of the dialectic of thought, a loss that permits the psychologizing away of social problems, also betrays its own historical predicament. Innis knew well enough that the biases of communication media are manmade and he understood as well the necessity of pointing up the ways in which biases also make men, systematically and usually without their knowledge and consent. Yet, if this distinction between the necessary and unnecessary enclosures of social reality could be lost on some humanist thought, it was certainly lost to much scientific thought as well.

When humanist and scientist traditionally diverged over the issue of what constituted a good society, what was often lost in the stand-off was the critical matter of what constituted a good science for achieving it. Like Weber and Veblen, Innis had tried to renew recognition of this epistemological conundrum. In his view, preoccupation with the "control of space" in modern societies had facilitated the suppression of a moral basis for social order in favor of technical ones. The type of knowledge most directly appropriate to a technically based social order was, perhaps self-evidently, the means-oriented logic of modern social science. This, in turn, suggested that the context-independent status of scientific claims might have more than coincidental affinities with the growing dominance of technologically mediated forms of communication over those more directly intersubjective ones.

In a designated age of communications it is understandable that the "advances" technology brings get analyzed and promoted less for their goals and more for their assists to the social process. And yet, these occasions, which may indeed serve to open up new possibilities for interpersonal relations, can also disclose to the more wary the suppression of important qualities of human interaction. Interaction patterns that seemingly can be constrained and directed by new developments in the technology itself systematically draw attention to "means-end" orientations. In such circumstances aspects of human interaction that fall outside these empirical enclosures can be devalued and repressed by the rationalized discourse of an operational science itself.

In the development of scientific knowledge and technological expertise the further development of society was considered by many to be automatic and desirable. Especially alongside the heady publicity-cum-ideology that "it works," claims that science and technology themselves eventually might become social problems were largely discounted. This denial, which accompanies the rise of positivist science generally in the twentieth century, locates also an aspect of its cultural contradiction.[10]

Because technologically mediated forms of interaction do alter aspects of intersubjectivity at the same time they extend it, communication media are significant not only by virtue of their assistance to the transportation of goods and ideas—which is well established—but also by their consequences for the conditions in which human social relations are constituted, that is, understood and undertaken. Yet, if technologically assisted media seem to entail transportation, the transportation model convincingly explained neither communication nor interaction. Technologically assisted communication could not be adequately accounted for as relationships entailed by the liberal marketplace because technological media enter into society as forms of interaction whose bias and pattern of influence have to be understood within the scope of socially constituted relationships.[11]

Where the science of communications wished to restrict itself to those aspects of human behavior fashioned internally by the messages and institutions of communication media, Innis' perspective serves to remind us that these behavioral enclosures, like their descriptive science, must also have a history. For some time now Innis' effort to ground this materially through a history of media has been obscured by the ambitious but separate project of McLuhan. In retrospect, the technological determinism, for which both have been severely criticized, seems inappropriate. Preoccupations with technology and constraint in Innis reveal a concern with the opposite—an interest in understanding the state of intersubjective relations in society. Like technology, intersubjectivity has its own unwritten history and Innis, through aspects of the former, was struggling for a necessary link to the latter. Placed against the merging self-image of a society considered technical and increasingly steered by science, his work remains revisionist. It challenges us to look again, this time not only for the control of social order but like the muse of history for some sense of its cunning.

Though Marx, Nietzsche, and Freud insisted upon it in different ways, much twentieth century thought has had trouble with the idea that the observer of phenomenal reality might not be as reliably detached from it as the data suggested. In fact the notion that the "data" of observations might be better described as the "capta" of particular theories has had a well-known impact on the division of disciplines in the present century. An epistemological issue here has been the perplexing question of whether some sort of intersubjective standards of rationality were needed to sort out objective claims from matters of prejudice and false belief. Moreover, since systematic human inquiry at a particular time was almost certain to be guided by some ideal of objectivity, it was at least probable that particular standards of objectivity might depend strongly upon the inquiring communities themselves. Such concerns, in turn, have raised questions about the very possibility of a logic of science. The denial of all such doubts about the nature of inquiry and observer and in its place the insistence that there is a significant body of hard empirical fact, a basic, final, knowable reality, is objectivism.[12]

This objectivist denial locates epistemologically the major division in modern communicational thought. On the one side a procrustean empiricism with monotonous unanimity remains unyielding to the possible weight of historical conditions behind its "facts" or the sounds of possible alternatives within them. On the other, there is a growing wariness among a diversity of scholars and researchers that it is not only the status of the facts that matters but also the status of the scientific communities that occasion them. Precisely because the beliefs communities share, even communities of pure inquiry, can never be completely independent of phenomena, there has been renewed interest in the process of scientific research itself. In the emergence of this latter point of view there was a dawning recognition of just how significantly beliefs could both reflect and distort conditions of social life. Against the more naive and mechanical forms of empiricism, such arguments seemed to suggest that the real force of ideologies in the modern experience might be shown to reside more cunningly in their subtler uses, for justification and legitimation rather than simply for promotion and propaganda. In this sense, it was not just naive forms of empiricism but any community with beliefs, assumptions, scholarships, methods, or heuristics operating as ideologies that placed important limits on what counts as rational choice.[13]

To account in part for the way epistemic communities prescribed earlier or competing forms of rationality, Innis had proposed the cultural monopoly of knowledge. Of central consequence to him was the manner in which knowledge monopolies were related to more complicated divisions of labor and more complex social orders. Especially in our modern epoch, as rational choice became vested in new knowledge elites, the accompanying growth of technical knowledge and new types of technical media appeared to have brought about the conditions for a systematic devaluation of those aspects of interaction identified by Innis with moral, political, and communal idealizations of life within oral traditions. In their place enfranchised occupations, classes, organizations, and even nation–states served to repress the more directly intersubjective modes of communication into a permanent and unequal dichotomy of information and practical public reason.

When knowledge in the form of information becomes the consequence of the gradual disappearance of more intersubjective grounds for reason, the erosion of such intersubjective grounds for rationality creates some initially tricky terrain for democratic societies. Political elites increasingly must claim authoritative access to information in decision-making that deflates public challenges and access to expert counsel in gauging popular sentiment that reduces the reciprocal process of civil understanding to the one-way street of public opinion and official explanations. Inevitably in a society where reasoning appears more vested in the detached observations of experts, rationality becomes more easily identifiable with expertise alone. In the future of such a scenario, where reason could be restricted to those able to speak the technical languages of expertise, the grounds and the occasions for rational discourse may well shift more dramatically from the public domain into the community of experts themselves. What results may well be seen as a structural inequality in which modern communication media and knowledge elites function to provide information about decisions— and do this increasingly for the purpose of manipulating opinion toward the dubious end of motivationless public acceptance. At such imagined extremities the dichotomy of information and public reason reveals its own betrayal: that forms of information no longer able to risk debate nor invite decision become eventually neither knowledge nor argument but mutatis mutandis, a measure of the domination possible in exchange.

It is perhaps only in the deeper logic of communication epistemology that such problems are of interest. Their solutions are a different matter. To give attention to the interactional perspective while renewing a commitment to the historical subject, it requires that we understand critically these problems that result from the hegemonies in our communicative interaction and exchange. If knowledge can itself become problematic through failure to recognize methodologically the organized means through which it is disseminated and the organized ends to which it is applied, this must be true of our knowledge of the communication process as well. This is why contemporary theorists of communications as diverse as Raymond Williams in England and Jürgen Habermas in Germany have argued emphatically that the discourse through which we understand the institutions of communication may be as consequential in the long run as the existence of the institutions themselves.[14]

As communication phenomena follow McLuhan's prediction and move closer to the center of concern for society, these aspects of its study begin to assume their significance, something Harold Adams Innis as a theorist of the margins from a marginal country may simply have sensed more directly than most.

NOTES

[1]The major communications texts of Innis that establish this argument are: *Empire and Communication*, Toronto, Oxford University Press, 1950; *Bias of Communication*, Toronto, University of Toronto Press, 1951; *Changing Concepts of Time*, Toronto, University of Toronto Press, 1952; and two unpublished manuscripts, *The Idea File*, and *A History of Communication*, University of Toronto Archives.

[2]Innis, *Bias of Communication*, pp. 137–138; *Empire and Communication*, pp. 153–154; *A History of Communication*, Ch. 4.

[3]Innis, *Empire and Communication*, pp. 4–5.

[4]Cox, Kirwan, and Crean, S. M. "An Interview with Marshall McLuhan." *Cinema Canada*, August 1976, Special Edition.

[5]Carey, James. "Harold Adams Innis and Marshall McLuhan." *Antioch Review*, Vol. 27, No. 1, 1967, p. 18.

[6]Jacoby, Russell. *Social Amnesia*. Boston, Beacon, 1975.

[7]It was the work of the Frankfurt School that inspired many of the critiques of philosophical behaviorism that emerged in the 1960s. In addition to Russell Jacoby's *Social Amnesia*, William Leiss' *The Domination of Nature* (Boston, Beacon, 1972) and Martin Jay's *The Dialectical Imagination* (Boston, Little Brown, 1973) are exemplary of the diversity of such second generation scholarship in North America.

[8]Innis, *Bias of Communication*, p. 61.

[9]The influential source of this presupposition is the development model pioneered by Wilbur Schramm, Lucian Pye, and Daniel Lerner in the 1950s. For its impact on UNESCO see Herbert Schiller's *Communication and Cultural Domination* (White Plains, International Arts and Sciences Press, 1976) and for a more varied revision of this thinking see the collection of articles in *The Journal of Communication* (Vol. 28, No. 1, 1978) and *Communication Research* (No. 3, 1976).

[10]This argument has been given important new recognition by Jürgen Habermas' *Knowledge and Human Interest* (Boston, Beacon, 1971) and Gerard Radnitsky's *Contemporary Schools of Metascience* (Chicago, Henry Regnery, 1973).

[11]The curiousness of communications research that focused exclusively on audience research is a matter that still needs attention, especially given its dominance in the United States until quite recently. Jeremy Tunstall's *The Media are American* (London, Constable, 1977) sets out some of the historical consequences of this scholarship on the spread and characteristics of large-scale media institutions.

[12]Del Hymes' collection of articles in *Reinventing Anthropology* (New York, Vintage, 1974) is the best source for these problems from the point of view of communication studies; Richard Bernstein's *The Restructuring of Social and Political Theory* (New York:

Harcourt, Brace, Javanovich, 1976) is the source for the broader argument and implications and the basis for some of the present characterizations.

[13]Gouldner, Alvin. *The Dialectic of Ideology and Technology*. New York, Seabury, 1976, pp. 56–59.

[14]This argument has its modern basis in C. Wright Mills. *The Sociological Imagination* (New York, Oxford University Press, 1959) and Jürgen Habermas, *Toward a Rational Society* (Boston, Beacon, 1971). In communications there is a diverse recognition of this argument: Gregory Bateson, *Steps to an Ecology of Mind* (New York, Ballantine, 1972), Anthony Wilden, *System and Structure* (London, Tavistock, 1972), Raymond Williams, *Television: Technology and Cultural Form* (London, Fontana, 1974).

18

INNIS AND THE HISTORY
OF COMMUNICATION: ANTECEDENTS,
PARALLELS, AND UNSUSPECTED BIASES

PAUL HEYER
Simon Fraser University

These tools have enabled workers in the historical field to distinguish various sedimentary strata; linear successions, which for so long had been the object of research, have given way to discoveries in depth. From the political mobility at the surface down to the slow movements of "material civilization," ever more levels of analysis have been established: each has its own peculiar discontinuities and patterns; and as one descends to the deepest levels, the rhythms become broader. Beneath the rapidly changing history of governments, wars, and famines, there emerge other, apparently unmoving histories: the history of sea routes, the history of corn or of goldmining, the history of drought and irrigation, the history of crop rotation, the history of the balance achieved by the human species between hunger and abundance. The old questions of the traditional analysis [What link should be made between disparate events? How can a causal succession be established between them? What continuity or overall significance do they possess? Is it possible to define a totality, or must one be content with reconstituting connexions?] are now being replaced by questions of another type: which strata should be isolated from others? What types of series should be established? What criteria of periodization should be adopted for each of them? What system of relations [hierarchy, dominance, stratification, univocal determination, circular causality] may be established between them? What series of series may be established? And in what large-scale chronological table may distinct series of events be determined?

—Foucault. 1976[1]

It might be useful, and provoking, to introduce some of the questions I wish to deal with in the work of Innis via the observations of a much discussed writer of the current generation who, from a quite different direction, has broached some of the same concerns.

In the above passage, French philosopher-historian Michel Foucault is describing approaches to history that have been growing in significance over the last several decades. However, his own historical perspective differs from those he is here describing. Foucault's historiography, which he calls an archeology of knowledge, is concerned with the communication process of knowledge as manifested in science, philosophy, the history of thought, and most preeminently, the history of discourse. Despite this focus, he accords the historiography that deals with economic and technological patterns a healthy respect. Both Foucault's perspective and those he is assessing are distinct from the kind of traditional history that deals with what he refers to as a "thick layer of events" and linear successions or, as Marx once put it, "the high sounding drama of princes and states." In his analysis, Foucault is assessing historical approaches that have risen to prominence since Innis wrote and he gives no evidence of or awareness of Innis. Yet there is a definite link between these approaches and what Innis tried to do in his work on Canadian economic history and in his comparative study on the role of communication technology in the development of civilization and extension of empire.

In his recent books, Foucault has been almost obsessively concerned with his own historical methodology. Innis, by contrast, was almost illusive when it came to outlining the methodology used in his later work. As a result he has left us with a bewildering, ill-defined and often contradictory legacy in this area, one a number of writers, including several in this volume, are trying to untangle. This paper will not be concerned with the Innis method per se. Instead it will comment directly on the nature of the subject matter of his later work and show how aspects of this concern were both anticipated by earlier writers and paralleled by several scholars of his own generation. I will deal with authors whose specific works were either unknown to Innis, or if known, of only negligible influence. In addition, instances will be pointed out where the contributions of some of these authors might have helped to rectify some unsuspected biases in Innis, biases that sometimes steered the implications of an analysis away from what was originally intended.

THE SUBJECT AND THE APPROACH

The fact Innis wished to devote the scholarly efforts of his later years to the study of communication in history should not be taken lightly. It was a bold and innovative step. Unlike his earlier ventures, which could be accommodated into political economy, history, or sociology, the later work did not find ready acceptance into traditional disciplinary structures. This, I believe, is largely responsible for the lack of recognition it received in his own time and in the years following his death. Several former colleagues were, and still are, uncomfortable with the entire research area. *Empire and Communications* and the *Bias of Communication* are eclectic works that draw from archaeology, anthropology, philosophy, and the history of science, as well as the traditional humanities and social science venues in which Innis was schooled. Although the writing style and many of the analyses in these texts are notoriously confusing, the subject area itself, communication in history and the relationship of communication to the social order, is no mere mélange. It constitutes a well-focused, unambiguously charted province for scholarly assessment. It also should be noted that at the time Innis wrote, there was no formal discipline called "communication" to house his effort, and although such a discipline now exists, it has yet to assimilate fully the Innis legacy.

Over the past three hundred years the relationship between communication, society, and history has been discussed by numerous writers who comprise what I have elected to call a discontinuous tradition in modern social thought, a tradition to which the work of Innis constitutes one of the most recent and definitive chapters. The tradition is discontinuous because the authors reflect different disciplinary affiliations, national traditions, and research goals, and their works do not form continuous stages in a conscious development. Very often whole arguments and conclusions are repeated. Questions resolved in one generation are raised again decades, even a century, later by writers unaware of the earlier contributions. Although this is in part true for the history of thought in all fields, it is more pronounced in the communication–society–history relationship than in any other problematic that I can think of in the history of social thought. For example, several questions central to Innis in the communication–society–history arena have an unsuspected ancestry that dates back to the Enlightenment.[2]

During his lifetime, the particular concern that Innis had for communication in the context of the history of technology was partially shared by several contemporaries, though their influence on his thought ranged from slight to nonexistent. For instance, during the first half of the twentieth century a number of writers with roots in the humanities and social sciences began to show concern with the impact on human life brought about by various developments in the machine industry. The pioneering work in this direction was Lewis Mumford's *Technics and Civilization*, first published in 1934.[3] More recently, the names of Siegfried Giedion, Jacques Ellul, and Marshall McLuhan have been associated with this tradition. William Kuhns has referred to these men as the postindustrial prophets and included H. A. Innis in the pantheon.[4] Although Innis' historical analysis and human concern doubtlessly link him to the tradition, his reluctance to be a prophet places him on its margins. Marginal status, however, is nothing new for Innis. As David Crowley aptly notes in concluding the preceding paper, marginality is a recurring theme in the life and thought of this interdisciplinary scholar.

More than any of his contemporaries or successors who have dealt with technology in history, Innis is steeped in paradox. Perhaps it is not an exaggeration to say he deliberately sought to be regarded in this light. This attitude both kept others from typing him—none in the tradition, McLuhan included, are as difficult to categorize—and prevented him from achieving intellectual stasis.

Few scholars have been, at one and the same time, as independent as Innis and yet as dependent. This ambivalence is especially pronounced in the later work dealing with the history of communication. Even a cursory examination of these studies will show they are characterized by an almost total reliance on secondary sources. On almost every page, he draws from and cites major figures in the humanities and social sciences, but he declares no overt affiliation, be it intellectual or political. To Innis, no name is sacrosanct, a situation that has apparently gone unacknowledged by writers endeavoring to synthesize the Innis–Marx legacies. Another Innis paradox is his discomfort with theory, a point raised by Liora Salter in the opening paper of this section. Despite this discomfort, his work evidences stronger ties to what is often called the nomothetic approach to history (a concern for regularities, laws, and necessary relationships) than it does to the contrasting ideographic approach (a concern for the unique, particular, and discrete). Yet Innis seems deliberately to avoid identifying with nomothetic theorists such as the classical social evolutionists, while at the same time being more theoretical than the humanist tradition to which he perhaps felt spiritually closer. This quandary notwithstanding, his work has been enormously suggestive with respect to theory, both in political economy and in communication.

FORERUNNERS

There is good reason to regard Innis as the first writer to create a distinct field of inquiry using the social and economic consequence of developments in communication as subject matter. He was not, of course, the first to discuss the relationship. In the nineteenth century Marx made reference, in *Das Kapital*, to the role of the telegraph and railroad in defining the social relations of production, and earlier in this volume Ian Parker has discussed the Innis–Marx parallel at some length. Although Innis was critical of and did not draw directly from Marx, it is obvious the Marxian presence is felt. This contrasts sharply to

McLuhan, who with a pontifical air totally alien to the Innis spirit from which he claims descent has dismissed Marx as irrelevant.

However, if we consider communication less from the technological side, and more from the context of language and its role in the history of society, the eighteenth century provides us with a body of material prefiguring some of the concerns of Innis, McLuhan, and other twentieth-century writers. Under the influence of earlier philosophers such as Hobbes, Descartes, and Locke, writers of the eighteenth-century Enlightment began to apply models inspired by the natural sciences to the study of the "natural history of mankind"—a field that would today include both our species' history in the biological sense and the history of society and civilization. Condillac, Turgot, Condorcet, Rousseau, and Monboddo, among others, dealt with questions pertaining to the origin of society. In addition, they often attempted to define the criteria governing social formation at various historical periods. Usually economic and technological factors, or else stages in intellectual development, were held to make up the essential charter of a given age. Yet to many of these writers, communication in the form of language, and to a lesser extent writing, loomed as crucial to any discussion of the history of human society and civilization. Even Adam Smith, a figure who at first glance appears an unlikely candidate, wrote an essay in 1761 dealing with the formation of languages and their role in the social process, though given the emphasis he would later place, in the *Wealth of Nations* (1776), on the social importance of exchange, it is perhaps not all that surprising.

Perhaps the most insightful of the Enlightenment thinkers to turn his attention to the role of communication in the history of society was Jean-Jacques Rousseau. In his discourse on the *Origin of Inequality Among Men* (1755), the subject is given due recognition. However, in another work dating from the same period, an essay titled *On the Origin of Languages*,[5] language and society are discussed in a context that includes an assessment of writing. In the chapter "On Script," Rousseau analyzes the social preconditions for the emergence of the various forms of writing and the role this skill played in the expansion of the societies using it. Of particular interest is the historical relevance to modern debates evidenced in a number of his discussions, especially his analysis of whether a medium such as writing merely preserves speech, or in fact transforms it and at the same time cognitive and social orientation. This issue is an important one to Innis, McLuhan, and members of the newer generation of communication historians such as Jack Goody. Rousseau was emphatic in his belief that writing changes language and therefore the context of communication; in fact, his analysis partially recalls what Innis said about writing facilitating the formation of monopolies of knowledge. And, like many modern communication historians, Rousseau was concerned with the implications of the difference between oral and literate traditions.

Moving again into the nineteenth century, it should be noted that, in addition to Marx, several other writers have discussed the role of communication in culture history. These were the social evolutionists who were frequently concerned with the relationship of writing to the emergence of civilization. For present purposes, only the most important one need be mentioned. In his *Researches into the Early History of Mankind* (1865)[6], Edward B. Tylor, a founding father of modern anthropology, extensively scrutinized what we might today label the history of communication. In *Researches into the Early History of Mankind*, Tylor focuses on gesture, the nature and origin of language, the development of notational systems and various forms of writing, and other systems of information dissemination such as myth and oral history. The emergence of new forms of communication is held by Tylor to comprise the essential matrix upon which subsequent cultural development occurs. Unfortunately, neither Innis nor McLuhan show evidence of having read Tylor. The omission is perhaps pardonable in the former, since Tylor discussed communication apart from its social and economic context. However, the latter might have drawn sustenance from the connections Tylor traced between human psychology, language, and writing.

CULTURE AND THE ORAL TRADITION

Although Tylor's important contribution to the study of communication has been largely unheralded, he usually is credited with framing the concept of culture, which has permeated subsequent social science. In 1871, he defined culture as "that complex whole which includes knowledge, belief, art, morals, laws, custom, and any other capabilities and habits acquired by man as a member of society."[7] The Innis culture concept has a different geneology, one Don Theall (earlier in this section) traces to a number of classical humanist sources, an exercise, that in future can receive invaluable aid from John Watson's recent work.[8] However, Theall highlights only the positive aspects of Innis' humanistically rooted concept of culture, such as its emphasis on balance and harmony, its use as a critical tool and its relationship to communication and community. Nevertheless, problems and pitfalls are connected with defining culture in an exclusively humanist context, which minimizes input from the social sciences. Not surprisingly, Innis was aware of this dilemma. In fact, he warns us against it, but in a moment of "do as I say, not as I do," he succumbed to an unsuspected bias he hoped others would avoid.

In the *Bias of Communication,* Innis states that each civilization tends to believe in its own uniqueness or superiority, that culture is often defined as "something which we have and others have not."[9] He may have unconsciously derived this definition from Greek writers such as Herodotus, who, when commenting on the lifeways of non-Greek societies in the *Histories,* often begins his sentences with "They do not . . ." or "Contrary to us they. . . ." Although Innis must have been aware of the descriptive and analytical use of the concept of culture in social science, the tradition of Tylor and subsequent anthropology, he chose to employ the humanist variant. The difficulty with the humanist concept is that it is usually value-laden (however, it must not be assumed that the social science concept is entirely value free) and grounded in a perspective that is hierarchical, idealist, and elitist. Innis, of course, tried to steer clear of, and often spoke out against, such attitudes—he would seem to be the last person one would accuse of snobbery. Nevertheless, his adherence to a humanist culture concept carried with it unsuspected ideological overtones that biased both the examples he chose to emphasize and his language of analysis. Before describing several instances, I would like to highlight three fundamental points of reference integral to a humanist culture concept that to varying degrees manage to seep into Innis' practice of social science.

First, culture in a humanist tradition is often used to define an enlightened, balanced (the term Innis often used), or privileged state of individual being—for example, as in the lyrics by Paul Simon: "the man ain't got no cultcha." This view implicitly divides individuals so endowed from those who are not, the latter usually occupying a lower rung in the class hierarchy. Second, culture to the humanist often refers to those transcendent outpourings of society such as art, religion, and intellectual life, rather than to the totality of lifeways as in the definition by Tylor cited earlier. Third, the humanist reference can be to those typically western and highly literate notions of freedom and the sanctity of the individual, notions that extensively preoccupied the avowedly oral-biased Innis. Not only are these attitudes absent in people who live in an oral as opposed to a literate tradition (in the former sociocentric categories, and in the latter egocentric, prevail), but also, according to Michel Foucault, they do not pervade western thought at all until after the Renaissance.[10]

A frequent consequence of the humanist assumptions regarding culture that I have just highlighted is ethnocentrism, a belief in the inherent superiority of one's nation or tradition. Almost all historians have such leanings. In the case of Innis it is covert, revealed by omissions in his analysis, rather than in the forceable imposition of a given point of view. By exposing these gaps it is not my intent to devalue his insights, but to build on and render more inclusive a project that frequently outstripped the tools at hand. A case in point is his view of the oral tradition.

The Innis "ideal type" or model of the oral tradition is based on the Greek experience, as several contributors have already noted. His work evidences no discussion of the phenomenon as exemplified in the pre-state societies of Africa, Asia, and the New World. Discounting the obvious limitations of model building from one source, the real oversight resides in the fact that he looked for enlightenment outside Canada when illustrations could have been drawn from the home front. For example, the oral tradition and democracy among the Iroquois were subjects elaborated by two well-known nineteenth century writers; Francis Parkman, the historian, and Lewis H. Morgan, the anthropologist. Both favorably compared the Iroquois to the early Greeks to whom Innis was so indebted.[11] Again, links to the humanist traditions and culture concept, with its ofttimes unintended racism, may have led Innis to this omission. Even in his regional studies of Canada and researches into policy, native peoples are almost invisible.

An interesting point of comparison is to look at the concept of the oral tradition as espoused by McLuhan. Although McLuhan's view of the phenomenon is rife with misunderstandings that cannot be dealt with here, it is nevertheless worth noting that his formulations are substantially more inclusive than those of Innis. This is largely a result of his collaboration with anthropologist Edmund Carpenter at the University of Toronto during the 1950s. For McLuhan, Hopi, early Greek, and Eskimo are all equally valid expressions of the oral tradition. Nevertheless, although lauding the tribal nexus, with its "acoustic space," he has been almost completely indifferent to the racial and cultural genocide of native peoples facilitated by the imposition of new technologies.

The contrast between the implications of living in an oral versus a literate tradition, which Crowley relates to a moral versus a technical social order in Innis, is not merely an idle historical exercise. As Rowland Lorimer has recently emphasized, it has a direct significance to everyday life situations such as interethnic relations and socialization through the education system.[12] It might, therefore, be useful to mention briefly two contemporaries of Innis who also dealt with the oral tradition and whose contributions in this area, although unacknowledged by Innis, can be used to extend some of his formulations.

In a profound and searching work, *Primitive Man as Philospher* (1927),[13] the German-American anthropologist, Paul Radin, dealt with the nature of the oral tradition and the contrast in world view between preliterate peoples and those dependent on what he referred to as the rule of the written word. Radin discussed the psychological consequences created by the invention of writing. He also assessed the impact of the various media that imbue the written word with permanence. Like Innis, Radin's bias was with the oral, not the written tradition; unlike Innis, Radin identified with nonwriting, tribal peoples, not the Greeks. Another contributor in this area was the noted linguist, Edward Sapir. His landmark article, "Culture, Genuine and Spurious,"[14] dealt with some of the contrasts later posed by Innis in his oral/literate, moral/ technical dichotomy. More than any twentieth-century writer, Sapir succeeded in weaving together, and using as a critical tool, the best features of the humanist and the social science concepts of culture. It is unfortunate that Innis, whose essay "Industrialism and Cultural Values" in the *Bias of Communication* has many features in common with Sapir's effort, never drew from that linguist's work. The oversight is especially puzzling when we consider Sapir's extended sojourn in Canada and his eventual faculty position at the school from which Innis received his doctorate, the University of Chicago.[15]

Perhaps the most thoroughgoing and perceptive work since Innis (and McLuhan) dealing with oral versus literature traditions, and the impact of literacy on human cognitive orientation, has been undertaken by Jack Goody.[16] Goody looks at a number of societies using a frame of reference he calls the "mode of communication." He is particularly concerned with the relationship between the "mode of communication" in a given society and the capacity of the individuals in that society to store and augment knowledge, knowledge that can in turn be used to extend the limits of the particular society. Although Goody is an anthropologist by training, the range of his analysis includes both prehistory and history. He places considerable importance on the role of writing in the framing of various taxonomies: the systems of classification that particular societies have elaborated during periods in their development. Even the oral versus literate dichotomy in academic discourse is considered. Although it comes from a tradition other than the one in which Innis is situated, and goes into detail on points Innis only touched, Goody's material constitutes an important contribution to a project for which Innis remains the definitive architect.

COMMUNICATION AND CIVILIZATION

Not only did humanism's limiting hand constrain Innis' concept of both culture and the oral tradition, it did the same for his view of civilization by imparting a definite western bias. I find this particularly frustrating in light of the significant connections he defines between historical epochs and the dominant mode of communication. In his preoccupation with the Babylonian-Egyptian continuum, he overlooks, and does not apologize for overlooking, the high civilizations of the New World—the Inca, Aztec, and Maya. Yet even to a nonarchaeologically trained eye, the history of these people can provide ample fuel for the Innis method. Considerable material now exists to render fruitful an application of his assumptions regarding the role of time and space in the development of civilization to the pre-Columbian context. For example, during the expansionist phase of the Inca Empire, how crucial was the quipu, a series of cords of different lengths, thickness and color that could be knotted at various intervals to indicate crop production, the population of regions and taxation? The quipu, with its capacity to record and frame, would almost certainly have been analyzed by Innis as a space-binding device. This brief example only serves to show how potentially rich a mesh might be between Innis' later work on the history of communication and contemporary archaeology.

Although the possibility of a link between Innis and archaeology has yet to be unveiled, a generation ago it was at least glimpsed by both Innis and archaeology. In an interesting exchange, *Empire and Communications* was reviewed by V. Gordon Childe,[17] probably the foremost archaeological synthesizer in the twentieth century, and Innis replied in a rejoinder entitled, "Communications and Archaeology."[18] Childe, without doubt the most knowledgeable critic Innis could have had in this area, praised the latter for dealing with the history of communication in terms of the media that convey information rather than making reference to the linguistic content of particular periods. Childe also brought to light several inaccuracies and misunderstandings on the part of Innis. He graciously noted that they were the result of Innis' unavoidable distance from first hand sources and expert advice and praised the Canadian scholar for his courage in pursuing and awakening Childe's own interest in such an important line of inquiry. Innis replied by thanking the British archaeologist both for the review and for being kinder than necessary. He complimented him for being a lucid writer and a popularizer in the best sense of the term (Innis was neither and at times must have recognized this deficiency) thereby helping to break down entrenched monopolies of knowledge. In conclusion, Innis stressed the strengths and shortcomings of first hand research in archaeology and highlighted the importance of Childe's contribution to his own sphere of interest.

In critiquing Innisian history, Childe, who had strong Marxian leanings, must have appreciated the fact that for Innis the technology of communication is materialistically rather than idealistically conceived. This materialism is relational, not mechanistic. To paraphrase Crowley, in the Innis view, the media of communication do not constitute a causal nexus but are an integral element in the way holistically distinct realities arise out of former ones. Similarly, a number of other papers in this volume have laid to rest the specter of Innis as a technological determinist, if indeed the specter ever really existed.

For Innis, communication technology never determines the character of an historical epoch; in his words it "hastens," "facilitates," or "helps to define" that character. Interplay, formation, and interaction are terms that can be used to describe his view of the historical process. Reflexive determinism is as inappropriate to Innis as it is to Marx. True, Marx once said that "the hand mill will give you society with the feudal lord and the steam engine society with the industrial capitalist,"[19] but he did not base a theory of history on such illustrative connections and nobody else would, except perhaps McLuhan. If Innis neglects the social relations of production in his communication researches, as he certainly does, and is somewhat naive with respect to the role of ideology, he nevertheless leaves suitable openings for their inclusion as a generation of Innis-inspired researchers are beginning to demonstrate.

EXTENDING PARTS OF THE LEGACY

In a number of areas Innis anticipated perspectives destined for later development by writers who, in all likelihood, have had no familiarity with his work. One case in particular is appropriate to this section of the volume. Recently, owing in part to the work of French theorist Roland Barthes, it has become avante garde to delineate the way academic institutions frame and control what constitutes acceptable knowledge in the human sciences.[20] Yet, in his communication studies two decades earlier, Innis generated a similar critique. He endeavored to apply the economist's concept of monopoly to the field of scholarship, and in so doing criticized tendencies that were creating rigid boundaries around academic disciplines in the social sciences. Innis did not want to drastically restructure or to do away with the traditional disciplines but to cultivate an exchange relationship between them. He sought to make the multiplicity of resources in the university accountable to relevant problems, both intellectual and practical, and not to entrenched interests. His efforts in these areas should serve as inspiration to contemporary researchers concerned with the increasingly precarious position of the modern university. The academic orientation and public role of this institution is now more in need of a self-reflective critique than when, over a generation ago, Innis first diagnosed its inadequacies.

Since Innis' death, a number of writers working in allied areas and independent of his influence have done research relating to the study of communication in history. In several instances, this work can serve to extend or complement, and, in turn, be extended and complemented by Innis' concerns. One such writer is Michel Foucault, with whose analysis I began this essay. As an historian, Foucault shares with Innis an antiheroic and antiprogressive view of the subject, but his points of focus are somewhat different. Because much of Foucault's work is concerned with the underlying framework that constrains the diversity of perceptions in a given age, he has been connected to the structuralist movement. Of particular interest to him are the assumptions that bias knowledge in the development of given disciplines; this he tries to reveal by analyzing the discourse used by the particular discipline. In dealing with the communication process of knowledge, Foucault confines his analysis to the thought system itself—the interrelationship of ideas to one another and to their subject. He does not stress the social relations underlying the communication acts, nor the kind of bias that developments in communication technology might impart to a specific kind of discourse, areas where the contributions of Innis can provide a valuable resource. Future historical studies that deal with the communication process of knowledge in particular periods would do well to draw from and relate the approaches expounded by Foucault and Innis.

In conclusion, I wish to note that the inadequacies of unsuspected biases I have alluded to in Innis' work result from the ambitiousness and courage of his venture. An interdisciplinary approach to the history of communication is a vision not easily embraced by a single scholar, not even a scholar having the thoroughness and imagination of H. A. Innis. It is to pay Innis the highest tribute to state that the critical method he outlined can be reworked in light of new knowledge and used to challenge some of the gaps and speculative assumptions that abound in his work. In part, this results from the fact that this work is perhaps more incomplete than that of any other major scholar. In fact, he was very much aware of the incomplete and provisional nature of many of his formulations and expressed himself openly on this in the rejoinder to Childe cited earlier. However, within Innis' incomplete researches are viable directions that can be freshly followed by a new generation of interdisciplinary scholars, as the preceding chapters demonstrate.

Conscientiously pursuing some of the directions highlighted by Innis will frequently lead to conclusions that are at odds with those Innis reached. Knowing what we know of his legacy—thanks in part to this volume and the conference that inspired it—would he have wanted it any other way?

NOTES

[1]Foucault, Michel. *The Archaeology of Knowledge,* New York: Harper & Row, 1976.

[2]This entire problematic is the subject of a work I am currently researching tentatively titled, "The Discontinuous Tradition: Communications and History in Modern Social Thought."

[3]Mumford, Lewis. *Technics and Civilization,* New York: Harcourt, Brace & World, 1963.

[4]Kuhns, William. *The Post-industrial Prophets: Interpretation of Technology,* New York: Weybright and Talley, 1971.

[5]Rousseau, Jean-Jacques. *On the Origin of Language,* New York: Frederick Ungar, 1966.

[6]Tylor, Edward Burnett. *Researches into the Early History of Mankind and the Development of Civilization,* Chicago: The University Press, 1964.

[7]Tylor, Edward Burnett. *The Origins of Culture,* New York: Harper Torch Books, 1958, p. 1.

[8]Watson, John. "Innis Communication Studies and Classical Scholarship," a study presented to the Canadian Political Science Association Annual Conference, Fredericton, New Brunswick, June, 1977.

[9]Innis, H. A. *The Bias of Communication,* Toronto: The University Press, 1973, p. 132.

[10]Foucault, Michel. *The Order of Things,* New York: Random House, 1973.

[11]Innis' indebtedness to Greek sources for his view of the oral tradition is well analyzed in Alison Beale's M. A. Thesis: "The Concept of Language in the Communication Theory of H. A. Innis," McGill University, 1979.

[12]Lorimer, Rowland. "On Orientation to Literacy," unpublished manuscript, Department of Communication Studies, Simon Fraser University, 1978.

[13]Radin, Paul. *Primitive Man as Philosopher,* New York: Dover, 1956.

[14]Sapir, Edward. "Culture, Genuine and Spurious." *American Journal of Sociology,* Volume 29, 1924.

[15]From 1920 to 1925 Sapir was Chief of the Division of Anthropology in the Geological Survey of the Canadian National Museum at Ottawa. In 1925, he took up his post at the University of Chicago, several years after Innis had left.

[16]Goody, Jack. *The Domestication of the Savage Mind,* Cambridge: The University Press, 1978.

[17]Childe, V. Gordon. "Review of *Empire and Communications* by Harold Innis," *Canadian Journal of Economics and Political Science,* XVII, February, 1951.

[18]Innis, H. A. "Communications and Archaeology," *Canadian Journal of Economics and Political Science,* XVII, May, 1951.

[19]Quoted in David McLellan, *Marx,* London: Fontana, 1975, p. 41.

[20]Barthes, Roland. "Science Versus Literature," *The Times Literary Supplement,* September 28, 1967.

AUTHOR INDEX

PROPER NOUN INDEX